1 MONTH OF
FREE
READING

at

www.ForgottenBooks.com

ISBN 978-0-484-69174-1
PIBN 10670524

COMMENTARIES

ON

THE LIFE AND REIGN

OF

CHARLES THE FIRST,

KING OF ENGLAND.

BY I. D'ISRAELI.

VOL. IV.

LONDON:

HENRY COLBURN AND RICHARD BENTLEY,

NEW BURLINGTON STREET.

1830.

LONDON :

PRINTED BY SAMUEL BENTLEY,
Dorset-street, Fleet-street.

CONTENTS

OF THE

FOURTH VOLUME.

CHAPTER V.

CHAPTER VI.

CHAPTER VII.

CHAPTER VIII.

CHAPTER IX.

CHAPTER X.

CHAPTER XI.

CHAPTER XII.

CONTENTS.

CHAPTER XIII.

CHAPTER XIV.

CHAPTER XV.

CHAPTER XVI.

CHAPTER XVII.

LIFE AND REIGN

OF

CHARLES THE FIRST.

CHAPTER I.

OF THE CONSPIRACIES OF THE SCOTS AGAINST CHARLES THE FIRST.

HUME closes a luminous view of the discontents in Scotland by a philosophical observation on the King's inflexibility in this great revolution. " In his whole conduct of this affair there appeared no mark of the good sense with which he was endowed; a lively instance of that species of character so frequently to be met with, where there are found parts and judgment in every discourse and opinion; in many actions, indiscretion and imprudence. Men's views of things are the result of their understandings alone; their conduct is regulated by their understanding, their temper and their passions."

The almost daily correspondence of Charles with the Marquis of Hamilton, during the Scottish commotions, betrays no deficient energy of mind at this period; indeed the reverse is true. These numerous letters are a striking evidence not only of the unwearied activity of the Monarch, but of the prompt acuteness of the man. These are not official dispatches, undersigned by a Secretary, where mechanical forms often cover a vacuity of thought; but with the conciseness of a man of business, regardless of all ornament, Charles often expresses himself with great force, and with too much earnestness to indulge in an idle page.*

* Since writing this, we have the opinion of one whose practised skill in the construction of artificial periods, is too apparent in his criticism on the Letters of Charles the First. Mr. Godwin has recently thus described them. " They are written in what may be called a royal style; no atten_ tion is afforded by the writer to what are regarded as the ar_ tifices of composition. They have nothing in them of cir_ cumlocution or ceremony; no colouring of the craft of authorship. The sceptered penman proceeds somewhat im_ patiently to his point; he is blunt and brief: we see plainly that he thinks it would be some sacrifice of his dignity, if he were careful of auxiliaries and expletives, and used words other than were barely necessary to convey an unambiguous meaning." Mr. Godwin must pardon me, if I tell him that

Doubtless the strangely concerted opposition which burst out at the reading of the Liturgy came unexpected to Charles, who seems never to have suspected the existence of that public opinion which so long had been creating in the Scottish metropolis, that it had reached even to the remoter provinces. Persuaded that he could accomplish that National conformity which his father had perhaps designed, but had avoided with prudence, in the establishment of Episcopacy in his native kingdom, and amidst delusions raised up by the interests and passions of so many, when Hamilton once im-

this criticism is the most unjust and therefore the most erroneous, that ever a partisan adopted in order to depreciate what in itself is commendable. We have many hundreds of Letters of Charles the First. The King was his own Secretary, but it was not therefore incumbent on " the sceptered penman" to use a Secretary's style. He was to command not to discuss. Most of his letters were written on urgent, and even immediate occasions — not always in the calm of his cabinet, but often in the hurry of a moveable camp — more frequently in vexation and trouble; with the cares of Sovereignty weighing on the spirits, involved in the most complex intrigues—and at times distracted by opposite interests. Whatever may have been the extent of his capacity, it was always in a state of tension, and perhaps there are few men who could have written with the promptness of thought, and the earnestness of feeling, which mark the correspondence of Charles the First.

parted his fears and his doubts, Charles replied
that his information led him to conclude that
the Episcopalians did not constitute the inferior party in Scotland.

In the Scottish affairs Charles always proceeded unconscious of the conspiracies and disaffection around him ; could he suspect the
creatures of his favour, or the associates of his
leisure ?   Many who were not with him, were
known to be his friends, and more who had
largely participated of his favours, he had a
right to imagine were such.   And indeed it is
only by a due observation of this very circumstance of their personal regard for the King,
that we can lift the veil which hangs over
every part of the conduct of the mysterious
Ministers of Charles throughout the whole of
the Scottish transactions.   To this personal
regard was often opposed their national feeling.
In the degree that their loyalty executed their
master's design, they felt that they were betraying their own cause ; and when they sacrificed the royal interests for that cause, they
were hurried into popular compliances which
threatened even a greater danger.

The father and the son from affection, or
from policy, had studied to reconcile their ancient and native Kingdom, to the absence of

their Court, by every Royal indulgence. That the national pride of Scotia, too often wounded by the gibes and taunts of their Southern brethren, should not be further mortified by any sense of dependance on England, Charles had placed the whole conduct of their affairs among two or three Scotchmen who attended at the Court for this purpose. There they held their councils, so that the affairs of Scotland were never brought before the Privy Council.* But the consequence of this tenderness for their privileges was, that Scotland and its affairs excited no curiosity in the English public; and while the Court and country were alive to any weekly news they received from Germany and Poland, no one ever inquired after any event which occurred in so considerable a portion of their own Kingdom. The result of the system which the Stuart dynasty had adopted was unfortunate also in another point. The numerous Scottish residents at the English court, on whom these Monarchs doubtless relied for their zealous exertions with their countrymen, entirely lost their personal influence over their distant brothers, nor were the honours lavished on these absentees valued by the Scottish people at large. These absentees however

* This fact is ascertained by Clarendon, i. 195.

remained Scottish in their hearts, and found as
little compunction in betraying the secrets of
their master, as the nation afterwards experienced in selling him. Nor did the English
people sympathise with their new friends, whom
they looked on as intruders on their interests,
and who perpetually were the burthen of a
ballad, or the jest of a tale. Thirty years could
not indeed allay the ancient prejudices of two
nations, since even a century and a half have
not extinguished them; so long can last the
idiosyncrasy of manners, and so long it is ere
popular malice becomes obsolete.

The presence-chamber, and the privy-cham-
ber, and the bed-chamber, were crowded with
Scotchmen, who formed a vast disproportion to
the Englishmen at Court. Carte has given a
list of officers of state all Scotch. The Marquis
of Hamilton was Master of the Horse, and had
filled the stables with Scots; the Earl of Mor-
ton was Captain of the Band of Pensioners;
the Duke of Lenox was Warden of the Cinque
ports; the Earl of Ancram Keeper of the
Privy-purse; Sir William Balfour, Keeper of
the Tower; Wemyss, Master-gunner of the
Navy. Numberless were the gentlemen ushers,
the grooms, and the carvers, and the cup-
bearers—who, creatures of the bounties of the

father and the son, and prospering in the
wealth of England, were betraying their Sovereign in continued intelligence with their distant compatriots, and with malcontents nearer
at hand.

There existed a Scottish faction at Court
closely connected with the Nobility, and with
the Commoners, Puritans, or Patriots. The
Earl of Haddington, brother-in-law to the Earl
of Rothes, who was the first conspicuous leader
of the Covenanters, and whom Haddington
afterwards joined — remained at Whitehall.
This Lord was busily intriguing with some of
our peers, such as the Earl of Holland who
was the visible head of the Puritans in town,
as his brother the Earl of Warwick, afterwards
the High-admiral of the Parliamentarians, was
considered the chief of the Oppositionists in
the country, and with Lords Say, Brook, and
Wharton ; while Mr. Eleazer Borthwick, the
able and statesmanlike agent of the Covenanters, and who passed twelve years in London,
held daily communication with the good citizens of the Puritanic party, and with Hampden, Pym and other patriots. The intercourse
seems to have been mutual. There is a remarkable passage in the preface to Burnet's
Memoire of the Hamiltons, where he tells us

that " a gentleman of quality of the English
nation, who was afterwards a great Parliament-
man, went and lived some time in Scotland
before the troubles broke out, and represented
to the men that had then the greatest interest
there, that the business of the ship-money and
the Habeas Corpus, &c. had so irritated the
English nation that if they made sure work at
home they needed fear nothing from England."
Burnet, it is to be regretted, has not preserved
the name of this "English gentleman of quality."
This " great Parliament-man," appears to have
been Hampden ; Echard mentions that he paid
an annual visit to Scotland to concert measures
with *his friends.*   We find by Nalson that this
celebrated person alluded to, whoever he was,
and " other principal men of the faction," as
Nalson calls them, " made frequent journeys
into Scotland, and had many meetings and
consultations how to carry on their combina_
tions." *   Wariston in Cromwell's time valued

* Nalson, ii. 427.   Dalrymple, 124, on this very point
observes, on the confession of Wariston, that the Scots had
kept up an intelligence with the English. " This is a very
remarkable circumstance," he adds ; " it cannot be fully ex_
plained unless we were certain what persons of the English.
nation corresponded with the Scots and incited and en_
couraged their measures.   He who can explain and illustrate
this particular from original papers will greatly serve the

himself on these intrigues, which had confused the councils and nullified the actions of the King, and ruined the Stuarts. The recent publication of Secretary Nicholas's letters to the King confirms these accounts of the private meetings of the Opposition to concert measures; and in writing to the King then at Edinburgh he remarkably observes, that " they were of late very jocund and cheerful by some advertisements out of Scotland, from whose actions and successes they intend, as I hear, to take a pattern for their proceedings here."* In fact, the party were holding a little parliament of their own, with their own lords, and their own commoners. At London, and in the country, they had their committees. Accounts have reached us of what passed at the seat of Lord Say in Oxfordshire, where company, unobserved by the house, often assembled in a particular apartment, which they entered by a secret passage in which no servant was allowed to appear, but their discussions were often loud.

cause of truth." We are not so entirely deprived of this knowledge as Dalrymple supposed, but we still want more original papers, which in this age of unburying manuscripts may yet be discovered. I have sometimes fancied that Hampden and Pym must have left some manuscripts and correspondence.

* Evelyn, ii. 28.

The same secret assemblies were held at Mr. Knightley's in Northamptonshire. In these and other places, the party had their council-chambers and leading speakers. In the metropolis some places have been particularised where they met to terminate their more important decisions; Secretary Nicholas has noticed Lord Mandeville's house at Chelsea; Echard one in Gray's-inn-lane;* and Clarendon indicates a kind of fraternity where the members of this party seem to have lived and boarded as in a private family.† We are told that Pym rode through different counties, and others did the same, to procure elections of members, and for other purposes. We may at least admire their diligence, but we rather perceive its spirit when the Earl of Warwick wrote from York to his friends in Essex " that the game was well begun;" and another leader, whose name has not come down to us, observed that " their party was then strong enough to pull the King's crown from his head, but the Gospel would not suffer them." It is lamentable to observe that Patriots should be constrained to assume the characters of conspirators, and to leave the open and honourable path, for dark and intricate plots; the mind

* Echard, 485.   † Clarendon, i. 319.

becomes degraded by the artifices it practises, and cunning and subtlety are substituted for those generous emotions and that nobler wisdom, which separate at a vast interval the true Patriot from the intriguing Partisan.

We know too little of the secret history of the parties who were so conspicuous in the civil war. Such active spirits as Hampden and Pym, though they lived in the age of Diaries, appear to have left no memorial of themselves, or of their transactions. They were probably too deeply busied in the plans and schemes of the day. One great man among them, Lord Kimbolton, afterwards Viscount Mandeville, and finally the second Earl of Manchester, wrote memoirs relating to this very party with whom he had acted many years. Even this authentic source of secret history remains imperfect, and is only known by a few important extracts in Nalson's collection.* The simultaneous movements of these parties, the Scotch and the English, sometimes betrayed their secret connexion. On the day the King received the Scottish petition,

* Nalson acknowledges receiving from " Sir Francis North, now Lord-Keeper of the great seal of England, a transcript of some memoirs of the late Earl of Manchester, the originals being written with the Earl's own hand." ii. 206. May not these memoirs be recovered?

there was also presented another signed by twelve English Peers for calling a Parliament, and the shrewd politicians of Edinburgh on this occasion surmised that Haddington and Borthwick had not laboured in vain, and that " the work would shortly begin in that king-dom."*

There is not wanting certain evidence that the King was surrounded by spies, prying into his movements, watching his unguarded hours, and chronicling his accidental expressions. Even in his sleep the King could not elude their scrutiny; his pockets were ransacked for letters to transmit copies to the Covenanters. This treachery was so well known, that Arch-bishop Laud on delivering some important communications requested the King not to trust the papers to his pocket.† We find Se-cretary Nicholas complaining that his own let-ters are seen by other eyes than the King's; and on one occasion, that the secret orders which he received from the King were known before he could convey them to the Lord Keeper.‡

---

* Bishop Guthry's Memoirs, 74. See the Petition in Nalson, ii. 437.

† L'Estrange, Charles I. 196.

‡ Evelyn, 42. Correspondence.

This low degradation of eminent men betraying the secret councils of their Royal master by such humiliating means, is not so rare a circumstance in secret history as one might imagine. The difficulty of procuring a private audience with James the First, induced the Spanish ambassador to watch his opportunity of slipping into his Majesty's pocket those extraordinary charges against Buckingham, which alarmed the King, and probably would have ended in the ruin of the favourite. Anecdotes are related of the Jesuits, respecting their discoveries, picked out of the very foulest papers which a great personage used, and which when he had used he imagined that he had destroyed. A remarkable fact of this kind has not, as far as I know, been published, and as it relates to two illustrious personages, and the transaction is itself as ingenious as it appears authentic, the reader may be interested by its preservation.

De Witt having taken the Prince of Orange (our William the Third) under his government and tuition, in order to be master of all his actions and motions, surrounded him by his own creatures. A *valet de chambre*, who had constantly attended the Prince from a child, was, at the Prince's earnest request, suffered to continue in his service. The Prince had then a constant and very secret correspondence with the English Court ; and on the receipt of these letters usually put them in his waistcoat pocket. One day De Witt in conversation with the Prince, warning him against intrigues dangerous to his Highness, let fall expressions from which the Prince inferred that the pensioner had seen some of his secret letters from England.

The Prince however, with his usual caution, took no notice to any one of his embarrassment, but pondering on the circumstance, when he went to bed, feigned sleep ; and after due time, detected the faithful operations of his valet, who taking out the letters copied them for the pensionary, and then carefully replaced the originals. The Prince still continued to conceal the discovery, but took care in his subsequent letters from England to receive such answers as he wished to have conveyed to De Witt. These by degrees changed the face of affairs, removed the pensioner's jealousies, and ever after kept him in a false security, with regard to his pupil's transactions and correspondences. When the Prince had overcome all his difficulties, and was made Stadt-holder, he confounded his valet by revealing one secret of the English correspondence which he had not yet copied; and complimenting him on the great service he had so unintentionally done his master, by his dextrous secretaryship of the waistcoat-pocket, he dismissed the traitor, not without the charity of a small pension.*

The Marquis of Hamilton was a person not less illustrious than the Pensionary De Witt, and he stands accused of practices not less insidious, actuated perhaps too by a less pardonable motive, the ruin of a rival, and that rival one as great as himself. The famous Earl of Montrose, whom we at first find among the Covenanters, himself acquainted the King with the real occasion of his having joined them. On his return from the Court of France, where he had been a Captain in the Scottish guards, Montrose intended to enter into the King's service, and was advised to make his way through the means of his countryman the Marquis of Hamilton. Hamilton professed every good-will, admiring that romantic gallantry which Cardinal de Retz has so forcibly and so classically described; but Hamilton cunningly insi-

---

* This anecdote was told by D'Allone, Secretary to Queen Mary, and long in the confidence of King William, to Lord ——, "the great friend" of the Rev. Henry Etough, who communicated it in a letter to Dr. Birch.

nuated, that the King was so wholly attached to the English, and so systematically slighted the Scotch, that were it not for his country, he himself would not longer submit to the indignities he endured. To the King, Hamilton in noticing the return of Montrose and his purpose to wait on his Majesty, insinuated that this Earl was so popular among the Scots by an ancient descent from the royal family; that if he were not nipped in the bud, he was one who might occasion much future trouble. When the Earl of Montrose was introduced to the King by Hamilton with great demonstration of affection, Charles too recently tutored to forget his lesson, gave Montrose his hand formally to kiss, but ungraciously turned away in silence. The slighted and romantic hero, indignant at the coldness of that Royalty which best suited his spirit, hastened to Scotland, and threw himself in anger and despair, into the hands of the Covenanters.* But the heart of Montrose remained secretly attached to his Sovereign—and at length he opened a correspon-

---

* This story is told by Heylin in his little curious volume of "Observations on the history of King Charles, by Hamon L'Estrange." p. 205. It is confirmed from other quarters. The subsequent conduct of Hamilton is itself a confirmation.

dence with Charles. A letter of Montrose was taken out of the King's pocket, and the copy transmitted to the Covenanters, which put an end to his influence with that party. The report-.was current, and the fact has been sanctioned by history, that the Marquis of Hamilton had done, or procured to be done, this " foul and midnight deed." Burnet, in whose folio Memoir of the Hamiltons, we never discover a single ambiguous act, or one political tergiversation — has attempted to strike out even this blot from the scutcheon of his hero. He tells us that the letter to the King, was inclosed by Montrose in one he addressed to Sir Richard Graham, who opening the letter carelessly dropped the inclosure, when Sir James Mercer, the bearer of these letters from Scotland, civilly stooping to take up the letter, silently marked the royal address, and hastened to the Scottish camp to tell the tale. This accident, resting on Sir James Mercer's testimony, may be true, but it would not account for the knowledge of the contents of the letter. For this purpose Burnet adds, on his own au. thority, for I find none given, that the council of war insisted that Montrose himself should furnish a copy of his own letter. If this were done, we may be sure it contained no treason.

Montrose in his defence showed that others were corresponding with the Court, and when Lesley accused him of having corresponded with the enemy, the dauntless Montrose in his chivalric manner asked " Who is he who durst reckon the King an enemy?" The affair at that moment had no result. Investigation would have implicated other leaders of the Covenanters. From other quarters indeed we learn that copies of letters addressed by Montrose to the King were transmitted to the Scotch by some bed-chamber men, who searched the King's pockets when he was asleep.* It is probable that the Marquis of Hamilton was not the only Scotchman who thus served his country's cause at the cost of his honour.

Whether it were love of country, or concealed ambition, or some motive less honourable, the insincerity of the Scotch about the person of Charles is very remarkable, from the nobleman to the domestic. The loyal Earl of Argyle advised Charles to keep his son the Earl of Lorn, afterwards the famous Argyle, at Court, and not allow him to return to Scotland, predicting to the King with an honest *naïveté*, that if Lorn once left him " he would

* Bishop Guthry, p. 75. This circumstance rests on other authorities.

wind him a pin." Charles thanked the father
for the counsel, but as the son had been called
up by his warrant, he considered that he ought
not forcibly to retain him, for Charles added
that " it behoved him to be a King of his
word."* Charles, it appears, had conferred many
substantial honours on Argyle—in places—
in titles—and even in donations of money.
As we advance in the investigation of the
Scottish affairs, and particularly in a following
chapter on the Hamiltons, we shall find an unparalleled scene of involved intrigues, of which
many can never be elucidated. But hardly
any surpasses the faithlessness of the son of
Argyle, who on more than one occasion displayed an absolute recklessness of his honour
and his word. It was in one of those ebullitions
when the heart of the perfidious, from its full-
ness, utters what it would at another time conceal, and gains nothing by the avowal, that we
discover his profound dissimulation. When
at length the Earl openly joined the Covenanters, in his maiden speech he assured them
that " from the beginning he had been theirs
—and would have held to the cause as soon
as any did, had it not been, that he conceived
that by attaching himself to the King, and

* Bishop Guthry, 31.

going along with his Council, he was more useful to them than had he from the first declared himself."*

Of the loose notions of Scottish gratitude and of the solemn asseverations of its perpetuity, we have a remarkable instance in the great Scotch General Lesley, who was created Earl of Leven, by the favour, or the policy of Charles. At this unexpected honour the old soldier was so transported that once on his knees he swore, " that he would not only never bear arms against the King but would serve him without asking the cause." This was the inebriation of his loyalty, for in less than two years after, he led the Scotch army against the creator of his honours.

Charles offended his English subjects by conferring on a Scotchman, Sir William Balfour, the Lieutenancy of the Tower. The Parliamentary party were not certain that this hardy Scot was staunch to their cause, and once obtained his removal. They needed not to have been jealous of the passive obedience of the devoted Lieutenant-Governor of the Tower; for Sir William Balfour took an early part with the Parliament; zealously rendered the captivity of Strafford inexorably severe,

* Bishop Guthry's Memoirs, 41.

and resisted the most considerable bribe ever
offered to a Governor, to connive at the escape
of a State-prisoner. Having thus manifested
himself to be worthy of the confidence of the
party, he became one of their ablest commanders, when he had the satisfaction of encoun-
tering his Royal master in arms.

Among the inferior Scots we find frequent
notices of this personal ingratitude to the Monarch. Even the menials of Whitehall de-
famed the Sovereign and the Court. Even
the common feelings of humanity were alien
to the hearts of Scotchmen; for they had all
drawn from the breasts of their nurses the sour
milk of Presbytery and democracy. " Little
William Murray" as Charles affectionately called him, of the bed-chamber, had from his
childhood enjoyed the particular confidence of
Charles, and transacted his most delicate affairs.
Yet on several occasions this mysterious man
raised suspicions of his conduct. It is not
only from Clarendon that we learn the faithlessness of this domestic companion and confidential agent of the manhood of the Monarch;
we draw it from an impartial witness in De
Montreuil, the French Ambassador, who accompanied Charles in the last critical period of his
life. At a moment when the unhappy Mo-

narch was meditating to emigrate, the plan was
entirely left to the care of William Murray,
who was ever flattering the King of its safety ;
yet, adds De Montreuil, Murray is very careful to hinder the King from employing those
who certainly are as able as himself, and far
more sincere. Murray persisted in reiterating
his doubts that Ashburnham would deceive
the King. The impartial Frenchman sarcastically concludes, " Thus I perceive that these
honest persons as zealous for their Prince had
two displeasures ; the one, that their master is
betrayed, and the other that it is not they who
betray him."*

The Scottish Archbishop Spotiswood was so
sensible of the infidelity of his countrymen
that he offered himself as a personal sacrifice,
advising Charles to have a list prepared of all
his counsellors, his household officers and domestic servants, and with his own pen expunge
all the Scots, beginning with the Archbishop
himself, which at least would prevent any complaint of partiality. The state secrets of the
privy-councils of Charles were betrayed. A
Royal Commission for " the discovery of re-
vealers of secrets in council " is surely an anomalous State-paper. One such however we

* Thurloe's State Papers, i. 85. 88. 92.

have from Charles, when the dissolution or continuance of Parliament was agitated in May 1640, with the simple confession that "by what ways or means they were revealed and disclosed, is not yet manifested to us." *

In Scotland, the Scotch were even less to be trusted. The King's Advocate, Sir Thomas Hope, was much more the advocate of the Covenanters. This subtle lawyer had great command over Charles. Having undertaken the restitution of those Church lands of which the nobles had formerly defrauded the Crown, none doubted that by his delays and evasions he was acting in concert with the nobility.† Hamilton, when High Commissioner, complained that all the skill of the King's Advocate only perplexed his resolutions. The King's Advocate could not appear openly in the cause he had secretly espoused, but he failed not to supply the legal points on which Lord Balmerino and Henderson proceeded in their opposition. Most of the Lords of the Council, and officers of State, were unquestionably Cove-

* This singular Commission is preserved in Nalson's collection, i. 344.

† Burnet's History of his own Time, i` 39. — Guthry's Memoirs, 71—89.

nanters, though openly acting contrary to their principles.

The faithlessness of the Scots in their own country may not be difficult to account for— " The Cause," as it was emphatically called, was national ; and the appearance of liberty was on their side — though often disgraced by the mutual intrigues of rivals, and above all by that religious fanaticism which enabled the crafty insurgents to kindle a war which can never terminate by a peace — a holy war !

It is more difficult to satisfy our curiosity on the infidelity of the Scots about the person of the King, and who were residents at the Court of Whitehall. Their ingratitude or their trea_chery could not originate in any contemptuous or unkind treatment of Charles, for we discover only his entire confidence and his confirmed partialities — and the best we can say in favour of these domestic treasons is, that the Scots at London were the same as the Scots at Edinburgh. Malcolm Laing, enlightened and acute, acknowledged that " seldom were the Scotch distinguished for their loyalty." * Did the feudal tyranny of their haughty aristocracy seem more tolerable than the rule of a Sovereign ? Was not the establishment of the

* Laing, iii. 187.

Presbytery the true origin of the spirit of their modern democracy?

There remains a paradox in this history. The devotion of the following generations of Scotchmen to their Stuarts, has been as romantic as that conduct which we have noticed was crafty and treacherous; it seems a problem in human nature and in Scottish history; and would be best solved by that enlightened genius of Scotia, who gives the value of history to fiction, and the charm of his philosophy to the severity of truth.

Thus surrounded by great and by minor conspiracies, and betrayed in his most secret councils — we shall hereafter see how the King himself became the secret object of the contests between the rival and involved intrigues of Scotchmen. The unfortunate King of England now proceeded on principles of State which appeared to him irrefragable — and for some time imagined that the show of his regal authority would put down the insurgency of a whole people.

CHAPTER II.

THE DIFFICULTIES OF CHARLES THE FIRST IN THE FIRST INVASION OF THE SCOTS.

THE system of these commentaries is to pursue our inquiries, independent of the chronological arrangement of events, with which every history of England will furnish the reader. It therefore sometimes happens that we have not only to allude to incidents already noticed, but must necessarily anticipate others which have not yet been told. One art of discovering Truth in history is that of joining its dispersed, but connected facts; facts which were furnished at the time by those who were often unconscious of this secret relation. Thus the horizon of history expands, and a brighter gleam darts through that hazy atmosphere in which past events are necessarily enveloped.

We have shown how the Scottish intrigues were closely connected with those in England;

we shall find that our own revolutionary measures were entirely modelled on those of the
Scots. This principle of discovery is of the utmost importance for the proper comprehension
of the history of this period ; and it is surprising, that none of the writers of our history
have yet struck into this vein. In detecting
the secret intercourse which existed between
the parties at Edinburgh and at London, we
shall obtain the most striking evidence of the
true origin of many obscure and mysterious incidents in the reign of Charles the First ; and
in comparing the proceedings of the Commons
in England with those of the Scottish leaders,
we shall find that the same designs became their
common object. When we come to develope
the character of the Marquis of Hamilton we
shall allude to those great events in the Scottish commotions in which he bore so conspicuous a part ; at present we turn our attention to
the King himself, from the beginning and
through the progress of that great revolution,
for such indeed it was, and the model which a
party at home servilely copied. His motives
and his perplexities may sometimes be ascertained ; and some incidents which historians
have erroneously denied, or have misconceived,
and others which time only has revealed, be-

come revelations of Truth. The personal character of Charles the First accompanied by all
his misfortunes and his errors, is of itself a
study for the painter of man. The inextricable dilemmas, the delusive designs, the wavering hopes and fears in which this unhappy Sovereign was enclosed as in a magical circle, may
excite the sympathy of those who wish not to
extenuate the errors of his policy, and yet who
would not at the same time be ignorant of the
passions of his age. The history of the man is
not less interesting than the history of the Monarch, and a tale of human nature is not less
precious than a history of England.

The moment the solemn " Covenant " was
taken, a term drawn from the inspiration of the
Judaic history, and every true Scotchman became a good Israelite—the moment that " the
Tables," as the Scots meanly called their assemblies of the four great classes of their people,
or as they are ably dignified in the *Mercure
François*, perhaps by Richelieu himself, " the
four Chambers," constituted a national Convention, holding itself independent of the Royal
Council, and assuming the office of Sovereignty,
the revolution became necessarily political. This
moment had been anticipated by the Marquis
of Hamilton in the preceding year. Address-

ing the King, he observed, " Probably this people have somewhat else in their thoughts than
religion. But that must serve for a cloak to
rebellion, wherein for a time they may prevail ;
but to make them miserable and bring them
again to a dutiful obedience, I am confident
your Majesty will not find it a work of long
time, nor of great difficulty, as they have foolishly fancied to themselves."*

In July 1637 the Liturgy was first read at
Edinburgh, and six months afterwards in February 1638 the Scots entered into their Covenant. We detect in the warm historian of the
great presbyterial revolution all the triumph
and exultation of the Militant saint. *" Our
second and glorious Reformation* in 1638, when
this church was again settled upon her own
base, and the rights she claimed from the time
of the Reformation, were restored, so that she
became ' fair as the moon, clear as the sun, and
terrible as an army with banners.'. It is hard
to manage a full cup, and I *shall not take upon
me to defend every step in that happy period.*"†

In January 1639 orders were issued by the
Covenanters for a general drilling throughout

* Lord Hardwicke's State Papers, ii. 118.

† Wodrow's introduction to History of the Sufferings of
the Church of Scotland, p. ii.

the kingdom. " Terrible as an army with banners," which appears only a metaphorical expression in the zealot, was in truth a simple historical fact. They divided and subdivided the kingdom. The Earl of Traquair writes from Edinburgh. " The writers and advocates are the only men busy here, in this time of drilling; and of the writers I dare say the most of them spend more upon powder than they have gained these six months bygone with the pen."* They had secretly supplied themselves abroad by the purchase of ammunition and arms, and had engaged experienced officers and commanders, from their absent countrymen who had been trained to arms in the school of the great military genius of the age. A small sum, and busy agents from Richelieu, had served to kindle the flame of insurgency, but such was the national poverty that it could never have maintained its army. The spirit of the people, long unused to war, was roused by those great leaders of demo_ cracy, the Presbyters in their pulpits, who pro_ nounced the curse of Meros on those who came not to the help of the Lord against the mighty. The enthusiasm flew from rank to

* The Earl of Traquair to the Marquis of Hamilton. Hardwicke State Papers, ii. 125.

rank ; all men pressed forward as volunteers.
When the Marquis of Hamilton anchored before Leith, he witnessed the gentry labouring
on a bastion, and ladies of the first condition,
busied in the trenches.

But if this enthusiasm had been caught by
the people, the leaders of the Covenant, and
their wary General, Alexander Lesley, were
proceeding with a more human policy. Conscious of their feeble resources in case of a defeat, or what would have proved as fatal, a
prolonged campaign, they studied to avoid the
appearance of an offensive war. They held
out no menace, but they urged a plea; they
had armed, not to invade England, but to defend themselves from an English invasion.
When the King issued a proclamation that
they should not approach nearer the Royal
camp than ten miles, it was dextrously obeyed.
Such was the infant strength of the Rebellion !
The Scots had taken the precaution to disperse
by their pedlars in their packs " an Information to all good Christians," about " the true
Religion" and " the Lord's own cause," which
were made palatable to the English Puritans
with sprinklings of Scriptural allusions, where
the Sanballats " and such like" were pointed at,
who opposed the building of the New Jerusa-

lem by Ezra and Nehemiah.* Such was the
style of those Scotch patriots, and such long
afterwards, was to be that of the English.
Letters had also been dispatched to some at
Court vindicating their proceedings, solemnly
protesting that they designed no harm to England, and expecting no hostility from them;
letters not ill received among some eminent
persons at Court.†

The Scots, in their first invasion, were long
influenced by motives of delicacy from ven-
turing to cross the Tweed. The insurgents
contented themselves in exercising their tactics
at home, possessing themselves of the forts of
their own country. They only made war by
acts of peace, and renewed their " humble desires" only by petitions, armed at once to strike
or to sign.

An unpublished letter, which is in the State-
paper office, from Edward Norgate, who followed the English army, exhibits the misery of
the country and the consequent confusion
which prevailed in a disorderly army.

            " Barwick, 29th May, 1639.
" The King made a halt at Alnwick, upon some alarm
that was in the camp, whereof he received information from

---

* This State-paper is preserved in Frankland, 739.
† Burnet's Memoirs of the Hamiltons, 116.

my Lord General, so that persons of great quality lay in
their coaches, carts from the town being little and company
great. So at Morpeth I staid, but the next day went on to
Alnwick, whence the King was gone that morning to the
army at Gaswick five miles short of Barwick, for the alarm
was false.

"The next morning passing through Belfort (nothing like
the name either in strength or beauty, it being the most
miserable beggarly sodden town, or town of sods, that ever
was made in an afternoon of loam and sticks), there I
stumbled upon Mr. Murray one of the cup-bearers to
his Majesty, who had taken up the very and only room
in the only alehouse. Thither he kindly invited me, to a
place as good as a death's head or memento for mortality,
top and sides being all earth and the beds no bigger than
so many coffins. Indeed it was for beauty and conveniency
like a covered saw-pit. Our host was a moving uncleanly
skeleton; I asked him who had condemned him thither.
He said, *durum telum necessitas.* That he with fourscore
other gentlemen of quality (a horse troop) being billeted the
night before at a little village three miles further, coming
to the place after a long and weary march, found no other
accommodation than a dark and rainy night; in all the
town not one loaf of bread nor quart of beer, not a lock of
hay nor peck of oats, and little shelter for horse or man;
only a few hens they roasted and eat without bread, but not
without water. Their horses had nothing. He told me I
should find the army in little better condition, the first com-
panies having stood in water up to the ancles by reason of
the rain; that in forty-eight hours they had no bread, nor
other lodging but on the wet ground, the camp being low
near the sea-side, nor any shelter but the fair heavens. After
dinner I rode to the army where I think there was not above

seven thousand foot; the horse elsewhere dispersed into villages about three thousand. Here I found the cause of the late want was for want of carriages to bring bread to the army, but now they were better accommodated, yet lay *sub dio.* The King was in his tent about where some of the Lords had pitched theirs. I think none that loves him but must wish the army ten times doubled, and those ten fifteen times better accommodated; especially seeing this town as ill provided as the other, and the hourly reports of the Scots advancing ten thousand in one place and fifteen thousand in another to second their fellows. Yet are we told they come with a petition, but it seems they mean to dictate the reference to themselves, wherein I believe Sir Edward Powell will have little to do.

"To this town (Barwick) I came last night, when Sir John Borrowes and I could hardly get a loaf of bread to our supper; a black-cake we got scarce edible. I went to Mr. Secretary's (Sir John Coke) to beg one, and had it given me with much difficulty, Mr. May protesting that his master was glad to send to my Lord Governor for bread for him and his, the day before, and that he got but two half-penny loaves. This day our host fetching us some to dinner, had it snatched from him by a soldier, who much complain. The people here say that if some present and speedy order be not taken, they shall want bread for their families, the soldiers devouring what can be got, and the Scots, by whom it seems the town was formerly supplied with victual of all kinds, and that in a plentiful manner and cheap, having declared they fear extremely the want of provisions, the country in Northumberland side being very barren, but plentiful beyond the boundary towards Scotland."*

---

* The writer Edward Norgate was Secretary to Winde_ bank. Birch transcribed this letter from one in the State_ paper office. Sloane MSS. 4176.

Both the armies at length were encamped opposite to each other, and found themselves in an extraordinary situation. At the time, the causes of the unexpected results of this formidable appearance on both sides, were not known, and were therefore misrepresented.

The Royal army had been hastily formed by the King; Charles relied on the imposing pomp of his splendid cavalry, the flower of the English nobility and gentry, and on the number of his troops, to awe the Scots into submission. Ludlow aptly describes this army as " raised rather out of compliment than affection;" and Clarendon, evidently with pain to himself, has confirmed this opinion. " The King summoned most of the nobility of the kingdom without any consideration of their affections how they stood disposed to that service, presuming that the glory of such a visible appearance of the whole nobility would at once terrify and reduce the Scots." Clarendon adds one of those profound reflections which we rarely find but in this " Lord Chancellor of Human Nature," that " such kinds of uniting do often produce the greatest confusions; when more and greater men are called together, than can be united in affections or interests, in the necessary differences which

arise from thence, they quickly come to know
each other so well, as they rather break into
several divisions than join any one public interest; and from hence have always arisen the
most dangerous factions."*   But a royal care
unknown to Clarendon lay hidden in the
King's breast.   Charles was aware of the moral
condition of his army.   The Marquis of Hamilton had in the gallery at Whitehall confidentially revealed to the King the fatal secret,
that the English nobility and general officers
were far from being heartily engaged in this
war.   They were not to be trusted; the Scots
at Court had succeeded in impressing on the
minds of some that they were little interested
in a *bellum Episcopale;* nor was it probably
unknown to Charles that the officers and pri-
vates in his army on their march had openly
declared that they would not fight to maintain
the pride and power of the Bishops.†   Many
also who took no interest in the factions of the
day, but consulted their own quiet and the
King's happiness, vented their contempt on the
poverty of Scotland; and as May tells us, the
younger courtiers were usually heard to wish
Scotland under water, or that the old wall

* Clarendon, i. 206.
† Whitelocke's Memorials, 33.

of Severus was re-edified. Others of graver thoughts, as Comines was then a favourite historian, pointed out the story of Charles the Duke of Burgundy's war with the Swiss, who, had he taken them all prisoners, could not have paid a ransom to the value of the spurs and ˙bridles in his camp. And a verse of Juvenal was frequent in their mouths:

> Curandum in primis ne magna injuria fiat
> Fortibus et miseris.*

It is certain that Charles was aware of the neutrality of some, and of the treachery of others of his commanders; for when the infidelity of the Earl of Holland, at a subsequent day, was noticed to him, the King replied " Had that army been in earnest he would have chosen other commanders." It is evident therefore that the King depended entirely on " the glory of such a visible appearance." Charles, in fact, was leading only the phantom of an army. Charles betrayed his alarm at the distempered condition of his army when he was reduced to the extraordinary expedient of requiring a *Sacramentum militare.* This was a subscription to a solemn profession of loyalty and obedience, and at the same time disclaim-

* Sat. 8—121.

ing any correspondence with the Insurgents.
"The Scots," sarcastically observes Lord Clarendon, "took it to a man without grieving
their conscience, or reforming their manners."
But an open refusal came from a quarter
whence perhaps it was not expected, however
it might be suspected. Two English noblemen, afterwards well known in the civil war
Lord Say and Sele and Lord Brooke, in the
King's presence sullenly refused their signatures. These Lords ingeniously averred that
it was against law to impose oaths not enjoined
by law ; and further, being ignorant of the laws
of Scotland neither could they decide whether
the Covenanters were rebels. The King indignant at this studied insult offered in the
face of his whole army, and doubtless dreading
that the example of these Lords might prove
infectious, immediately ordered them to be
put under restraint. Charles desired that the
Attorney and the Solicitor should be privately
consulted, whether these Lords could be proceeded against criminally, but the King found
that "the cunning and jesuitical answers," as
Secretary Windebank calls them, "only concealed their malignity and aversion to his
Majesty's service." The sturdy refusal of these
Lords threatened alarming consequences at that

critical moment—they indeed had only anticipated the unhappy day that was shortly to
befall England ; and their conduct had instantly
operated, for those who had willingly subscribed this bond of loyalty now signed another
paper declaring the sense in which they had
accepted it. This vain expedient of securing
the fidelity of the faithless was thrown aside.

While the mind of the perplexed Monarch
was suspended between doubt and fear, amidst
the disaffection and reluctant duty, which prevailed in the Royal camp, a far different scene
broke forth among the joyous tents of a people
who once more beheld their native hills covered
with a national army. There a veteran and
unlettered soldier, aged and weather-beaten,
deformed and diminutive in his person, but
renowned for his skill in all military affairs, was
recalled from foreign campaigns to the land of
his fathers. His sagacity was prompt to master
difficulties, and his enterprise was too prudent,
ever to have failed in good fortune. But the
military virtue now most to be valued—the
knowledge of the human heart—was eminently
his own. Lesley was a Scotchman who in
foreign lands had never forgotten the native
humours of his countrymen, and now marched
with them as if he had long been their neigh-

bour and their companion. In the plain simplicity of his language, he told the Noble, and
the meanest gentleman, that " volunteers were
not to be commanded like soldiers of fortune.
Brothers they were all, and engaged in one
cause." He flattered to command. Even the
haughty nobles, whose rivalries had been dreaded, loved the wisdom and authority of " the
old little crooked soldier" as Baillie naturally
paints him—and his undisciplined levies acquired at least that great result of all discipline, a love of obedience. The gentleman was
nothing the worse lying weeks together on the
ground, or standing all night in arms in the
storm, and the lusty peasantry raised their
hearts as they mingled with the nobles of the
land, and their own " Men of God." Their
eyes watched this " Captain of Israel." Lesley
had called on his country in the name of God,
and the Scottish camp seemed the tabernacle
of the Lord of Hosts. Crowded with spiritual
pastors, these sent forth their heralds to all their
Presbyteries, exhorting the absent, or reproach-
ing the loiterer. As the army advanced, its
numbers multiplied. Every company had a
new banner waving before the tent-door of its
captain, blazoned by the Scottish arms and inscribed " For Christ's Crown and Covenant."

The reveil called them to solemn prayer at the dawn; the drum beat to a sermon under the roof of Heaven, which twice a-day convinced them of the righteousness of their cause; and as the sun went down in the still repose of evening, the melodies of psalmody—the extemporaneous inspiration of some prophesying pietist, or exhortations from some folded page of the sacred volume, refreshed the spirits of these patriotic enthusiasts, who in combating on earth seemed to be possessing themselves of Heaven itself. " True," says Baillie, " there was swearing and cursing and brawling, whereat we grieved," but as the good Principal walked through their tents he caught the contagious fervour of this singular union of insurrection and religion. " I found the favour of God shining upon me, and a sweet, meek, humble, yet strong and vehement spirit leading me all along." The valiant Saint was ready either to start to battle, or to chorus a psalm.

The assumed humility in the supplications of the Covenanters induced Charles to imagine that they were intimidated at the view of the English army. A second proclamation more authoritatively commanded their submission; but one day when a very inferior Scotch force put to a shameful flight the whole cavalry of

Lord Holland, the determined spirit of the Scots was confirmed, as well as the suspicions and the dread of the King of the disposition of his own troops. The Marquis of Hamilton lay inactive at sea, and Lord Holland was a fugitive on land. At London the King was censured for not more vigorously quelling the Scotch revolt. Those indeed who were distant from the scene, and knew little or nothing of the state of both armies, wondered at the King losing this opportunity of chastising his rebels. Contemporaries rarely possess the secrets reserved for their posterity. The Covenanters were alike surprised at the inactivity of the English, which they ascribed to a refined policy designed to waste by delay their limited resources. They were acquainted at that moment neither with the indifference of the whole army, nor the disappointments of Charles in a foreign negociation for Spanish troops, who, it was rumoured, had landed in England, and also in some expected levies from Ireland. The Scots in this first incursion were awed too by the fear of rousing the jealousy of the English people. A secret intercouse indeed had already been opened with some English friends, but no party, however, had yet risen in strength openly to espouse their cause. We learn this

from Baillie—" the hope of England's conjunc-
tion is but small, for all the good words we
heard long ago from our friends." This is a
pointed allusion of the earliest intercourse of
the Covenanters with some of our own patriots.
He proceeds—" all this time when their occasion was great to have kythed their affections
both to us and their own liberties, there was
nought among them but either a deep sleep or
silence."* They knew they wanted not for
friends at Court, nor among the citizens, who
were not displeased to see the Scots in arms
against the King, and who were not desirous
of an English victory, supposing, says May,
that "the sword which subdued the Scots must
destroy their own liberties." But these friendships of the parties were yet callow, and not to
be too roughly handled. So jealous was our
Parliament at times of their invading friends,
that when the Scottish army after the pacification of Berwick intended to march through
this garrison town, a wooden bridge was ordered to be thrown over the Tweed at some distance from the town that they might be separated from the townsmen. The day had not
yet come, although it was fast approaching,
when the English Parliamentarians were to

* Baillie, i. 183.

vote their Scottish invaders " a friendly assistance," and that the Scots were to return their
solemn thanks for the style of " brethren" given
to them in the vote of the House.*

As the King from the first had never contemplated a war, and as the Scots did not know
whether they might begin one, both armies
were precisely at that point which would admit
of a treaty. Lesley decided on a great move_
ment. " He gave not out obscurely his pur_
pose to approach the English camp," says
Baillie. The enthusiasm of the people had
daily augmented his forces, but, destitute of
the resources to support a defensive war, this
sagacious general foresaw that his forces would
have dispersed as rapidly as they had assembled,
in the inactivity of a prolonged campaign ; and
that even his numerical strength might be fatal
in an impoverished land. The approach of
Lesley excited an alarm in the Royal camp.
At this critical moment an ancient page of the
King's was permitted to pass over to the Scottish camp on a visit to his friends. There he
hinted that if they would please to supplicate
the King, the happiness of peace might yet be
obtained. This light motion was not neglected
— an intercourse was granted, and the King's

* Rushworth, iv. 152.

honour was thus saved. Some English historians have presumed that the Scots were the first who solicited the peace, but Baillie has preserved the name of the old page who doubtless was the messenger of the pacific overture.

Four Scotch Commissioners, among whom were the Earl of Rothes, a voluptuary, and Lord Loudon, an able intriguer and necessitous man, both long afterwards gained over by Charles — met in the tent of the Earl of Arundel the English general, to confer on the adjustment of the minuter points in dispute. An extraordinary scene opened. Unexpectedly, at least to the Scottish Commissioners, the King himself entered — and taking his seat at the end of the table, the others then standing up, a remarkable conversation ensued. It was taken down at the time in notes, and sent by the Earl of Arundel to Laud.

This is a very dramatic narrative, and in some respects leads us to an intimate acquaintance with the manners of Charles the First. The propriety of the King's appearance at this conference may be doubtful; it would check the necessary freedom of discussion; but Charles on various critical occasions too easily flattered himself that he could compose all differences by his own presence; his sincerity might be greater than his prudence. On the present occasion the King seems not to have been more peremptory than a man who delivers himself without reserve, patient though dignified; and since we know that this meeting was not concerted, the spontaneous language of the King will show that his capacity was no ordinary one, and that his earnestness was not a mere form and show of obtruding royalty, designed more to gratify its own vanity than inspired by any deeper interest in the affairs of the people.

Dr. Lingard truly observes that "Charles for several days debated every point with an earnestness of argument and a tone of superiority which seems to have imposed on the hearers of both nations." This penurious commendation hardly does justice to Charles. We have a warmer account from Baillie. "The King was very sober, meek and patient to hear all. The King missed Henderson"—(with whom Charles at a distant day was to hold a famous controversy on Ecclesiastical polity)—"and Johnston"—(afterwards the hot Covenanter Wariston.)—"The King was much delighted with Henderson's discourse, but not so with Johnston's. Much and most free communing there was of the highest matters of

State. It is likely his Majesty's ears had never been tickled with such discourses, yet he was most patient of them all, and loving of clear reason. His Majesty was ever the longer the better loved of all that heard him, as one of the most just, reasonable, sweet persons they ever had seen." Of this remarkable conference which occurred on the first day, unknown to Clarendon and Hume, I shall select such passages as most enter into the character of Charles the First.

THE KING. — My Lords, you cannot but wonder at my unexpected coming hither ; which I would myself have spared, were it not to clear myself of that notorious slander laid upon me, that I shut my ears from the just complaints of my people in Scotland, which I never did, nor shall. But on the other side I shall expect from them, to do as subjects ought ; and upon these terms I shall never be wanting to them.

ROTHES.—The Earl of Rothes answered but with a low voice, that his sentences could hardly at any distance be understood. The effect of his speech was a justification of all their actions.

THE KING.—My Lord, you go the wrong

way in seeking to justify yourselves and actions ; for though I am not come hither with
any purpose to aggravate your offences, but to
make the fairest construction of them that
they may bear and lay aside all differences ;
yet if you stand on your justification, I shall
not command, but where I am sure to be
obeyed.

ROTHES.—Our coming is not to justify our
actions, or to capitulate, but to submit ourselves to the censure (judgment) of your Majesty, if so be we have committed any thing
contrary to the laws and customs of our
country.

THE KING.—I never took upon me to give
end to any difference, but where both parties
first submitted themselves unto my censure
(judgment), which if you will do, I shall do
you justice to the utmost of my knowledge,
without partiality.

ROTHES.—Our religion and conscience is
now in question, which ought to receive another trial.   Besides, neither have we power of
ourselves to conclude any thing, but to represent it to our fellows.

THE KING.—If you have no power to submit it to my judgment, go on with your justification.

ROTHES.—This is it which we desired, that thereby the subjects of both kingdoms may come to the truth of our actions; for ye know not the reason of our actions, nor we of yours.

THE KING.—Sure I am, you are never able to justify all your actions; the best way therefore were, to take my word, and to submit all to my judgment.

ROTHES.—We have reason to desire liberty for our public justification, seeing our cause hath received so much wrong, both in the foundation, relation, and the whole carriage of the business.

LOUDON.—Since your Majesty is pleased to dislike the way of justification, we therefore will desert it; for our purpose is no other but to enjoy the freedom of that religion which we know your Majesty and your kingdom do profess; and to prevent all alterations of that religion which we profess. Which finding ourselves likely to be deprived of, we have taken this course, wherein we have not behaved ourselves any otherwise than becometh loyal subjects. Our sole desires are, that what is point of religion may be judged by the practice of the church established in that kingdom.

THE KING.—Here his Majesty interrupted this long intended declaration, saying that he would not answer any proposition which they made, nor receive any, but in writing. They withdrew themselves to a side-table and wrote a supplication—to ratify the acts of the assembly at Glasgow that all Ecclesiastical matters be determined by the Kirk — and that a peace be granted and all incendiaries suffer punishment.

This supplication having been read, his Majesty said he could give no sudden answer to it — in fact it included the great point of the abolishment of Episcopacy.

THE KING.—Here you have presented your desires; as much as to say, Give us all we desire; which if no other than settling of your religion and laws established, I never had other intentions than to settle them. His Majesty withal told them that their propositions were a little too rude at the first. (Charles alluded to the ratifying the democratic acts of the Glasgow assembly.)

LOUDON.—We desire your Majesty that our grounds laid down may receive the most favourable construction.

THE KING.—I protest I have no intention to surprise you, but I withal desire you to consider how you stand too strictly upon your propositions.—I intend not to alter any thing in

your laws or religion which has been settled
by Sovereign authority.   Neither will I at all
encroach upon your laws by my prerogative;
but the question will be at last, Who shall be
the judge of the meaning of those laws?   His
Majesty then further told them that their pretences were fair, but their actions otherwise.

ROTHES.—We desire to be judged by the
written word of the laws.   Here he proceeded
in justifying the assembly at Glasgow.

THE KING.—You cannot expect the ratification of that assembly, seeing the election of
the Members of it were not lawful, nor was
there any free choice of them.

ROTHES.—There is no other way for settling
differences in religion but by such an assembly
of the Kirk.

THE KING. — That assembly was neither
free nor lawful, and so consequently the proceedings could not be lawful.   But when I say
one thing, and you another, who shall judge?

The Earl of Rothes offered to bring the book
of the assembly to the King to prove its legality—Lord Loudon explained the nature of
the presbyterial government—by the book of
discipline—the work of the earlier Puritans.

THE KING. — The book of discipline was
never ratified by King or Parliament; but

ever rejected by them. Besides this, there were never in any assembly, so many lay Elders as in this.

ROTHES. — In some assemblies there have been more lay Elders than of the Clergy. In this assembly every lay Elder was so well instructed as that he could give judgment of any one point which should be called in question before them.

THE KING.—To affirm thus much in truth, seems very ridiculous; namely that every illiterate person should be able to be a fit judge of faith and religion. This indeed is very convenient and agreeable to their disposition, for by that means they might choose their own religion.

The King in closing the present conference observed, " I have all this while discoursed with disadvantage, seeing what I say I am obliged to make good; but ye are men of honour too, and therefore whatever ye assent unto, if others refuse, ye are also obliged to make it good."

Lord Loudon once affirmed the power of the Glasgow Assembly to punish any offences —Rothes, at a later conference, in plain terms affirmed the power of the Assembly to be so great that were he the King, it had authority

to excommunicate him also.*   Against this
principle, perfectly papal, the note-writer observes that his Majesty excellently disputed,
could reason have satisfied them.   Charles here
had. certainly the strongest argument.   It is
curious to .observe the advocates for popular
freedom eagerly contending for passive obedience, and a Monarch supposed to be a stickler
·for arbitrary government exposing the absurdity and injustice of a dangerous despotism.   So
contradictory seems human nature, when man
acts on his own temporary views or individual
interests.   We may regret that we have no
notes of the conference of the fierce republican
Wariston with Charles, though at a distant day
we have the King's sentiments on Republics
in a conversation with Harrington, the author
of the Oceana, and which at the time impressed

* This was no oratorical flourish of the Earl of Rothes,
but the avowed principle of the Presbytery.   Our first English Puritans under Cartwright, had maintained, not only
that " the Church could inflict its censures on Royalty,"
but that it possessed a supremacy of power.   Calvin's policy
was to make the Church an independent power in the state,
but this seems to have been but a first step ; there are
passages in his " Institution" which have an evident ten-
dency to Cartwright's and Knox's system.

that singular Commonwealth's man with a high notion of the King's character.

The peculiarity of this state of warfare was terminated by a treaty as peculiar; a treaty consisting more of verbal explanations in vague conversations, than of written agreements, or articles afterwards ratified. The Scots desired to have their religion and liberty according to the laws of the Kingdom—intending those that were in force before James's accession to the crown of England, and Charles, such as had been enacted since that time. Both sides must have perceived the ambiguity, but both were desirous of not coming to extremities. The Scots with twelve thousand men had not imagined that Charles could have raised an army of twenty thousand; but Charles was in no less perplexity than themselves, as he feared treachery among his own troops. The Scots wished delay in their negociation, and the King hoped the day would come when he could explain the terms. The Scots would only swear to the true religion of 1580; Charles insisted that the true religion was in 1606, and was more manifest in the present year of 1638. The King would not acknowledge, and the Scots would not disclaim the Glasgow Assem_bly. This difficulty was obviated by the King

consenting to call another assembly to decide
on Ecclesiastical affairs.   From that tender
subject the removal of Episcopacy, Charles con-
vulsively shrunk; while the Scottish Commissioners on their knees in vain implored that
great boon, it was evaded on the plea that the
King would not forestall the decision of the
future assembly.   Some harsh expressions in
the King's declaration were softened, but when
the Scots complained that it represented them
as if they had struck at the Monarchy, they
were answered that so much was due to the
Royal honour, and that the King's reputation
abroad required that his style should preserve
the regal authority.   Ambiguous sentences
were explained in conference, and the Scots on
their return to their camp set them down in
writing, which in due time, says Baillie, " shall
see the light in their own royal and noble
phrase."   " There were not two present," says
Clarendon, " who did agree in the same relation
of what was said and done, and which was
worse, not in the same interpretation.   An
agreement was made in which nobody meant
what others believed he did."

Malcolm Laing has severely charged the
King with dissimulation on this treaty ;* but

* Laing's Hist. of Scotland, iii. 171.

he does not lay the same charge on his own countrymen. When the treaty was signed, if treaty it can be called, an intercourse took place between all parties, and the result shortly appeared on both sides. The Scots cemented their secret friendships and excited the sympathy of many new ones; and under the tents where they had signed the peace, they concerted future plans of more successful invasion; a clearer understanding between some of the English and themselves appeared to all the world on their second incursion. Nor was the King less active in his accessions; Montrose now first discovered himself to Charles; several of the Scottish Lords were mollified by Royal condescensions, and the ambiguous Hamilton had so adroitly insinuated himself into the favour of the Covenanters, that he had slid into their secrets, and with admirable fidelity betrayed them to the King.

It is evident that the pacification of Berwick was as little sincere on one side, as on the other; and as is not uncommon, the parties with great truth reciprocally accuse each other. Equally impatient for peace, both dreaded the dubious issue of a battle, and both were alike unprovided with the means of maintaining their strength, even at the cost of a victory. The

exhausted exchequer of Charles had levelled
him to the poverty of the Scots. The determination to combat, rather than to retreat, was
probably as strong on one side as the other.
The language of the ingenuous Baillie is affecting,—though a Covenanter he had a great
reverence for Majesty. " Many secret motives
there were on all hands that spurred on to
this quick peace. What to have done when
we came to Tweed-side we were very uucer-
tain. The King would rather have hazarded
his person than have raised his camp. Had
he incurred any skaith (harm) or been disgraced
with a shameful flight, our hearts had been
broken for it; and likely all England behoved
to have risen in revenge." The Scots, it is
evident, at that moment feared the English
nation as much as the King.

This "quick peace" leaving unsettled the
great contending points, and every condition ambiguous or indefinite, could only be one of those
delusive treaties, which serve to prepare the
strongest party for war. It was a breathing
space for two armies who could not separate
without a determination to conquer; it was
a pacification, but it was not a peace. A treaty
in which more was explained verbally than
was written, could be but a patched-up peace,

not made to hold long together. The ink was scarce dry ere the treaty was broken. At Edinburgh they reproached their chiefs with apostasy; at London they lamented the disgrace incurred by an inglorious campaign.

At this moment we may be curious to discover the real feelings of Charles. They may be deemed romantic! Pleased probably with his partial interviews with Montrose and other Scottish Lords, he fancied that the presence of Majesty had not lost its charm over the people. In the warmth of his emotions, Charles, often hasty in his resolves, proposed to accompany his Scottish subjects on their return to Edinburgh — to hold the Parliament in person. He imagined a popular triumph to awaken the affections of a whole people. Charles becomes a self-painter in writing to Wentworth from Berwick.

" As for my affairs here, I am far from thinking that at this time I shall get half of my will, though I mean by the grace of God, to be in person both at Assembly and Parliament; for which I know many wise men blame me, and it may be you among the rest. And I confess not without many weighty and considerable arguments, which I have neither time to repeat or to confute — only this believe me, nothing

but my presence at this time in that country
can save it from irreparable confusion; yet I
will not be so vain as absolutely to say, that
I can. Wherefore my conclusion is, that if
I see a great probability, I go; otherwise not,
but return to London, or take other counsels."*

There is no dissimulation in this confidential
communication. The sorrowful and perplexed
state of a mind so variously agitated; the impulse that hurries him in his own person to
pacify the troubles of a people, and above all
the modest check which his own judgment
imposes on his sanguine hopes, are the characteristics of the man — and when we pause
on many similar effusions, we may at least
wonder how it was possible for such a man
ever to have been the absolute despot, which
the injustice of party and historical calumnies
so often set before us.

Charles did not pursue his romantic progress
to fill Fergus' chair in the palace of his ancestors. A fresh revolt had broken out in the
streets of Edinburgh on the surrender of the
Castle to the former royalist governor. "The
devout wives," as Guthry calls them who were
not apt to go on these messages without being
sent, again opened their campaign of Presby-

* Strafford's Letters, ii. 362.

tery, by an onset upon the Royal Commissioner the Earl of Traquair, with " their
neaves," (fists.) They broke my Lord Treasurer's White Staff in pieces before his face;
a circumstance which more endeared him to
the King, says Baillie, at the moment his credit
was cracking. When the Representative of
Majesty appealed for the chastisement of the
ringleaders, the Magistracy solemnly voted the
Treasurer a new staff!—thus estimating the
indignity the Crown had suffered—at the
damage of sixpence!

The King, still intent to open the Scottish
Parliament in person, required fourteen of the
Scottish Leaders to attend him at Berwick.
Rothes, Montrose, and Johnston came, but the
rest with Argyle contrived to raise a mob at
the moment of their pretended departure. At
the water-gate they were stopped on the pretence that the King would detain them. The
King repeated his summons, but he found
himself distrusted. These Lords feared that
Charles knew more of them than probably at
this moment the King did.

The ministers of Charles were alarmed at
these continued tumults; Secretary Windebank could not think without horror of the
King exposing himself to the mercy of a people

weary of monarchical Government, " who know your Majesty's sacred person is the only impediment to the Republic, liberty and confusion which they have designed themselves." Wentworth's caution had perhaps more weight. . " So total a defection in that people is not to be trusted with your sacred person over early, if at all." The distrust of the Scottish Lords was indignantly felt, and Charles could no longer confide in them who had no confidence in him. The King returned home from the dream of the pacification of Berwick, melancholy and unsatisfied, convinced that he had carried no single point, while from Hamilton and Montrose he was but too well informed of the dark designs of his enemies. The triumphal march which he had once promised himself, had only closed in an interview of two hostile armies, but it had shown the world, at home and abroad, that the Scottish insurgents were a nation.

Charles seems to have vented his disappointments in the graceless manner with which he disbanded his own army; he suddenly dismissed the gentry without any acknowledgment of their loyalty in leaving their homes at his call; nor did he scatter honours on those who had aspired to them. This impolitical conduct of the King was not forgotten when in the following year he had another army to collect — few cared to attend, and many abandoned him in the civil war. If Charles be often accused of dissimulation, it must also be acknowledged that he too often acted from spontaneous feelings, hasty and undisguised.

CHAPTER III.

CHARLES THE FIRST RESISTS THE SEDUCTIONS OF CARDINAL RICHELIEU.

THE vindication of the maritime rights of England formed the most glorious period in the reign of Charles the First. The King seems to have found himself more master of events, following only his own dispositions in asserting the independence of the British Crown and the security of his people. From 1630 to 1637 he probably anticipated none of those dark evils which lay brooding among his northern subjects and his dismissed Parliamentarians. Before the troubles broke out in Scotland, perhaps the most secret agents in the approaching revolution possessed as little foresight as Charles the First and his ministers.

It was at this period in 1637 that another political event occurred of not inferior importance than the Sovereignty of the Sea; it was

an event in which Charles the First maintained the independence of his Crown, among
foreign powers, guided by the true interests
of England. Those state-interests, I presume,
must ever be an unremitting watchfulness over
the growth of her neighbours' influence, and
the secret intrigues of their cabinets ; hence to
keep down the stronger, and to strengthen the
weaker, but above all things to preserve England from becoming a passive instrument of
the dangerous projects of an ambitious rival,
or a seductive enemy.

In the present case, Charles the First performed the duty of an English Monarch, however fatally the event terminated for his own
happiness.

Our popular historians, some of whom, it
must be granted, were not supplied with the
copious materials we now possess, and some of
whom would certainly have wanted both the
necessary diligence and candour, had they possessed them, have accused Charles the First
of a blind and sometimes of "a Popish" inclination towards Spain. On this prejudiced
principle, they have not hesitated to charge
as "a mere pretence" the danger into which
Charles considered the nation was thrown by
a secret league between France and the United

Provinces. Of the reality of this secret league
we can no longer doubt. We find it was discovered to Charles by the Spanish resident in
July 1634. France however had been busily
intriguing with the States-General two years
earlier, in 1632.

It was however not before five years afterwards, in 1637, that the project matured by
Cardinal Richelieu, assumed a tangible shape,
presenting itself openly to the English King.
The gestation of a great political design is
sometimes painfully slow, the birth is delayed
by its secrecy, and the pangs seem proportioned to its magnitude.

The plan of Richelieu, which we saw at
work by the intercepted dispatches in 1634,
and which was now settled in 1637, was in concert with the Prince of Orange, to seize the
maritime towns of the Spanish Netherlands,
the last remains of the ancient dominion of
Spain, from which important conquest, resulted
nothing short of the annihilation of the Spanish name and influence among the Flemings.
But before this bold enterprise could be opened, and even before it could be well resolved by
the Prince of Orange, the Cardinal deemed it
necessary to secure the neutrality of England;
and to ascertain the disposition of the cabinet

of Whitehall, the Cardinal dispatched the
Count D'Estrades with very particular instructions.

Richelieu, aware that he stood not in the:
good. graces of the Queen of England, whose
mother Mary of Medicis he had abandoned
to her destiny, commissioned the Count D'Estrades to offer Henrietta every possible proof
of his devotion to her, and intreating immediately to be put to the test, he desired the
honour of being made acquainted with her
wishes, that they might be instantly accomplished. Should the Count find the Queen
favourable, he was to deliver the Cardinal's
letter written by his own hand—but should
Henrietta continue unfriendly to the Cardinal,
D'Estrades in that case was to present the letter of her brother, the King of France.

D'Estrades, who on his arrival in England
had to execute with the utmost promptitude,
as we shall see, affairs of the most opposite
nature, hastened without a day's loss to the
Queen. He found Henrietta greatly indisposed against the Cardinal. The letter of his
Eminence was therefore suppressed, but her
brother's referred her to Count D'Estrades,
who acquainted her with the object of his
mission, requesting the Queen would use all

her influence to persuade her Royal husband to preserve a strict neutrality. Henrietta declared that " she never intermeddled in affairs of this nature," but in compliance with her brother's wish she would mention the subject to the King her husband, appointing the Ambassador, who pressed for time, to return at five o'clock.

When D'Estrades came he found the Queen in ill-humour; she complained that " he had been the occasion of her suffering a severe reprimand for having proposed to the King to remain neuter while the sea-ports of Flanders were to be attacked, but the King himself would expect the Count at six o'clock.

The Queen's reception was no favourable prognostic. The Ambassador was however graciously received by Charles. D'Estrades having opened his negotiation, laid great stress on the numerous advantages the King of England would derive from preserving a rigid neutrality. Masters of the sea, the English would have the whole commerce of Flanders at their disposal, and the supply of all the armies, both the Allied and the Spanish, which could only be carried on by English shipping. But his Eminence offered, apparently a less resistible seduction, for the Cardinal not only assured

Charles that he was most desirous of preserving
an union of interests with the two Courts, but
that his Eminence would pledge himself to
persuade his Royal Master to aid and support
Charles against any of his rebellious subjects.

Charles's reply to the French Ambassador
was prompt and decisive. " He wished for the
friendship of his brother — but friendship there
could be none if it were prejudical to his honour, or injurious to the interest of his people.
Should the ports of Flanders be attacked by
France and Holland, the English fleet would
be in the Downs ready for action, and with
an army of fifteen thousand men." Charles
thanked his Eminence for the offer of his aid,
" but he required no other assistance to punish
rebels, than his own regal authority and the
laws of England !" · ·

Such was the noble answer of Charles the
First to the political seduction of Richelieu ;
such was the strength of character which at
critical conjunctures he invariably displayed ;
and such was his fortune and his fate that the
greater his personal distresses rose on him, the
greater the energy which he seemed to derive
from their excitement. On this incident even
the sullen Presbyter Harris felt a transient
glow, exclaiming, " This answer was worthy a

British Monarch!" We must also recollect that this offer from the Cardinal was made in November, and that Charles had already in June been menaced by the rising troubles in Scotland. His own personal condition strangely contrasted with his magnanimity; to be plunged into a war with France while he was preparing a northern army to act against his own malcontents, required in the spirited Monarch that fortitude and moral courage, which in truth never failed him in his " hour of need."

But Charles probably did not know that D'Estrades, who remained here but a few weeks, and then hastened to the Prince of Orange, had a double commission in coming to England. He was to offer the King of England the aid of France, or rather of Cardinal Richelieu, should Charles be disposed to act as his Eminence desired; but should Charles prove adverse to his scheme, the ambidextrous agent was to address himself secretly to the heads of the Scotch party. The fact is, that D'Estrades had not been five days in London, ere he had already opened a communication with two Scotchmen, and in his dispatches congratulates the Cardinal on " this favourable conjuncture for embarrassing the King of England's affairs." Such then was the great *coup d'état*. The neu-

trality of the King was to be bribed by the destruction of the rebellious Scots, or enforced by
the necessity of devoting his whole powers to
their suppression.

The reply of the Cardinal to D'Estrades is
very remarkable. Sarcastically approving of
the openness of the King and Queen of England, in their conduct towards him, he owns
" that France might have been embarrassed
had the royal couple had the address of concealing their sentiments — but now *the year
should not close* before both should repent of
their refusal of his proposals. It shall soon be
known that I am not to be despised." He desired D'Estrades to assure the two Scotch deputies of his friendship and protection, and that
in a few days he will dispatch one of his chap-
lains the Abbé Chambres, who was their fellow
countryman, to hasten to Edinburgh and open
a negotiation with their party. This wily Statesman would have Scotchmen appear to govern
Scotchmen. The Abbé Chambres, whom
Whitelocke calls Chamberlain, and who had
probably gallicised his name, was accompanied
by a confidential page of his Eminence, also a
Scot, of the name of Hepburn—and probably
serving, in the present instance, in the capacity of a spy on the other spy. To mortify

the haughty Henrietta and to inconvenience
Charles, by rendering the English court still
more unpopular, the vindictive Cardinal within
a few months of the interview of D'Estrades
with Henrietta, drove by his persecutions the
exiled Mary of Medicis to her daughter. In
vain had Charles repeatedly urged his foreign
agents to prevent the Queen-mother directing
her flight to England—there seemed to be no
other resting-place for the royal fugitive. The
fortunes of Richelieu had been the creation of
this hapless Princess; but he never forgave, as
is usual with great politicians, the Patroness,
who was herself alarmed at the mighty being
her own feeble hand had formed.

Mary of Medicis, was the weakest of women, but she was a Queen of Sorrows; the
daughter of Tuscany, the wife of Henry IV.,
the mother of Lewis XIII. and of the Queens
of England and Spain, and the Duchess of
Savoy. She it was whom on her landing in
England, Waller addressed

" Great Queen of Europe! where thy offspring wears
   All the chief crowns; whose Princes are thy heirs."

This eminent personage, the victim of political
intrigue, was now, wherever she came, a wandering spectacle of melancholy,—the presence

of the ill-starred woman was looked on as a
prognostic of public calamity.   Here the sight
of her person inflamed the popular prejudice
against her daughter, and the season in which
she arrived turning out wet and stormy, the
common people called it " Queen-mother weather !"

Charles the First thus incurred the vindictive artifices of Richelieu ; and it is unquestionable that the royal fortunes were greatly
influenced by the mysterious policy of this
hardy and inventive Statesman.

The Cardinal accomplished his prediction or
malediction on Charles's head about the period
assigned.   We have found Richelieu instigating the Hollanders to violate the neutrality of
the British ports, at the very moment Richelieu
was holding a secret intercourse with the Scottish Covenanters, and subsequently with the
English Parliamentarians.   Thus by an extraordinary combination in his Cabinet, the hand
of Richelieu was directing the fate of Charles
the First at once in his maritime Sovereignty
and his Scottish dominions.

It would seem that Charles the First had
yet no notion that the disgrace of having incurred an insult in his own ports was the work of
the Cardinal, nor did he probably imagine that

the papistical Prelate could ever coalesce with the Calvinistical presbyters, or that the Minister of an absolute monarchy could ever cordially blend with the Commonwealth-men of England in the abolition of monarchy itself.

The influence of Cardinal Richelieu over the fortunes of Charles the First is a subject not unworthy of our inquiry.

CHAPTER IV.

OF THE INFLUENCE OF CARDINAL RICHELIEU ON THE FATE OF CHARLES THE FIRST.

THE famous Cardinal-Duke de Richelieu, was one of those great ministers on whom panegyrics and satires equally abound. It is hard to say of Richelieu that in his passion for glory he would have sacrificed his own France to Europe, if by that fatal pledge, Europe had prostrated herself to the Cardinal-Duke. In his political imagination he had contemplated on vast designs, which the ordinary date of human life only had interrupted, for when Richelieu was no more, a youthful Monarch and a minister trained in Richelieu's school, astonished and alarmed the world by the sparks which had fallen from his genius.

The master-genius of Richelieu had wrestled with domestic factions, and trodden down rivals. His mightier despotism had annihilated

the multiplied tyrannies of a haughty aristocracy who had usurped an authority over the
laws.

Richelieu must not be classed among those
rare and patriotic statesmen, who are the fathers
of their country. He first conquered his own
people—crushed his own nobility—and concentrated in his Sovereign the despotism he
himself required. Louis XIII. was jealous
even of the minister, in the absence of whose
genius, he would probably have ceased to reign;
but though the Prince was weak, the majesty
of the Throne was greater than it had ever
been. It was indeed an iron rule—state-prisons,
scaffolds, and garrisoned towns deformed the
fair face of " pleasant France."

It is said to have been a state-maxim of this
famed politician, who we must candidly remember lived in troubled times, that to keep
the people in subjection it is necessary to
depress them. An anecdote has come down
to us which in some respects describes the actual state of the French people during his formidable ministry. An Englishman was de-
claiming against the tyranny of this minister.
" Don't talk so loud," said his friend, " lest
some of his creatures there, should hear you"—
pointing to a crowd of beggars in their sabots.

At his death there were public rejoicings in
the more distant provinces, and the people by
their fireworks, and their dances, proclaimed to.
the world that the death of the tyrannical gives
a holiday to the people. . Yet when the Czar
Peter the Great visited the magnificent tomb
of Richelieu, contemplating the statue, he en-
thusiastically exclaimed, " Great man ! wert
thou living I would give thee half of my empire, wouldst thou teach me to govern the
other." Must we therefore consider that one
of the arts of government may consist . in
making a nation great, at the cost of its happiness ?

By the strength and unity of his government, Richelieu made the nation tremble while
he secured its power. A general rumour prevailed, and it was the favourite topic of conversation, as I learn by a manuscript letter of
the times, with " the brave Monsieurs in
France," that " their King must be Emperor,"
and it appears that to have ventured to con-
tradict them would have been at the hazard of
a duel. So early had the national egotism anticipated its glorious infirmity !* Thus while
France bowed under its severe master, with
secret pride she looked on her ascendancy in

* Harl. MSS. From a letter of the times.

the great family of European governments. A nation, like an individual, has often sacrificed 'its happiness to its splendour.

Richelieu conquered France—the greater conquest was in view. Force, remorseless force had mastered his native land, subtile intrigues were to weaken every other European kingdom. This great minister was now to strike out.amidst the most complicate obstacles and cabals, the elements of grandeur and prosperity, to create a political cabinet, which was to survive its creator and hold Europe itself in an equilibrium to be guided by the arm of France. His recruited armies were to encounter the Imperialist and the Spaniard, his miserable marine was one day to meet the fleets of England and Holland; and his silent genius was at the same time busied in Spain, till he struck out from its dominion an independent Kingdom in Portugal; and in England, whose alliance with the French Huguenots and whose invasion of Rhé were indelible on his implacable memory, till he subdued its independent Monarch by a revolution which he lived to witness, and, we are told, long enough to regret; for De Brienne, his confidential secretary of state, acknowledges that matters went further than the Cardinal had designed, and than he desired.

This confession of Brienne was sincere. Père d'Orleans, who had access to the papers of the Marquis de la Ferté-Imbault, who was the French ambassador in England in 1642, informs us that " Richelieu began to be alarmed at the consequences of his own successful intrigues, which menaced the destruction of a Monarch, whom France was only desirous of embarrassing, to wean him from his inclination to unite with Spain. The French Monarch offered to become a mediator between the parties; after three or four journeys to Windsor, the French ambassador found that the offer of the French Cabinet was received with equal suspicion by the King and by the Parliament." * Cardinal Mazarine in his correspondence with Sabran, the French agent in England in 1644, whose papers I have examined, was earnestly desirous of pacifying the English troubles. This is confirmed too by a conversation of Mazarine. with Lord Digby, in which the Cardinal told him that " France found too late their own error, that they had been well content to see the King's great puissance weakened by his domestic troubles, which they wished only should keep him from being able to hurt his neigh-

* Père d'Orleans, Revolutions d'Angleterre, iii. 34.

bours."* Such has ever been the human policy of political cabinets, who have sought for their own security by inflaming the intestine disorders of their neighbour; or to obtain some temporary advantage, provoke a lasting evil. Richelieu, by the Covenanters of Scotland and the Parliamentarians of England recruited his armies against Austria, and neutralised the ally Spain possessed in Charles. When the revolution burst forth, it was too late to undo the web of his own subtle work. How far, or if at all, the conduct of England towards the French Revolution in its early stage affords a parallel case, I know not. Accusations were raised by some of the French against Pitt. Pitt, like Richelieu, had his recollections, and our American Colonies might have been to Louis the Sixteenth, what the Isle of Rhé and La Rochelle were to Charles the First.

The politics of Richelieu may be paralleled with the system of Napoleon. Richelieu was forming an invisible alliance with the disaffected of every government; thus his own genius presided in their counsels, and all the members of his diplomacy served as the active agents of the revolutions of his age. We are

* Clarendon's State Papers, Suppt. iii. lix.

struck by the parallel of Richelieu and Napoleon in their secret principles. Pliant, as well as unbending, the Prelate of the Papacy could confirm the edict of Nantes for his own Huguenots, granting toleration at the moment he meditated their extermination;* to check the house of Austria the Romish Cardinal could confederate with the Protestant princes to maintain the Protestant cause; and the Minister of an absolute monarchy was the faithful ally of the new Republicans of Holland!

The intrigues of this politic statesman could not pass untraced amidst the gathering troubles of Charles the First — the serpent, however wary, still leaves the trail of his crooked motions in the dust he passes over. The Irish insurgents were supplied with arms by the

* It is a curious fact exhibiting the awkward dilemma into which great politicians sometimes thrust themselves, that at the moment the articles of peace with the French Protestants were to be signed at the council-table, both the Cardinals Richelieu and de la Rochefoucault withdrew, that they might not appear publicly to sanction a truce with Heretics—although this very peace was the favourite work of the great Cardinal himself. It may possibly be alleged that the departure of the Cardinals at signing this treaty with Heretics, might have been a mere form which grew out of their priestly character. Le Clerc unquestionably gives the anecdote in the spirit of a Protestant. It was certainly a dilemma.

Cardinal; the agents of the Covenanters were at Paris, as well as the agents of the French at Edinburgh.

Besides the political influence of Cardinal Richelieu over the fortunes of Charles the First, I think there was a more latent one, the result of which was not less important in the affairs of the English Monarch. Charles admired Richelieu, and many of the interior transactions which had occurred in France, the disorders composed, the difficulties overcome, often presented an image of the state of England. The disaffected Princes appeared to Charles, greatly to resemble some of our Patriots; the remonstrances of the French Parliaments, though these are but courts of law, had sometimes approached the lofty tone of our Commons, and the strong republican party of the Huguenots, could not well be separated in their conduct and their principles from our own Puritans. Charles had a mind too reflective, and too personally interested in these events, to pass over regardlessly the conduct and success of the great French minister. Charles the First, and Strafford, and possibly Laud, who has been idly compared with Richelieu, were close observers of the Cardinal-Duke; and Richelieu, unquestionably of them. Ministers

like jealous traders, keep an observant eye on each
other. Olivarez, the great Spanish Minister,
when some Frenchmen complained of the libels
and satires on Richelieu profusely spread in
Flanders, declared that as a Minister of State
it was his own interest not to countenance such
unworthy methods, but he had himself often
told his master that his greatest misfortune was
that the King of France possessed the most
skilful minister who for a thousand years had
appeared in Christendom; but as for himself he
would willingly submit to have whole libraries
printed every day against himself, provided
that the affairs of his master were as well conducted as those of France!

This secret sympathy, or this mutual influence among these great parties, was often indicated by circumstances accidentally preserved.
That Charles the First had long admired the
genius of Richelieu, appeared on the famous
day of the Dupes, when news arrived of the
dismission and fall of the French minister.
Henrietta rejoicing at the Cardinal's removal
from power, which had been so long desired by
the Queen-Mother, Charles the First checked
the feminine petulance, expressing his highest
admiration of the unrivalled capacity of the
minister. " Your mother is wrong," he ob-

served to the Queen; " the Cardinal has performed the greatest services for his master.
Had I been the Cardinal I would have listened tranquilly to the accusations of the Queen
your mother, and remembered those against
Scipio before the Roman people, who instead
of replying, led them to the Capitol to return
thanks to the gods, for having defeated the
Carthaginians. The Cardinal might have told
the King, within these two years Rochelle has
been taken, more than thirty towns of the
Huguenots have submitted, and their fortifications are demolished; Cazal has been twice
succoured, Savoy and a great part of Pied-
mont are in your hands : these advantages
which your arms have acquired by my cares,
answer for my industry and my fidelity."*

That Strafford was attentive to the proceedings of the French minister, appears by his

* Griffet, Hist. de Louis XIII. ii. 77.   From Richelieu's
Journal. That Charles had expressed himself to this purpose we cannot well doubt; it would not otherwise have
been entered into the Cardinal's Journal. But I suspect
that the latter part, where the Cardinal enumerates such a
variety of his own memorable acts, was added by himself,
as an illustration. Had Charles detailed such a series of
events, it would show a more particular attention than was
necessary ; in speaking to the Queen he would merely have
alluded to the general results of Richelieu's administration.

alleging the conduct of the Cardinal in appointing commissioners to enter the merchants'
houses at Paris to examine their accounts and
to cess every man according to his ability to
furnish the King's army.   And that Richelieu
was well acquainted with English affairs is
evident from the remarkable discovery mentioned in our former volumes of the minute
and secret correspondence the French minister
held with some courtiers at Whitehall.   Had
the political personages of the Court of England not been well known to Richelieu, he
would not have thrown out that striking observation, when hearing of the fate of Strafford;
he remarked that " the English had been foolish enough 'to take off the ablest head among
them."*

Charles the First, driven by his necessities
and the perpetual opposition of his Parliaments, could hardly avoid admiring the energies, which for some time he seems to me to
have fatally imitated.   English lawyers, in
their vague and florid style, had declared that
no Monarch was so absolute as an English Sovereign, and " the right divine" of kings was
not only upheld by kings themselves, but by
the divines of Christian Europe.   I have often

* Trial of Strafford, pp. 30. 592.

thought that by the vain struggle and confusion of the principles of the absolute Monarchy of France under Richelieu, with those of the constitutional forms of England, Charles the First fell a victim, as I have before expressed it, to strong measures in a weak Government.

CHAPTER V.

HISTORY AND TRIAL OF THE EARL OF STRAFFORD.

SIR THOMAS WENTWORTH, as we have already noticed, was an independent country-gentleman, who opened his political career by a patriotic opposition to the measures of Buckingham; he spoke seldom, but always with effect, and the ability which awed the minister taught him also the strength of its support. Severe scrutinisers into Wentworth's conduct have considered that there was a political coquetry in his patriotism, which rather sought to be won, than cared to be obdurate.

Wentworth, however, endured with magnanimity the petty persecutions of the day: he suffered confinement as a loan-recusant, but when having enlisted in the ranks of Opposition he suddenly hesitated in the march, when his opinions wavered, and he began to discuss

rather than to act with those whose confidence
he possessed, whose designs he comprehended,
and whose artifices of faction were not unknown to him, in a word, when Wentworth
gave signs of what in the modern political cant
is called *ratting*, he incurred the hatred of the
impetuous and the sorrows of the gentle. Noy
had deserted the popular cause, but he had
crept out like a groveling lawyer, calculating
on the most advantageous client; but Strafford,
for the Earl is best known in history by his
title, great and independent, whatever might
be his motive, was about to devote the most
elevated efforts of his nature and ascend into
the highest sphere of action; his wisdom was
to govern the Royal councils, and his heroism
to maintain the public safety.

Pym in parting from Strafford did not shed
the generous tear which Fox is reported to
have let fall for Burke. The enraged leader
of Opposition vowed perpetual enmity, and, as
if he had already contemplated in the long
perspective of his political vision that axe which
was so often to be raised, declared that " he
would never quit him while Strafford kept a
head on his shoulders." And when the fatal
hour arrived, Pym the patriot indulged his
personal rancour, and flew with indecent haste

to denounce Strafford as "the apostate who was the greatest enemy to the liberties of his country that any age had produced."

Charles at first urged his new minister to take his seat in the House. The presence of Strafford in Parliament inspired the King with confidence, but the Earl himself foresaw that it would irritate the parliamentary party, and their secret allies the Scots; out of their sight he would less occupy their thoughts, and should they persecute the Lord-Lieutenant of Ireland, at that safe distance he would be found at the head of his army. The statesman observed, prescient of his fate, "if any difference should happen between your Majesty and the Parliament, it would disturb your Majesty's affairs, and in that case I should prefer suffering myself, than them." But Charles professed that "as King of England he was able to protect his minister; whatever danger might happen, not a hair of his head should be touched." At that moment Charles the First unquestionably deemed himself possessing more independent power than by the sequel appeared. It is no rare case in political history, that when men are reduced to great weakness, they exist on the remembrance of the power they once possessed.

The magnanimous Strafford resigned the

army, who, were devoted to him, to attend in Parliament. Warned indeed by his friends at Whitehall of some impending design, he came not unprepared with evidence to impeach some of "the Scotising-English" in both houses of Parliament, whose intrigues with the Covenanters had already brought an invading army into England. Strafford particularly intended to impeach Lord Say. But the party more vigilant than he, who yet had never failed in vigilance, hurried to strike the first blow.* This act at least would exhaust the talents, the temper, and the industry of their dreaded adversary. Buckingham had crushed his enemy, Bristol, by the great advantage of reducing his accuser first to defend himself.

* There is no doubt that it depended but on the turn of a moment, that the political game would have been reversed. I shall quote as a proof, the most partial and uncandid of all our historical writers, Oldmixon, whose style debases even his perpetual misrepresentations. He makes the avowal. "Strafford had prepared matters for an impeachment against those Lords and gentlemen who had encouraged the Scots to march into England, but Mr. Pym was beforehand with him, and not many hours after he arrived in town, carried up to the House of Lords an accusation of high treason against Strafford," 157. This is a material fact, to which we shall again have occasion to allude. It is authenticated by Rushworth in his Introduction to Strafford's Trial, 2.

Whenever a political storm happens, an observer often recollects the prognostics of the
horizon.   Some days before the meeting of
Parliament, " Mr. Hyde"—as Clarendon then
designates himself, noticed " a marvellous elated
countenance in many of the Members."   The
conversation of Pym startled the young politician.   Now Pym avowed that " they must
be of another temper —they must not only
sweep the House clean below, but must pull
down all the cobwebs which hung in the top
and corners — and to remove all grievances they
must pull up the causes of them by the roots."
A radical reform hardly seems. the coinage of
our own days.

On the first day of the opening of Parliament, Pym, preluding with an awful solemnity,
declared that he had a business of great weight
to impart, and desired that the lobby should be
cleared.

This unusual proceeding in the Commons
reached the Lords, who dispatched a message
to desire a meeting in the painted chamber to
consult on the Scotch treaty.   The messengers
appear to have been sent on an errand of discovery respecting the impending debate.   The
House returned an answer by the same messengers, that they were in agitation of very

weighty and important affairs, and they doubted whether they could give a meeting to the
Lords, as early as was desired.

The debate proceeded with closed doors.
The key of the House was ordered to be laid
on the table. Pym, whose education had been
chiefly in the office of the Exchequer, accustomed to business, with nervous compressed
sense, and acute argument, displayed an austere
eloquence in his invective, different from the
elevated appeals to their imagination with
which the Ciceronian Eliot had formerly thundered in the Senate against the favourite Buckingham. Our orator had discovered the cause
of the calamities which had fallen upon the
nation in "the reign of a pious and virtuous
King who loved his people." He opened the
fountain whence flowed these waters of bitter-
ness — the very person who had perverted the
King's excellent judgment — he named! But
surely the declared enemy of Strafford sunk
from the dignity of the patriot into the malice
of the libeller when a British Senate listened to
the volatile rumours of a scandalous chronicle,
and personal malignity touched on the lighter
vanities of a great man, and even on his secret
amours! The party orator aggrandised his
victim into colossal power to alarm the true

patriot—while he shrunk him into a diminutive object of familiar contempt to gratify the
meaner spirits. But the plot was concerted—
the parts were prepared—the actors followed
each other. A knight who had posted from
Ireland, delivered a confused tale of the tyrannical measures of the Lord Lieutenant; another from Yorkshire alleged an arbitrary expression which had fallen from the Earl, that
" they should find the little finger of the
King's prerogative heavier than the loins of
the law." At this, the flame burst around—
passion, prejudice, and patriotism spoke but
with one voice, and raised but one hand! An
instant impeachment was moved and carried.
Even " Mr. Hyde" did not oppose it, and
when the immaculate Lord Falkland, who felt
no personal kindness for the Earl, and who
agreed on the propriety of the measure, conceived however that they should pause till
they had digested the articles against the accused; his Lordship was silenced by an argument of Pym, that were the moment lost, a
dissolution would follow. To those who were
doubtful whether the charges could amount to
high-treason, Pym replied that the House of
Commons were not judges, but simply accusers.
It proved however in the result that they were

to be both. But the principle itself, that they were not judges but merely accusers, seems to expose any individual to sequestration on the charge of any party who are bold enough to lay the imputation. Was not the impeachment of Hastings a persecution of many years?

Pym, that " ancient gentleman of great experience in parliamentary affairs and no less fidelity to his country," as " the Secretary of the Parliament' describes him; Pym, the declared enemy of Strafford, accompanied by his friends, hurried to the Lords, and abruptly " in the name of all the Commons of England accused Thomas Earl of Strafford, Lord Lieutenant of Ireland, of high-treason." The Lords, it appears, were startled by this unexpected intelligence, unexpected at least by most of them. The indecent haste which Pym betrayed on this occasion is said to have been occasioned by some knowledge that Strafford would have anticipated him in an impeachment, and we shall find hereafter that the subsequent attempted arrest of the five Members of the Commons, which proved so fatal to Charles, was probably connected with the presumed conspiracy of which Strafford imagined that he possessed sufficient evidence.

The impeachment having been communicated to the Earl, who was at that moment with
the King, he hastened to the House : finding
the doors closed, he struck it impetuously, and
inattentive to the remonstrance of Maxwell,
the Usher of the Black Rod, Strafford passed
on to his seat.   At his entrance his eye glanced
around with the accustomed haughty contraction of his brow—but his fate was before him !
A clamour rose " which suited not the gravity
of that supreme Court."   The Earl was already
a fallen Minister ! Called on to withdraw, Strafford in confusion retreated to the door, and
there awaited their summons to learn their decision.   When recalled, he stood before them,
but was commanded to the bar of the House
to kneel as an accused man.   The Earl protested against a general charge without the specifi-
cation of a single act of treason.   He was silenced, till he should clear himself of the charges
laid on him, and was consigned to the custody
of the Usher of the Black Rod.

The impeachment originally consisted of nine
articles, but their eager diligence set to work
in every obscure corner, and their encouraging
invitation of grievances made to every malcontent, had accumulated twenty-eight charges,
involving the conduct of the accused Mi-

nister during the long interval of fourteen years.*

The trial of the Earl of Strafford presented a more imposing spectacle than had ever been exhibited to the nation. Never had a greater actor appeared on the stage of public justice. " The pompous circumstances and stately manner of the trial," as May describes them, were

* After the charges had been delivered to the House of Lords, Strafford was conscious that they contained no act of treason. This appears by a letter which the Earl addressed to his lady on that occasion. This letter having fallen into the hands of a print-seller, he engraved a facsimile, and sold the original to some Collector, and no doubt it still exists. I shall preserve it here, both as an historical document, and as a remarkable evidence of the sagacity and the feelings of the eminent personage.

" SWEET HARTE.

" IT is long since I writt unto you, for I am here in such a trouble, as gives me little or no respett (respite). The charge is now cum in, and I am now able, I prayse God, to tell you, that I conceave ther is nothing capitall, and for the rest I knowe at the worste his Maᵗʸ will pardon all, without hurting my fortune, and then we shall be happy by God's grace. Therefore comfort your self, for I trust thes cloudes will away, and that wee shall have faire weather afterwardes. Farewell.

" Your lovinge husband,
" STRAFFORDE."

Tower of London, 4th Feb. 16⁴⁰⁄₄₁.

not here the only awful splendour; it was not
merely the outward solemnity of judicial forms
which affected the public imagination ; the passions of every class of citizens, from the Sovereign himself to the humblest of the people,
were alike agitated in the cause of this great
Minister. The trial of the Earl of Strafford
seemed no longer the trial of an individual—it
was the trial of the Sovereign's affections, and
the Sovereign's influence—it was the trial of
the kindled spirits of three rival nations—it
was the trial of a great man, whose very virtues
were his defects, and whose defects were to be
his crimes.

Westminster Hall was the scene. Scaffolds
nearly reaching the roof were erected on either
side, eleven stages high, divided by rails ; in
the upper ranks were the Commissioners of
Scotland, and the Lords of Ireland, who were
joined with the Commoners of England in
their accusations. The Members of the Lower
House sate uncovered ; but that punctilio of
etiquette had passed through a stiff debate and
had been conceded with great difficulty. In
the centre sate the Peers in their Parliament
robes, and the Lord Keeper and the Judges in
their scarlet robes were on the woolsacks. At
the upper end beyond the Peers, was a chair

raised under a cloth of State for the King, and another for the Prince. The Sovereign did not occupy this throne; for he was supposed not to be present, and reasons were alleged for this legal fiction. Two cabinets or galleries with trellis-work were on each side of the cloth of State. One the King, the Queen, and their Court occupied during the whole trial; the other was filled with the French nobility and other foreigners. At the foot of the State was a scaffold for ladies of quality; and at the lower end was a place with partitions and an apartment to retire to, for the convenience of the managers of the trial, to hold their consultations; opposite to them entered the witnesses; and between was a small desk where the prisoner stood or sate, the Lieutenant of the Tower beside him; at his back stood his four Secretaries carrying papers and assisting him in writing and reading. Strafford, in the midst of noise and confusion, was compelled to draw up his answers instanter, and was allowed but short intervals.

" It was daily the most glorious assembly the isle could afford; yet the gravity was not such as I expected," observes the grave and zealous Principal of the University of Glasgow. The coarseness of our national manners at this pe-

riod was not concealed by their magnificence,
and when compared with the conveniences, the
decorum and the refinement to which a more
polished state of society has given rise, it has
occasioned some misconceptions of the gross-
ness of the Court, and of the habits of Charles
himself—even with the philosopher, and far
more with those whose minds are but ill constituted to enter into distant times and strange
manners, with the feelings of a contemporary.

This awful solemnity, except at the moment
the prosecution was proceeding, exhibited such
a noisy and indecorous scene, that had it not
been detailed by the faithful memorialist we
could not have suspected such degrading occurrences, while turning over the copious folio
which Rushworth has devoted to this famous
trial.   There was always a great clamour about
the doors ; but at those intervals when the illustrious prisoner was busied in preparing his
answers, a distracting hubbub broke out; the
Lords were walking and chatting—the Commons, whose apology must rest on their multitude and their zeal, were more offensively.
loud.   They ate " flesh and bread," and " bottles
of beer and wine were going thick from mouth
to mouth."   The aristocracy of England were
not yet delicate enough to procure drinking-

cups; their indelicacy indeed was extraordinary, such as had never been witnessed within Westminster Hall, and would not have been pardoned in an assembly without. From eight in the morning till sometimes late in the night they were not allowed to retire, and " the bottles were going thick." Baillie, Covenanter as he was, had very elevated notions of ancestry as a Scot, and he treats contemptuously this Senate of English Peers, for he says of the single Marquis we then had, the Marquis of Winchester, " England hath no more Marquises, and he but a late upstart, a creature of Queen Elizabeth ! Hamilton goes here but among the Earls, and that a late one ; Dukes they have none in Parliament; York, Richmond, and Buckingham are but boys."

When it was proposed that the axe should be carried before the prisoner, the King expressly forbade it, assigning a legal distinction.

The illustrious prisoner appeared in deep mourning wearing his George. His dark countenance with its heavy brows retained the habitual commanding look, but the gracefulness of his gestures, and solemn thought softened his stern dignity. There was a sickly hue in his countenance ; for his complicated disorders were of a nature to be greatly increased by the

anxiety and the labours of his mind; his body
slightly bowed down, not by age, but by infirmity and care.   This was so evident, that he
alluded to it in one of his pathetic appeals,
when he drew the attention of the spectators
to his person.   " They had here, he said, this
rag of mortality before them worn out with
numerous infirmities, which if they tore into
shreds there was no great loss; only in the
spilling of his, they would open a way to the
blood of all the nobility in the land."

The physiognomy of Strafford may afford
a triumph to the votaries of Lavater; we have
all contemplated its masculine spirit in some
admired portraits;* even the prints retain the
dauntless austerity, the deep solemn thought,
and the lofty air of this great man—in his full
and contracted brows, his ample forehead, his
dark thick hair wore short, which added one
more stern characteristic to his countenance.†

* The portraits of Vandyke at Wentworth and Petworth
are well known; the latter appears eminently characteristic.
                                                        Hallam.

† A poet of the day, who had doubtless viewed the great
deputy of Ireland at the bar, has poetically delineated his
noble physiognomy.
                        ————On thy brow
          Sate Terror mixt with Wisdom, and at once
          Saturn and Hermes in thy countenance.
                Shepherd's Epigrams, lib. iv. ep. 39. 1651.

Although without a handsome feature his person was not disagreeable—the dark physiognomy of Strafford, or as Whitelocke calls it " the countenance manly black," did not prevent the Earl from being admired by the fair sex, especially at his trial. A woman's eye could detect some secret graces in his air, and the volatile Henrietta noticed that " he had the finest hands of any man in the world." * The grace of his action was in harmony with the eloquence which melted his auditors, and even disturbed the hearts of those who were watchful over their prey, and contemplated on the axe they had prepared for their victim.

* It could however hardly have been the personal attractions of Strafford which fascinated the women — it must have been their own sensibility in the high conception they had formed of his character, his awful magnanimity, and the superiority of his genius among all his accusers. The women were enchanted. The once courtly and refined May tells us, that " They were all of his side, whether moved by pity, proper to their sex, or by ambition of being thought able to judge of the parts of the prisoner," and with all the elegance of a poetical mind happily applies these verses : —

Non formosus erat, sed erat facundus Ulysses
Et tamen æquoreas torsit amore Deas.

Ulysses though not beautiful, the love
Of Goddesses by eloquence could move.

And

A writer of that day, no admirer of Strafford, was so deeply agitated at the Earl's last powerful appeal to his Peers, and to the public, that he acknowledges that Strafford was one of the most wonderful actors he had ever seen ; he ascribes the affecting breaks in his speech, all the tenderness of his domestic emotions, and the confusion of his thoughts, in the pause and forgetfulness of what he had to say—all this he ascribes to the arts and practices of an accomplished orator. Few orators, however, have drawn reluctant tears down the cheeks of their persecutors. When this " great actor" threw out these pathetic appeals to the domestic feelings of his auditors, they flowed from that sacred fountain of all true feelings, the heart of the man who uttered them—his lips trembled, and his eyes moistened with his own eloquence.

We may indeed ascribe to that discipline of the mind which Strafford had habitually prac-

And the rough covenanting Principal of the University of Glasgow, alluding to Strafford's eloquence, confesses that " With the more simple sort, especially the ladies, he gained daily much." May and Baillie, excellent judges of human nature, whose own bosoms were heated by political passions, seem to have forgot, that these had not yet contaminated the softer bosoms open to more generous emotions than their own.

tised, the promptness of his replies, his luminous statements, the force of his arguments,
and that imperturbable calm amidst the distractions of the crowd and the malignity of
lawyers, when his life at times seemed to be
hanging on the thread he himself was to weave.
This self-possession, those "gathered thoughts"
and government of his mind, we may indeed
consider as the practical results of his former
studies.

Some modern statesmen may smile at the
previous studies of this great minister. Certainly the Earl of Strafford did not derive his
greatness from the mere exercise of power.
Unremitting industry in his official duties was
one of his characteristics, but he had once practised another sort of diligence, in disciplining
his mind by severe studies. He had long accustomed himself, before perusing some eloquent writer in English, French, or Latin, to
compose on the subject in his own manner, and
then by comparing his own production with
the one which had suggested it, to fertilise his
own barrenness, or to prune his own luxuri-
ances by the more perfect production of that
writer who had composed more at leisure and
for glory.

At this moment the Archbishop, who lay in

the Tower, was forgotten! The result of every
day's trial furnished the prevalent conversation
or controversy, in every company; and the
Court-ladies were not less deeply engaged than
their grave Lords in taking notes, and arguing
in the confusion of words, whether the fundamental laws of the kingdom had been subvert-
ed, or only diverted in their course, by the
Lord-Lieutenant of Ireland. Another party
would maintain that misdemeanours, though
never so many, could not make one treason,
unless one of them had been treason in its own
nature; and a third would assert, as Strafford
did, that a hundred misdemeanours could not
make one felony, nor a hundred felonies one
treason, being a crime of a different kind.
Others would ask, as Pym asked, what use
were his Parliaments without Parliamentary
freedom? What praise was due to him for
making good laws in Ireland, if he made his
own will above all law?

The trial of the Earl of Strafford is well
known, by the folio volume of Rushworth.
Among many heavy charges of severe measures and arbitrary rule,* many were drawn

* The most arbitrary persecution was that of Lord Mountnorris, to whom evidently Strafford bore a strong personal
dislike, though he had formerly indulged a close intercourse

from hasty and unqualified language; many
expressions were asserted to have been misconceived; some were reports of reports, and as
the honest Scotchman in his journal describes
them, " chamber and table-discourse, flim-flams,
and fearie-fairies." The remarkable language
which when it was first delivered to the House
of Commons had kindled their spirit, that "they
should find the little finger of the King's pre-

with him. Mountnorris from a very humble station rose to
be a Viscount, but his manners were sordid, petulant, and
troublesome. For these he suffered too heavily. It is not
the object of this note to enter into any inquiry concerning
this affair. It may be worth a word to defend our illustrious
Hume from one of the unjust and hasty strictures of Mr.
Brodie. Hume notices that Mountnorris was a man of *infamous* character. Mr. Brodie observes that Hume " gives
no authority whatever, and that it is perfectly clear to me
that he had no other than the character from Lord Clarendon, and the reader will be able to judge how far he has
kept to it," iii. 69. It is indeed true that no such term as
" infamous" is applied to Mountnorris by Clarendon. But
Hume recollected that Mountnorris is also described by
Strafford in a letter " as one extremely given to good fel-
lowship, who sat up all night to play for large sums, very
meanly pursuing his advantage upon young noblemen and
gentlemen not so good gamesters as himself;" i. 403. Mr.
Brodie, who appears at times to have written in haste, has
himself furnished this very passage in his following page.
There is a comfort in Mr. Brodie's work, if carefully read ;
It is, that many parts will be found to correct others.

rogative heavier than the loins of the law," was
asserted by the prisoner to have been inverted;
Strafford declaring that the little finger of the
law would be heavier than the loins of the prerogative.　Besides that the observation applied
to a circumstance of itself innocent, while the
witness had placed it to another which might
seem criminal.　Incidents long passed — conversations forgotten—and the equity, or the
iniquity, of many of his acts of government
called in question, were so many charges heaped on the head of this political victim.　To all
these he was compelled to find an immediate
answer.　Sometimes he implored leave to retire to recollect himself, but this was denied,
and half an hour only was allowed in the open
Court, amidst the incessant din of voices and
the tumultuous movements of a crowd.　As
soon as his adversary had closed his charge,
Strafford would turn his back to the Lords,
and abstracting himself from the confusion
around, assisted by his secretaries read his
notes, and wrote or dictated his observations.
Composed of such hasty materials, Strafford
delivered his eloquent defence.　Baillie acknowledges that " he oft triumphed that they alleged
crimes against him which they were not able
to make good."

As the trial proceeded, the life of Strafford seemed in no peril from his accusers.* The great object of the Earl was to ward off the blow of treason ; and that he succeeded in this respect is evident by the extraordinary and desperate conduct the enemies of Strafford afterwards adopted to obtain their purpose. There are eloquent passages in his defence which perpetuate the sympathy which they excited in the hour of his agony. It is said that at some of our public schools parts of his speech have served for the practice of declamation.† He has described the cruelty of retailing familiar conversations, accidental expressions, and idle rumours to criminate a man.

"If words spoken to friends in familiar discourse, spoken in one's chamber, spoken at

* It evidently was the public opinion that Strafford would clear himself from all the heavy charges. This we gather from an impartial witness, the illustrious Grotius, who gives this intelligence to his brother, in a letter dated March 30, 1641.

† It is to be regretted that we do not possess a corrected copy of this far-famed speech, or oration. It appears differently in Whitelocke, Rushworth and in the State-Trials. Does a well-authenticated copy exist? A critical editor blessed with the right feeling, might still supply a more genuine copy than any, by melting the present copies into one, taking from each the most felicitous expressions and the

one's table, spoken in one's sick bed, spoken
perhaps to gain better reason, to give himself
more clear light and judgment, by reasoning;
if these things shall be brought against a man
as treason, this, under favour, takes away the
comfort of all human society; by this means
we shall be debarred from speaking, the principal joy and comfort of society, with wise and
good men, to become wiser, and better our lives.
If these things be strained to take away life
and honour, and all that is desirable, it will be
a silent world, a city will become a hermitage;
and sheep will be found amongst a crowd and
press of people, and no man shall dare to impart his solitary thoughts or opinions to his
friend and neighbour."

Thus he who was himself accused of straining an inquisitorial power to silence the free
thoughts of others, could pathetically plead for
that liberty which he himself had denied.
And now a criminal at the bar, in his own
person, offered a terrible example of the remorseless cruelty of misinterpreting, misquot-

most forcible conceptions. We may be certain that such
must be the most genuine, for the reporters of that day had
neither the talent, nor the disposition to improve the speeches
they imperfectly took down.

ing, and misapplying the words of another, to torture them into treason.

When the business was proceeding unfavourably to the real purpose of the prosecutors, a considerable difference arose between the two Houses. The Committee of the Lower House in order to render one of their charges more effectual than it turned out to be, were desirous of producing additional evidence — while the Earl craved the same liberty for himself, having other testimonies in his favour. This, Glyn the lawyer loudly protested against, inferring from this request that " the prisoner at the bar presumed to prescribe to the Commons." The Lords deemed it reasonable. On this they shouted " Withdraw! withdraw!" The Commons furiously rose and standing up with their hats on, " they cocked their beavers in the King's sight." The House broke up in tumult and dismay without even adjourning the court. Strafford slipped away in his barge, glad to be gone lest he should be torn to pieces — the Lords withdrew — and the King went home in sadness and silence. In the afternoon the Commons violently resolved to bring in a bill of Attainder. This was on a Saturday; Sunday was passed in terror by the town, who augured a final separation between the two Houses ; and it cannot be denied that the public feeling was a sort of political second-sight, whose melancholy vision was hastening the sad catastrophe on which they were meditating. Some of the Members of the Commons declared they would draw up a bill of Attainder against the Earl as well as every Lord who adhered to his cause — they would not pause till they had obtained his execution. Monday was spent in a conference between both Houses, for this discussion had suspended the trial in Westminster-hall. On this occasion there were yet remaining some of the Nobility who addressed the Commons in the lofty spirit of the aristocracy. These, it is said, told the Members of the Lower House that "it was an unnatural motion for the head to be governed by the tail ; that rebellion was as hateful as treason ; that the same blood that ennobled their ancestors ran still in their veins, and therefore they would not be suppressed by a popular faction." * Probably, for the last time, the Committee of the House of Commons

* Thus Eachard in his useful compilation. Though he usually does little more than transcribe from his originals yet he never gives his authorities. I have not discovered

seemed to give way to the Lords; or rather
in the present case were not hardy enough to
maintain the glaring injustice of denying the
prisoner the power of self-defence.

The evidence indeed had fallen far short of
involving Strafford in a capital crime, as he
himself had anticipated. It was also clear that
the Lords would not join in pronouncing an
illegal condemnation of death. The Commons
dreaded that their great victim of State should
escape from their grasp, whose immolation they
had vowed to their Scottish friends, and by
whose blood they proposed to open their meditated revolution.

It was then that an extraordinary incident,
the subtle contrivance of Pym, practising on the
dormant vengeance of the Vanes, took all parties
by surprise. The Secretary of State, Sir Henry
Vane, the father, had long been irreconcileably
indisposed against the Earl. Among minor
causes of personal dislike, Strafford in assuming
the title of the Barony of Raby, the castle
being the seat of the Vanes, had inflicted a
wanton insult on the Secretary, who had not
been without hopes himself of acquiring that

whence he drew this lofty style of the aristocracy. Baillie
is my authority for the picturesque passions of the Commons.

cherished title.* There existed other irrita-
tions against Strafford, who had treated Vane
with levity. But the caution and fears of a
weak man had taught Sir Henry to suppress
his indignation while Strafford was in power.
Even after, Vane hesitated to be an informer,
or an accuser, against the great man, for the
Secretary's views did not extend beyond the
horizon of the Court. This personal antipathy
however probably influenced the evidence he
gave. Some advice of the Earl at a Cabinet-
council for the transport of the Irish army, Sir
Henry understood was designed for England
to reduce the country to obedience. No other
Privy-Counsellor present confirmed this deposition. The subject of discussion was whether
to maintain an offensive or a defensive war, and
related to Scotland, and not England; his ear

---

* This assumption of a title which gave such offence to
another person, is clearly stated by Heylin in his anonymous
observations on L'Estrange's " Reign of King Charles," a
small volume curious and scarce. " Sir Henry Vane had
obtained of the King not long before, the Manor of Raby in
the Bishoprick of Durham, not without hope of being made
Baron of that place. The Lord Lieutenant deriving his descent from the Nevils, Earls of Westmorland, whose hono-
rary seat that was, procured himself to be created Baron of
Raby in those letters patent by which he was invested with
the Earldom of Strafford." p. 228. Heylin.

as he declared had caught the relative *that* kingdom referring to Scotland, for *this* kingdom, which would have referred to England. His first recollection was however so imperfect, that he declined to accuse Strafford with the charge in hand. At another time, on a second recollection, preluding with a formal declaration of his love of truth, he rather improved the meaning—but it required a third opportunity for Pym to extract from no unwilling witness, whatever he desired. Strafford argued against this heavy charge, that Sir Henry Vane was an incompetent witness—that he could not remember the words but at the third time— that words might be like in sound and differ in sense—that no such project which he had supposed had ever been proposed, for which Strafford appealed to the whole Council—and finally the Earl took a legal exception that no one could be arraigned for the crime of treason on a single testimony, which the law required to be attested by two sufficient witnesses.

It was then Pym broached a dangerous legal paradox, that "several concurring circumstances did make one witness as effectual as two." And therefore to give Sir Henry Vane's single evidence the competency of two witnesses, Pym opened a piece of secret history, that he might be enabled to produce as competent evidence, a certain document, which bore on its face the ugly feature of violated confidence.

Sir Henry Vane the younger was of a bolder temper than his father ; he had long been in close intercourse with Pym and the patriotic party. On the occasion of the son's marriage —so was the tale told to the Commons —the father being absent, sent the son the keys of his secret drawers at Whitehall to look for some title-deeds. The young patriot and the future mystic, indulged his statesman-like curiosity in ransacking all the state-secrets so carelessly confided by the Secretary, and in a red velvet cabinet he found, so he said, a paper of rough notes which his father had taken of a Cabinet Council. They were entitled " Notes taken at the Juncto," or as elsewhere marked, " No danger of a war with Scotland if offensive, not defensive."* These were in fact

* How are we to account for the difference between these notes, as they appear in the Earl of Manchester's Memoirs, in Nalson, ii. 208, and in Whitelocke's Memorials. It is more remarkable that such an extraordinary incident as the scene between the Vanes should not have been preserved by Rushworth, that assiduous collector. Did he consider the absurdity as well as cruelty of Pym's argument as not honourable to his masters the Commons ? Rushworth has also silently passed over the case of Lord Loftus, which we only

rough heads of notes of a debate in Council, consisting of fragments of sentences. It was doubted by some whether the Secretary ever did take notes at the board, the King having desired that all notes of Cabinet Councils should be destroyed, that opinions not adopted should never appear against their advisers. " This paper," as the Earl of Manchester notices in his memoirs, " either from his own curiosity, or his father's direction, he opens and reads, and *hastens to Pym* with great expressions of a troubled mind, not knowing what way to clear

know from Clarendon, and where certain private letters of Strafford to his lady, not designed for the eyes of a third person, were brought into court. These are but a few of the castrations and voluntary omissions of the Clerk of the Commons.

I have had frequent occasions to detect the incorrect state of many of our historical documents, or state-papers as they are called, owing, I suppose, to the hasty carelessness of our early transcribers, who gave them rather in their own way than in the exact state in which they found them. I took great pains to copy from the autograph letter of Lord Carleton the paper found in Felton's hat, and which had been variously given to the world. His Lordship's letter was sent to the Queen, and yet he gave this paper which he pretends to have transcribed, very incorrectly, as now appears by the identical paper itself which I have examined in the autograph collections of Mr. Upcott, and which Dr. Lingard has recently published.

himself betwixt the discharge of his duty to
the Commonwealth and his faithfulness to his
father."* The younger Vane could not have
applied to any one who with greater facility
could ease his scruples. Pym takes a copy of
the notes, and promising a tender care for the
son's reputation and the father's security, the
original is replaced in the velvet cabinet, and the
father knows nothing of their late abstraction.
To complete the imperfect and confused evi-

* Such pieces of secret history are often told differently by
the parties concerned; there is great art in turning a tale.
In the present instance, to infer that there was no premeditated plot, it is stated that Pym visited the younger Vane
during a severe indisposition, when the paper of notes was
produced; that Pym insisted on taking a copy. It was
some time afterwards, when the elder Vane's testimony was
considered incomplete, that Pym then produced this copy
as a substitute for the original. Mr. Brodie is my sole authority for this statement respecting " the severe indisposition" of the younger Vane, and his " reluctance" in suffering Pym to take a copy. (Brodie, iii. 91.) Even Oldmixon
doubts not that " all this was theatrical, and the notes were
taken to do Strafford a good turn some time or other, and
the key was sent on purpose to have this paper found among
others." And concludes " it is no matter how we came by
them," (166, 167.) It would have been scarce credible that
history in our own times could have been composed in this
manner, had not Oldmixon furnished his extraordinary specimen of party-writing, and his fierce vulgarity, through all
the solemnity of a large folio.

dence of the elder Vane, Pym unexpectedly brings forward a transcript of these notes which concurred with the particular charge the Secretary had after his two former hesitations witnessed against Strafford. No originals could be produced, as they were declared by the father to have been destroyed in pursuance of the King's desire. At the same time the father considered that the copy which Pym had just delivered in, was ".like those Notes."* The point now pressed was that since Sir Henry

---

* Sir Philip Warwick calls these notes, what probably the original was, " Sir Henry Vane's blotted and blundering paper." We see even by Sir Henry's third extorted testimony that he only considered Pym's copy " like those notes," a most vague mode of authenticating it! Mr. Brodie, here the advocate of a very weak cause, labours to colour the want of recollection in Vane by recriminating on " the memories of the other witnesses of the Privy Council, which continued incurable to the last." How could the other members recollect what Vane had misconceived, namely, that the Irish army was designed to be transported to England, and not to Scotland. I do not deny that when the Irish army had conquered the Scottish, the patriots in England would have been endangered. Mr. Brodie also urges that " the previous want of recollection in Vane proves that he had no understanding with the prosecutors." It is very possible that Vane the father might have found himself entrapped by the infidelity of his son, and the subtilty of Pym.

Vane believed that the present was a true copy, his former written testimony, and his present evidence amounted to the validity of two witnesses, which are legally required to prove an act of treason. This extravagant position, that one person could become two witnesses, was not rejected by the Commons !

A remarkable scene now opened between the father and the son. The younger Vane rose apparently in great trouble, as if this discovery had for ever lost him his father's confidence, and with that air of earnest enthusiasm, which afterwards stamped such a singularity on all his proceedings, he cast himself on the compassion of the House to pardon this trespass on his natural parent, and to recollect that he had acted from his abundant zeal for their common cause. All this while the father sternly looking on his son, declared that he now too clearly saw the unhappy object who had been the source of his troubles in those pressing interrogatories to which he had been put to the torture. However he did not deny that the copy was as good as the original. The House, thus taken by surprise, admiring this conflict of feeling between the father and the son, and more the conscience of the youthful patriot, " a very gracious youth," as the Scottish Co-

venanter designates him, they interfered to reconcile them. But long after, in public, they
appeared to act separately and in opposition to
each other. The old courtier, the Secretary,
retained his office, lifting up his hands and his
voice against the hardier proceedings of his
son, who proved afterwards so remarkable a
personage in the approaching revolution; but
we cannot doubt that he secretly hugged himself that the Vanes at last had struck their
vindictive blow at the great man in whose
presence he had not dared even to imagine
those thoughts of revenge, which lay rankling
in his soul, for contempt so long endured.

We have every reason to believe with Clarendon that the whole scene had been precon-
certed between the Vanes and Pym — and the
political juggle was played off with all the de-
lusion so grateful to those who look to be deceived. Vane the father, on various occasions,
proved to be a faithless or an inept servant to
Charles, and was at last expelled. He went
over a proselyte to that party among whom his
son was to act so conspicuous a part, but no
change of party could elevate his spirit. His
natural abjectness having crept into a bolder
line of conduct, quite alien from his character,
through the instigation of his aspiring son, the

Secretary lived at last to be contemned by all men, and to endure that heaviest curse of bustling ineptitude and unprincipled selfishness—the contempt of his own son!

Strafford was still reserved before he withdrew from the bar to the block, to listen to the two speeches of Pym and St. John. These are both memorable. Baillie considered that " the King never heard a lecture of so free language against his idolised prerogative :" yet the speech of Pym, divested of its personal rancour, is not so democratic but that every constitutional Englishman at this moment would assent to many passages of its condensed and masculine eloquence. It is worthy of our observation that the orators of every party, when laying down the principles of the British Constitution agree in substance, and even in words. The Earl of Strafford delivered himself in a style as constitutional as Pym. It is only in the application of the principles, or in that mental reservation which party advocates permit themselves, or in the different associations of ideas on general terms, that we discover the fallacy of principles and the ambiguity of words.

An interesting incident occurred which interrupted the speech of Pym, but which does

not appear as the speech is printed in Rushworth. The close of Pym's speech is a cruel
personal invective; he labours from the depths
of his imagination to aggravate the pretended
crime of treason — he says, alluding to Strafford,
his death " will not be a new way of blood;
there are marks enough to trace this law to the
very original of this kingdom, and if it hath
not been put into execution, as he (Strafford)
allegeth, these two hundred and forty years, it
was not for want of law, but that, all that time
hath not bred a man bold enough to commit
such crimes as these — he is the only man that
in so long a time hath ventured upon such a
treason as this."

It must have been, we may imagine, at this
passage that the illustrious prisoner raising his
head, fixed his disdainful and indignant glance
on the orator — and it convulsed the speaker's
whole frame. Pym betrayed a sudden confusion — his memory deserted him — his hands
trembled over his papers — he could no longer
find either ideas or notes *— and he abruptly

* It is maliciously observed by Nalson that the famous
reply of Pym to the Earl's defence was " not an extempore
product of his parts and abilities." Nalson too notices that
Pym "fell into a great disorder and confusion, and pulled
out a paper to refresh his memory, which occasioned one of

closed his speech. " To humble the man, God let his memory fail him a little before the end," observes Pym's warm eulogist the Scottish Covenanter.

Strafford indeed often displayed all the silent expression of eloquent gesture. His glance quickly discovered what was passing in his mind — and his motions seemed often a comment on the living text.

Unquestionably Strafford had obtained the secret suffrages of the Lords by his forceful appeals to their better feelings, and by enlightening their political wisdom — and the party who were athirst for his blood, were more than once in despair. The great lawyers, such illustrious names as Selden, Holborn and -

the noble auditors to smile." It certainly does not detract from the merit of a speech to be delivered to the public that the speaker had premeditated it; it would be better that many were so. We may wish that Nalson had been more explicit on the cause of the confusion of ideas and the abrupt close of Pym's speech. It was reported to have been occasioned by the high and disdainful look which Strafford suddenly fixed on Pym, and so disconcerted the orator that he could not recover from this electrical shock given to his feelings. We discover nothing of this in the speech of Pym as given by Rushworth, no more than we do of the remarkable incident of the Vanes which occurred during the trial.

Bridgeman, had declared that there was no law of treason which could reach Strafford. The Commons basely degraded themselves in a debate by menacing those lawyers who dared to plead for that person whom they accused of high-treason.* They actually prosecuted and sent to the Tower the Counsellor Jeffrey Palmer, some time afterwards, not for not urging his points with all possible force, but for the decency and respect with which he had treated "the wicked Earl," as Pym called Strafford. Such are the passions of Parliament! The revolutionary tribunal of France hardly offers an act of more inhuman injustice.

The dark and the sullen St. John, in opposition to his more eminent brothers, now came forward, with his " Argument of Law" to satisfy the scruples of those Members, for many had actually left them, who might oppose the fatal bill of Attainder. In a speech of three hours, replete with the curious erudition of cases of treason, as if still doubtful whether the dusty volumes of a Law-library might fail

---

* Clarendon in noticing this fact adds, "This matter was too gross to receive any public order, and so the debate ended — but it was no doubt their intention to let those gentlemen know how warily they incurred the anger of that terrible congregation."—i 394.

in convincing his auditors, our lawyer argued from the *Lex talionis,* and introduced his famous barbarous comparison—" He that would not have others to have a law, why should he have any himself? It's true we give law to hares and deer because they be beasts of chase, but it was never accounted either cruelty, or foul play, to knock foxes and wolves on the head, as they can be found, because these be beasts of prey." Such was the spirit that hunted down the fallen Minister! Strafford silently betrayed his deep attention—and often by the solemn elevation of his hands and eyes to Heaven, he appealed against the merciless State-Advocate. The indignant emotions of the great man were the only reply the Court could not refuse him, to the invective of this " Law-Argument," which lasted so long, that nothing more was heard on that day. These emotions were not the less dignified nor the less affecting; the auditors of St. John were the spectators of Strafford; his silent gestures had so deeply penetrated their hearts, that a contemporary historian regrets that the pathos of his action could not be preserved from oblivion, as well as that other eloquence whose immortality makes posterity the auditors of Strafford.

The Commons hurried the ferocious bill of

Attainder through their House, by a second reading in one day. On the third reading, Lord Digby forcibly opposed it, and some of the most illustrious names in our legal history protested against it. Lord Digby, the son of the Earl of Bristol—that extraordinary and accomplished man, who had all along proceeded with the popular party and had wound himself into all the secrets of its leaders—on a sudden, and as Clarendon tells us, "before he was so much as suspected,"* left them, as Digby said, "at the final sentence unto death or life of a great Minister of State." He did not hesitate to declare that he continued the same in his opinions, that the Earl of Strafford was a most dangerous Minister, insupportable to free subjects—his rare abilities had only aggravated his practices—Strafford was the grand Apostate of the Commonwealth who must expect no pardon in this world till he be dispatched to the other—but as my conscience stands," added Digby, "my hand must not be to that dispatch."

Digby, when he consented to Strafford's accusation, had been assured by Pym that the notes of Sir Henry Vane would prove his treason; but a transcript of disjointed frag-

* Clarendon Papers, iii. Suppt. liii.

ments, of which even the original did not exist,
containing only " the venomous parts of speech,"
could be of no use but to bring men into danger. At first the Secretary positively denied
the charge about the Irish army—pressed a
second time, he seemed doubtful—yet he who
twice upon oath would not remember, might
well on the third time misremember, where the
difference of a letter *here* for *there*, and *that* for
this, quite alters the case.

" God keep me from giving judgment of
death on any man upon a law made *à poste-
riori*; let the mark be set on the door where
the plague is, and then let him that would
enter die.

" Let every man lay his head upon his heart
and sadly consider what we are going to do,
with a breath either justice or murder—the
danger being so great and the cause so doubtful that I see the best lawyers in diametrical
opposition concerning it; let every man wipe
his heart as he does his eyes when he would
judge of a nice and subtle object.

" Away with personal animosities, away with
all flatteries to the people, in being the sharper
against him because he is odious to them;
away with all fears lest by the sparing of his
blood they may be incensed; away with all

such considerations as that it is not fit for a Parliament, that one accused by it of treason should escape with life."

Digby is accused of volatility of character, but he surely delivered himself on this occasion with earnestness. As for the speaker and the speech, the one with difficulty escaped being sent to the Tower, and the other was honoured by being condemned to the flames. His old party was so enraged, that they would gladly have prepared a block for his head as determinedly as they had decided on one for Strafford. The House expelled Digby. Those who had intimidated the lawyers who offered to plead for the prisoner, and at last would not reply to the legal argument of Lane, the Earl's Advocate, assigning this curt reason that " it was below their dignity to contend with a private lawyer," in the same " public spirit," decided that none of their own Members should be allowed to differ from themselves! It must be confessed that those who were advocating the cause of public liberty, were violating all personal freedom ; and, to say the least, were as partial to the practices of arbitrary government, and even to tyranny itself, as he whom they had condemned.

This memorable trial, which had opened on

the 22d of March, closed as far as the evidence,
on the 13th of April, but these charges not
amounting to a capital conviction, it became
necessary to urge their arguments on legal
points, but on the 30th of April the trial was
abruptly interrupted by the bill of attainder.

One party asserts that the Commons suddenly declined the prosecution by *Trial* from
a failure of the evidence, but the Parliamentarians insist that the votes of the Lords on
two particular charges, that of billeting soldiers and another, had sufficiently convicted the
Earl of treason without any need of their bill
of Attainder. Thus on their own showing their
illegal and anomalous violence was a gratuitous
exercise of the worst tyranny. To obviate the
odium of this conduct, an artful reason has
been alleged. The Commons resolved to make
the King himself as judge a party in it; and
though the common way of process would have
convicted Strafford capitally, as they assume,
yet then the King would have been passive
only in his punishment; but they had resolved
that he should be a participator in the condemnation of death, in terror to all future evil
counsellors.* Such is one of those insolent
avowals of a party, when, to extricate them-

* Oldmixon, 169.

selves from being implicated in one heavy charge, they have the effrontery to assign another motive, which though it gives a different turn to the circumstance, is not inferior to it in baseness. Were that true, which is denied, that the Commons could have convicted Strafford capitally without having recourse to their bill of Attainder, their present proceeding was only a personal persecution of their unfortunate Monarch. *

The truth is more manifest than the evidence of party-writers on either side. Long before the trial a formidable party in the Commons had decided on the public execution of the Minister. The Scots were implacable, for Strafford's decision respecting them was well known ; and their army was now maintained by " the brotherly assistance " of the Scottised English, who were at once their masters and servants. So intimate was the mutual dependance ! The immolation of their arch-adversary, the Minister of Charles, was a bond of blood which was to seal this dark and secret alliance.

That this public execution had been resolved on appears as early as the second of April, long before the first part of the trial had closed. The famous Wariston confided to his Scottish correspondent, Lord Balmerino, the settled scheme. Wariston, the great head of the Covenanters, was deep in the secrets of his English friends. The whole passage is remarkable. " Strafford's business is but yet in the fifteenth article. The Lower House, if they see that the King gains many of the Upper House not to condemn him, will make a bill of *teinture*,* and condemnation formally in their own house, and send it up to their House as any other act of Parliament, to be voiced (voted) formally." Twenty days afterwards, on the 22d of April, he writes exultingly " The Lower House has given up their bill (delivered)—grow in daily strength—*We have Strafford's life!* They are thinking on monies for us. Lord encourage and direct them !"

During the progress of the trial, the Commons appear to have discovered that public opinion, when not under the guidance of party, and even that of their own supporters, was more divided than ever. A month had elapsed and little had been gained by their " accumulative evidence " and their " constructive trea-

* Dalrymple's Memorials, 117. So Wariston spells *Attainder;* a plain proof that though he relished the thing, the Scotch lawyer was not acquainted with the word. Or is this the term in Scotch law ?

son ;" and now, since their proofs did not amount to legal evidence, they determined on a legislative power; at once decreeing Strafford guilty of treason, every one might eagerly vote for the execution of the attainted man, without requiring any further testimony than his own vote.

This doubtless hastened the bill of Attainder; which bears the indelible stamp of that perturbation with which it was framed. After it was brought to the Lords, it languished in the Upper House, for few of the Peers were disposed to consent to a verdict of death on the illustrious State-prisoner, who, though not blessed with many friends among his Peers, stood however strangely condemned for a capital crime of a novel and uncertain treason; the unheard of treason of a post-facto law, so that that was made treason in the case of Strafford which could not have been treason at the time it was done; and whose conviction was considered so anomalous, even by the Commons themselves, that they had providently introduced a proviso that their act should not be held as a precedent in after-times.

This extraordinary clause has proved a sore point with the Anti-Straffordians. From the first it was considered by most persons who

trusted to their common sense, that it must
stand as a perpetual evidence of their injustice.
It is obvious that the Commons never intended
to have stigmatised their own bill — and it has
therefore been attempted to explain away the
monstrous absurdity of the declaration that
the Act of one Parliament should never be
a precedent for another. I shall throw into a
note a remarkable specimen of the length to
which party-purposes may drive some who dis-
honour any which they join.*

* The present instance of literary depravity would be difficult to parallel unless we search for others in the same
writer of history. Oldmixon gives as from Rushworth the
following passage. " This Proviso hath occasioned the common discourse and opinion that the judgment against
the Earl was enacted never to be drawn into precedent *in
Parliament*, whereas *it expressly respects only Judges in inferior Courts*." Rushworth by a marginal note marked the
mysterious proviso, but he offered no explanation whatever.
All that here appears in italics is a villainous interpolation
of Oldmixon, who, blending his own explanation with Rushworth's note, to a careless reader it becomes authenticated.
Oldmixon took the notion from Wellwood, who affects to
call the general opinion "a silly mistake which has gained
some credit in the world, but it relates only to Judges and
inferior Courts, who notwithstanding the present act, shall
not adjudge or interpret any treason in any other manner
than they should have done before the making of this act."
It is extraordinary that this explanation which explains
nothing, could be adopted by successive writers of the same

Hitherto the King throughout the trial of Strafford had preserved a silence as deep as his sorrows. Every morning was Charles seen in the trellised cabinet reserved for him half an hour earlier than the Lords. There sate the pensive and dejected Monarch often occupied in taking notes. Though constitutionally absent, the idea that his personal presence would animate his unfortunate Minister, or at least testify to him the deep anxiety of his royal Master, probably led to this un-

political school. The state of the question remains unaltered : they, the Commons, declared that the act which themselves had done should not be considered as a precedent. Yet this mystifying explanation has been repeated by Mrs. Macaulay ; but as if she were not quite satisfied with it, she draws from her alembic a more rectified spirit, asserting that " this decree of the Commons shows a very laudable attention to the preservation of public liberty." (ii. 454.) Mr. Brodie tells us that " it is an usual clause in a bill *pro re nata*, that it should not be drawn into a precedent, as a proper restraint upon the ordinary Courts to which alone it is applicable." (ii. 130.) Mr. Brodie, no doubt, is a skilful lawyer, and may solve historical and moral enigmas technically ; but to those who are apt, as Wellwood says, to fall into " a silly mistake," or as Oldmixon explicitly calls it, " this general error in the histories of disaffected authors," that is, authors who are not for striking off people's heads for a party-purpose — our difficulties remain as great as ever. We do not contemplate on two kinds of Justice — the one remitting attention. Charles and the Queen never returned to their palace, as Henrietta assured Madame de Motteville, without aching hearts, and often in tears.

At this crisis, Charles for the first time in this eventful cause was induced to appear openly in it. The King addressed the Parliament from the Throne. He confided to them his secret and oppressed feelings. He implored them to spare his conscience in this awful trial.

for the nonce.—Are there two kinds of Justice as well as Courts? Is that which is proclaimed to be treason in the Higher Court not allowed to be so in the Inferior?

Our last philosophical historian on this topic has more deeply penetrated into the designs of the actors in the present scene. Mr. Hallam has said nothing on Wellwood's explanation, but I believe he has assigned the real motive of this obscure and ridiculous proviso in the bill of Attainder. " It seems to have been introduced in order to quiet the apprehensions of some among the Peers who had gone great lengths with the government, and were astonished to find that their obedience to the King could be turned into treason against him." (i. 566.)

The truth seems to be, that the Commons, determined to accomplish their great deed, in the heat of passion were entangled in difficulties—and got over them as well as they could. Historians who write in the calm of leisure appear sometimes to forget that many important events have been transacted not with the wisdom of Legislators or the purity of Patriots, but with the heated haste of Partisans.

He had never intended to have spoken on this business, and *had they proceeded according to law*, the law should have taken its course, but by adopting the way of attainder they had forced him to become a party in his quality of Judge. They well knew that he had been present from the opening to the close of this great affair, and therefore he could not pretend ignorance of what had occurred. He assured them what no one could know so well as himself, that never had Strafford suggested bringing over an Irish army into England—nor to alter in the least any of the laws of England, much less to alter all law itself. " I must tell you this, that I think no body durst be ever so impudent to move me in it; for if they had, I should have put a mark upon them and made them an example to all posterity.

" I desire to be rightly understood. I cannot condemn him of high treason, but I cannot say I can clear him of his misdemeanour.— I do think my Lord of Strafford is not fit hereafter to serve me, or the commonwealth, in any place of trust, no not so much as to be a constable.

" Find a way to satisfy justice and your own fears, but do not press on my conscience. I have not so ill deserved of the Parliament at this time that they should press me on this tender point. I leave it to you, my Lords, to find some such way as to bring me out of this great strait. Certainly he that thinks him guilty of High-treason, may condemn him of misdemeanour."

Such was the speech Charles the First was induced to deliver either to relieve his long harassed feelings or deceived by the advice of others; but whether he was mistaken, or had been deceived, it is quite certain that he was in earnest. The apologists of Charles tell us that it was either a sinister project of the enemies of Strafford, Bristol and Saville, to hasten the catastrophe, which is not probable, for neither of these Lords were present when it was voted, or the treacherous counsel of Lord Say, who the King was now weak enough to imagine had become his friend since his recent admission into place and power.* Strafford himself protested against the King's interposition, and at once saw through all the mischief.

* Clarendon sarcastically alluding to Lord Say, observes, " Those who believed his will to be much worse than his un- derstanding had the uncharitableness to think that he in- tended to betray his master, and put the ruin of the Earl out of question." Father Philips, the Queen's Confessor, who was likely to be informed, also alludes to Lord Say.

The Commons, who had already counted on
their own triumph when they saw the King
still doubtful to act, were in no temper to
retrace their steps, but raising a more violent
clamour insisted that the Royal interference,
during the progress of a Bill in Parliament,
forejudging their councils, had more openly
violated their privilege than ever!

All historians have censured, or lamented,
the ill-timed interposition of the King. In
the humbled tone of supplication, we perceive
only the language of the heart, and all those
distracted emotions which were still more evident in those two fatal concessions, immediately to follow, when Charles, as if insensible
by despair, with an utter carelessness of self-
preservation, signed the commission for the execution of Strafford against " his conscience,"*

---

* The remembrance of that act embittered his after-days
with the most melancholy contrition. In a letter among
the Harleian MSS. 6988. fo. 106. to the Queen, Charles
writes that " He had sinned against his conscience, for the
truth is I was surprised with it instantly after I made that
base sinful concession concerning the Earl of Strafford. I
hope that God will accept of my hearty repentance." I
quote this as I have shown that Henrietta could not have
advised from herself Charles to an act which he has noticed
to her in this manner, and which evidently shows that the
advice came from a different quarter.

and that famous bill which hurried in a few hours through the House, perpetuated the Parliament independent of the King. An act by which the Sovereign virtually dethroned himself.

There was no political wisdom in the King's address from the throne; but whether he had delivered that speech, or remained mute in despair, the result had been the same. The trial of the Earl of Strafford, either from matter of fact, or matter of law, was only assuming the forms of justice to perform an unjust act. Ere his conviction was recorded, his doom had been sealed, for the execution had been pronounced before the arraignment.

The secret history of this momentous period more deeply interests us than almost any in our domestic annals; the trial of the King himself hardly exceeded it. The execution of Strafford was but the precursor of that mighty and yet distant event.

Here let us pause, to view the state of men's minds on the trial of Strafford, and the secret causes which were at work, hastening on his fate. Ireland had been ruled, and she called that rule tyranny; Scotland would have been conquered, and she called it treason; England beheld a Minister whom she dreaded, as the vast instrument of the regal prerogative. The fate of the great Minister, whether he was to be snatched out of the hands of the merciless who stood athirst for his blood, or whether the state-victim was to bleed on the altar of the nation, involved so many principles of policy, so many duties of moral justice, and such sympathies of our common humanity, that it was not only the King and his Minister and the leaders of Opposition who were at variance, the intense interest pervaded the recesses of domestic life, and the opposite views of individuals separated for ever in opinion and in act, the most ancient friendships. Anecdotes recorded of independent men reveal the feelings of the times. The members for Cornwall, neighbours and friends, acting usually in concert, are an instance. Sir Bevil Grenville begged his colleague Sir Alexander Carew not to have a hand in this ominous business of the death of the Earl of Strafford. Carew fiercely replied, " was I sure to be the next man that should suffer upon the same scaffold, and with the same axe, I would give my consent to the passing of the bill." The Earl of Essex complained that he was weary of arguments. After listening to Mr. Hyde, who would have saved the life of the Minister but have deprived him

of all political power, the Earl waived any
farther discussion, and shaking his head, exclaimed " stone-dead hath no fellow."   We
may believe that such honourable men were
perfectly free on this occasion from all partici-
patiou of mere party-purposes, and yet we see
how opposite were their consciences.   But this
was an unhappy time for consciences, since
they talked much of a public and a private one.
There was a new doctrine, that the King is
obliged to conform himself and his own understanding to the advice and conscience of his
Parliaments; or as Warburton clearly discri-
minates this invasion of the Sovereign's veto,
" it was taking away the King's negative voice,
and therefore this *public* conscience was as
absurd an idea as it was a wicked one."

The King had pleaded for his " conscience,"
but in that day of political passion, and in that
dark struggle of Prerogative and Privilege,
even men of the purest principles dreaded the
one, and feared to lose the other.

Could we enter into the palace of Whitehall, observe its disturbed movements, and
penetrate into the cabinet of the afflicted Monarch, wavering in doubt and dismay ; could
we see the House of Lords resisting the popular
clamour till they flew from their seats in ter-

·ror; could we pass into the City and discover a sudden irritation in the public mind acted on by artifices till then unpractised; could we join the party of Pym, under his secreting roof, where the Scottish Covenanters, Hampden among them, held their conclaves and ratified their indissoluble covenant — we should contemplate an unparalleled scene of the disturbed state of a whole nation.

In some respects we are not unfurnished with certain outlines of these intrigues and manœuvres on both sides; and by connecting so many distinct but simultaneous movements, we may form a tolerable conception of that secret history of this period which otherwise we do not possess.

It is remarkable that when the Earl of Strafford at the beginning of his persecution appeared among the people, this fallen Minister was looked on with awe, and was courteously saluted, both on his landing from the Tower and on his return.* As the trial pro-

---

* Some writers, and others, had reported that at first the crowd had betrayed their inveterate hatred of the Earl, and had declared that " if Strafford passed the stroke of justice, they would tear him to pieces." This is positively denied by Rushworth. " In this report, as in all others of this nature, more is thrust upon the vulgar than they did justly deserve at *this time*." (viii. 42.)

ceeded, the public opinion was oftener in favour of this state-prisoner than against him;
and as we see by Grotius's letter and by many
other authorities,* candid and honourable men
had concluded that the Earl must stand ac-
quitted of the high charges of acts of treason.
It is evident that the people had not yet caught
the contagious feelings of the ruling party.
In a few short weeks we discover the populace
pushed on by some unknown impulses, bar-
barously clamouring for Strafford's execution,
and marching in open insurrection under the
eye of the Sovereign. We cannot account for
this extraordinary change, unless we suppose
that very extraordinary means had been adopted to organize this *mobocracy*.

* Very many, were it necessary to produce them. I shall
however quote the words of Baxter, a contemporary; they
take a comprehensive view of an important topic. " Those
that connived at these tumults were glad to see the people
of their mind in the main, and thought it would do much to
facilitate their work and hold the lower members to their
cause ; for though the House was unanimous enough in condemning ship-money and the Bishop's innovations, &c. *yet it was
long doubtful which side would have the major vote in the matter
of the Earl of Strafford's death.*"---Baxter's Narrative, fol. 19.

CHAPTER VI.

THE ARTS OF INSURGENCY.

LORD CLARENDON, in a curious narrative concerning that extraordinary genius Lord Digby, would insinuate that his Lordship abandoned the party of Pym not only for "their desperate designs," as Clarendon stigmatises them, but from his indignation at the artifices of faction which they practised. On these his Lordship has taken this general view. " The uningenuity of their proceedings, and the foul arts they could give themselves leave to use to compass any thing they proposed to do; their method was first to consider what was necessary to be done for some public end which might reasonably enough be wished for that public end, and then to make no scruple of doing any thing which might probably bring it to pass, let it be of what nature it would."* This

* Clarendon's State Papers, iii. Suppt. liii.

charge is heavy, and Clarendon is an adversary ;
but justly has Dr. Lingard observed that " his
assertion seems to be fully supported by the
facts." The description of Clarendon may be
considered as the secret principle of those arts
of insurgency which we must ever regret were
so ignobly practised by the lofty advocates of
freedom. It is this which has sometimes
clouded over with suspicion their integrity,
and polluted their patriotism with artifices
which we only afterwards discovered among
the criminals of France. The political doctrine that the end sanctifies the means, is the
casuistry of the worst part of mankind, and is
a principle which while it allows of every base
and dishonourable act, will also include the
barbarous crime of assassination.

The arts of insurgency practised by the popular party under Pym, were very various,
and by the skill of their practice seem to have
been refined into a system. Their Scottish
masters had taught more than one successful
lesson to their imitative pupils. One of the
most dextrous of these arts is that of marshall-
ing a troubled multitude, inflaming the passions
of the people whom yet they control. Whenever the heats of the House seemed to abate,
and patriotism loitered in the ardent course it

had to run, to strike a new terror in the Government, and spread dismay among the members who had not embraced the designs of the
prevalent party, the mob which had triumphed
at Edinburgh seemed to have been transferred
to the English metropolis. The system was
adapted to a larger scale, suitable to the magnitude of the theatre where the political drama
was now to be acted.

The PRESS, no longer being under restraint,
a people unaccustomed to its freedom would
naturally riot in its licentiousness, and it
swarmed with portentous pamphlets. Pamphlets and Tracts are the production of political freedom and of an agitated people. They
never are more abundant than in disturbed
times, when men think what they list, and
write what they think, and all seem ready to
govern, and none to obey. Of the nations of
Europe, our country long stood unrivalled for
the rapid succession of these busy records of
men's thoughts—these suggestions of their opposite inferences and their eternal differences.
Of these leaves of the hour and volumes of a
week, the labours of the passions, the wisdom,
or the folly of our countrymen, during the Revolution of Charles the First, in that single
period of twenty years, from 1640 to 1660,

about thirty thousand appear to have started up. We have been a nation of pamphleteers. The French in their Revolution, which so often resembled our own in its principles and its devices, could not avoid the same impulse of instructing, or corrupting, their fellow-citizens; but the practice seemed to them so novel that a recent French biographer designates an early period in the French Revolution as that one when " the art of pamphlets had not yet reached perfection."* The collection of the French revolutionary pamphlets now stands by the side of the English tracts of the age of Charles the First; as abundant in number and as fierce in passion; rival monuments which exist together, for the astonishment and the instruction of posterity, for whom they reveal so many suppressed secrets in the history of man.†

The pamphlets of this time were usually directed to prepare men's minds to the impending changes in the Church and State. Charles the First, by his constant notice of these ensnaring pamphlets, appears to have been most sensitive

---

* Mirabeau, Biog. Universelle, xxiv. 96.

† Most of the thirty thousand English tracts were collected by the order of Charles the First, and became the gift of George the Third to our national library. The French collection has been a recent acquisition.

to these "poisoners of the minds of his weak subjects;—amazed by what eyes these things are seen and by what ears they are heard.' He answered the mightier pamphlets published by the-Parliament itself. "We are contented to let ourself fall to any office that may undeceive our people and to take more pains this way by our pen than ever King hath done." Charles was such an attentive observer of these pamphlets, that he once paid ten pounds only for the perusal of one, which could not otherwise be procured. The custom now began of printing the speeches of the leading members in the Commons, and sometimes by the order of the House. Some of the speakers avowedly printed their own speeches.* These fugitive leaves were every where dispersed and every where eagerly read. Baxter, in the curious folio of his auto-biography, tells us they were " greedily bought up throughout the land, which greatly increased the people's apprehension of their danger."† I have seen some which doubtless recommended themselves by bearing the authentic stamp of the well-cut portrait in wood

* "Five speeches by Sir Benjamin Rudyard, printed according to his own true copies, the former being absurdly false."

† Baxter's Narrative of his Life, fo. 18—1696.

of the portly Pym, who then reigning with
absolute power, bore the nick-name of " King
Pym." But it seems that more were written
than were published. Many Royalist tracts
remain in their manuscript state, no one caring
to print books out of fashion, or had the courage to brave the authority of the men in
power; and Nalson complains that the speeches
in favour of Episcopacy were so completely
suppressed or discouraged, that when he made
his collection, but a few years after, they were
utterly lost, while those on the other side by
passing into so many hands were easily procured.

The pulpit was a state-engine of not inferior
magnitude to the press. The Presbyter, and
the Puritan, had not always complained unjustly of what they styled " Court Divinity,"
inculcating in the indissoluble alliance of devotion and politics,—the strictest conformity,
and the most passive obedience. In truth however they themselves did not find these servile principles irreconcileable with their own.
Our Non-conformists only aspired to change
their direction; for they insisted on as strict
conformity and as passive an obedience to
themselves, in remodelling the mighty fabric
of the Hierarchy and the Kingdom, by the

petty Calvinistical republic of their own Presbytery.

In London a new scene opened. Here the Scotch Divines with rigid sanctified looks, talking in scriptural phrases of every-day occurrences, and with gestures, as of men in ecstasy, disordered, but impressive, thundered their novel doctrines in St. Antholine's church; the first whith was assigned in England for the Covenanters. The Puritans, who had long held themselves as their cousins in insurrection, but had lived in secrecy and seclusion, now acknowledged a closer affinity; and in their fraternal embrace gave precedence to their more active and triumphant elder. The patriotic party had often denounced the Clergy for meddling in temporal affairs; but their own clergy, for such now the presbyterian may be called, were in fact their chief agents in acting on the people. They sermonized like the venal "leading articles" of the present day, trumpeting forth the most desperate alarms, and vomiting the most violent menaces. These persons, like the retainers of our party-papers, we are told in one of the royal declarations, " were all the week attending the doors of both Houses to be employed in their errands." And in their " Lectures," or seven-hours Sermons, all the

news of the week was divinely commented on
from their pulpits. These their personal invectives made palatable, and their heated imagination, bewitching to " the corner-creepers"—
the secret malcontent—the straying lounger—
and all that disaffected populace which hang
loosely on society, and among whom the seditious will always obtain a majority. Their
religion inflamed their politics. The convulsed
bosoms of the crowd were electrified by the
new saints; then was seen the mob without,
clinging to the doors and windows, when ex-
cluded by the mob within, catching the barbarous accents of a provincial messenger of
heaven. " We pray, preach, and print against
them what we are able most freely. Many a
sore thrust got both men and women thronging into our sermons"— says Baillie. The voice
of the Covenant no longer cried in the wilder-
ness. " We hope a harvest of fruits are coming," exclaims our covenanting zealot. The
extirpation " root and branch" of the Bishops,
and the ominous spectacle of a headless Lord
Lieutenant of Ireland, were to anticipate the
planting of that " Rose of Sharon," and those
" lilies of the valley," the sour intolerant Scotch
Presbytery.

Arts of more subtile nature even than this

combination of pamphlets, speeches, and preachings, were practised in those fugitive chimæras
—rumours and reports. These shook with
their hot and cold fits an aguish populace.
The calumny which was either too vague to
grapple with, or which took long to remove,
always left something sticking behind it, which
repeated till believed, has, I fear, sometimes
become history for all parties. Assuredly there
are historical calumnies! The lie which pros-
pered through its morning was forgotten at eve
only to be supplied by another. In distempered times that which is not intelligible, every
one interprets for himself; and such bruited
news by their very extravagance, are rendered
the more effective, for the ignorance of the
people often exceeding their credulity, every
one in imaginary dangers is prone to think
the very worst that is possible. It was news,
that the Papists with cavalry, burrowed under
ground in Surrey, but were more openly gathering together in Lancashire; it was news
that there was a plot to blow up the river with
gunpowder in order to drown the city ;* it was

* Mr. Brodie, almost ashamed of these artful rumours spread
abroad by a party, says " they were cunningly exaggerated,"
and particularly censures Clarendon, as retailing " stories
which appear to be pure fiction ;" undoubtedly he would

news that the French and even the Danes
were preparing for a descent, though the Covenanters had reason to be certain that the cabinet of the Louvre were in no mood to lend
their aid to that of Whitehall. A sanctified
tailor sitting under a hedge, " mending the
notes he had taken of some sermon," informs
the Commons that he had listened to two sol-
dier-like-men, who were acquainting one another with a settled employment of some of
their comrades, to dispatch several members of

consider the present ludicrous one as such. I find it however confirmed by Fuller. He assures us that one of the
most prevailing dangers among the Londoners was " a design laid for a mine of powder under the Thames to cause
the river to drown the city." The people had a public thanks-
giving on its discovery. The plot in truth was not so much
at the bottom of the Thames, as at the bottom of their purses,
which the Scots long drained. The tricks of this nature
which were practised, were more numerous than we care to
trouble the reader with. Could it be imagined that the
House of Commons, I would rather say, a party in it, sent
forth an order to the Justices of Peace at Dorchester, " to
make diligent search for a barrel of gunpowder which had
been sent down for a barrel of soap," and " to send an account of the matter to the House." Even Mrs. Macaulay
has confessed, that the Commons affected many panics
which they did not experience,—she will not, however, confess that the mobs of five and six thousand citizens in arms,
was any thing more than the " Vox Populi."

both Houses; the Commoners at the rate of forty shillings, and the Lords at ten pounds! This worthy's name has even been chronicled; and his notable discovery enters into English history, for on this occasion, the Commons emitted several orders for the security of the Houses, as well as the Members. It was still worse when a midnight alarm shook the city that the King was coming down with horse and foot, and all the citizens started up in their warm night-caps and rushed to arms.

The people were cast into political delusions, and self-tormented by imaginary horrors. A ludicrous but authentic incident of the times is scarcely credible. So susceptible was this diseased state of the public mind, that Sir Walter Earle, one of the zealous but weakest adversaries of Strafford, and a creature of Pym's—rose to make a report of a design to blow up the House of Commons! The news acted as if the explosion had taken effect. In the pressure some alarmed listeners suddenly leaning forward, part of the flooring in the gallery gave way—at the cracking many hurried out—Sir John Wray, an honest Lincolnshire patriot, exclaiming that "he smelt gunpowder," and another leaving the House saying "There was hot work, and a great fire within"—the simple

words of the panic-struck knight, and the metaphorical orator, were too literally caught up
by the persons in the lobby, who sent them
to the people on the river. Before carriages
were in general use the river was a great tho-
roughfare; boats were used ere hackney-coaches
were projected; a considerable portion of the
busy populace were always on the Thames —
these re-echoed the report to the city — the
drums beat, the train-bands marched, "a world
of people in arms" flew to Westminster, and
this ridiculous incident* satisfactorily confirm-

---

* I hesitated for some time to record this incredible incident, though I found it in Nalson, very exactly dated with
the names of persons. The particulars I afterwards discovered amply confirmed by a contemporary and a Covenanter present in London —Baillie, i. 296. It is equal to
any of those retailed by Clarendon, which Mr. Brodie must
have known, as well as myself, were NOT "cunningly exaggerated" and "pure fictions." In two or three months
these "treasons" amounted to thirty-nine, according to the
account of a venerable Member of the House of Commons.—
History of the English and Scotch Presbytery, Villa Franca,
1659.

Since writing this note in examining "the Diurnal Occurrences," I find that so far from this gunpowder-plot
being considered as too extravagant for the popular credulity, that five days afterwards "the Commons appointed a
committee to search about the Parliament-house lest any

ed to the Commons their own absolute power over the people.

These rumours indeed, as Clarendon describes them, "upon examination always vanished; but for the time, and they were always · applied as useful articles of time, served to transport common minds with fears and apprehensions, and so induced them to comply in sense with those who ever like soonest to find remedies for those diseases which none but themselves could discover.

The source of these rumours must be traced to that *surveillance,* to use a French term for a French practice, under which the town seems to have been placed, and the patriot Pym must now figure in the degraded form of a *Lieutenant de Police.* Spies and informers were daily conveying to Pym the table-talk of taverns, and even of private society; by such secret intelligence, perpetually renewed, his sleepless vigilance preserved his ascendancy in the House of Commons. There he ruled so despotically that the royalists at length nicknamed the man they most dreaded, "King

plot should be in agitation against them." Either they had really frightened themselves, or they forgot to stow in the cellar some barrels of powder.

Pym." The art of raising these popular commotions, and the greater art of regulating them,
depended on a double contrivance. The people were to terrify the Government, but they
were themselves to be thrown into an occa-
sional panic, for the affrightened are the most
docile to be led.

But pamphlets, speeches, preachings and
rumours, had not exhausted the invention of
these agitators of the people ; they were to be
taught something more hideous, in the cry for
blood ! One more deadly arrow lay in their
quiver — it was their petitions !

The most humble petitions had always preceded the most decisive acts of the insubordina-
tion of the Covenanters. Here again we discover how closely Pym's party copied their model.
The first striking evidence of the manœuvres of
the Scottish party in the House of Commons,
as far as appears publicly,—for what passed in
private has been only partially detected — was
a petition of the citizens to both Houses for
justice to be executed on the Earl of Strafford.
This petition was presented on the 23rd of
April, immediately after Lord Digby had
offended them by the reasons he alleged for his
desertion of their cause. The Aldermen and
Common-council, who afterwards were so alert

on these occasions, here only make their chief
lament on the decay of trade and the difficulty
with which country tradesmen pay their debts
in London, — in consequence of the delay in
sending Strafford to the block.   This petition
is said to have been subscribed by twenty thousand of good rank and quality.

Improving on the art of petitioning, in
time we come to petitions of " the Apprentices" and " those whose apprenticeship had
lately expired."   In that day, when there existed no police in the City, and no regular
military environed the Court, not the least formidable part of his Majesty's liege subjects
were those " Operatives" as they have since
styled themselves,—the apprentices of London.
An insurrection of " the London boys," as the
Spanish Ambassador called them, frequently
alarmed Whitehall ; nor were their number,
at least, contemptible, for when they once
offered to attend on the Parliament, they were
said to amount " to ten thousand who offered
their services with warlike weapons."*   It was
a militia for insurgency ready at all seasons,
and might be depended on for any work of
destruction, at the cheapest rate.†

* Nalson, ii. 831.

† We have the deposition and an information of some of

The number of the present subscribers from the City is so considerable; and as these shortly after sallied forth with daggers and bludgeons, the inference is obvious, that this train of explosion must have been long laid, else the combustible line could not have ignited at a touch.

Clarendon has related an extraordinary artifice in getting up these addresses. A petition was first prepared, modest in its form, and not unreasonable in its matter. Such a petition was certain of being well received at a public meeting, and a few hands instantly filled the paper. As numbers multiplied, many sheets were required to be tacked to the pe-

these apprentices. When one of these had boastingly returned from Whitehall, and was asked the reason of his joining with the mob, he said that " They were sent for by some Parliament-men"—that " his master was a constable, who gave him a sword and bid him go," and that other apprentices had received the same directions from their masters. One Captain Ven, of the City, appears to have been their Marechal-de-Camp, for one evening he issued his orders to apprentices to repair to Westminster with arms, for there was an uproar in the Parliament-house ; " Mr. Lavender's man," who was at that moment " taking tobacco with a party," instantly threw his pipe away, to the surprise of the honest citizens, who had not been aware of the military genius of " Mr. Lavender's man."

tition. The original petition was then cut off
and supplied by a new one, framed more suitable to the design in hand, and the long list
of names was annexed to the amended address.
Persons saw their names appended to petitions
they had never heard of, and when they complained, were engaged by threats or promises
to sit still, and trust to those who, they were
told, knew better than they which petition
should have been preferred.

Such invidious practices sometimes betrayed
themselves. A petition was presented to the
House from Herefordshire, which referred to
certain matters which had been debated on the
preceding night, signed by many thousand
hands. It is evident that this petition must
have been one of those which were substituted
for the original; and was presented in their
hurry some days before it was intended that it
should make its appearance.* These petitions
thus were often the single work of a faction,
in the name of the county, whose real sub-
scriptions were put to that which they had
never subscribed. Scenes of petitioners more
ludicrous occurred when the porters, said to
be many thousands in number, with great eloquence protested against " a malignant, blood-

* Husband's Collections, 537.

seeking, rebellious party, insulting the privileges of Parliament, which if not punished,
they should be forced to make good the saying that necessity has no law." The climax
of petitioning was, however, all the beggars,
who declared that by means of the Bishops
and Popish Lords they knew not where to get
bread—their religion and their lives were in
danger; " but as they never doubted the
House of Commons, and understood that all
stuck in the Lords' House, they wished to
learn the names of those Peers who opposed
the Commons." A deputation of tradesmen's
wives, headed by Mrs. Stagg, a brewer's wife,
was as courteously received; Pym came to the
door of the Commons, and at last with great
political gallantry, told the " good women" that
it had come " at a seasonable time," requesting
them now " to turn their petition into prayers,
for the members of the House, who were ready
to relieve their husbands and children." A
people are sometimes excited into follies, which,
when they are once forgotten, their historian
incurs the risk of being suspected of gross credulity. When the day arrived that the ruling
faction of the Independents found the petitions of the people troublesome, although they
allowed of all which suited their measures,

according to Lord Hollis, they fined and committed the petitioners of whom they disap-
proved; and on a petition for peace, some
horse were sent out to run over the people, and
the Trained Bands fired among the petitioners.*

Minuter artifices were the usual practices
of Pym, for to his adroit management the
more subtile manœuvres must be traced. One
was the impeachment of persons whose evidence, it was suspected, might favour Strafford,
not one of whom were afterwards prosecuted.
This remarkably appeared in the case of Sir
George Radcliffe : no charge was afterwards
brought forward; it was sufficient that the
Earl lost the benefit of the aid of his confidential friend. On the same principle, the Irish
Chancellor, the Chief Justice, the Bishop of
Derry, and others were alike impeached, which
disqualified them as witnesses at Strafford's
trial, but the impeachments themselves were
all dropped. When we recollect that on one
occasion, when an Irish witness was so mean
a personage that Pym, ashamed to bring him
forward before the Committee, had him dressed up for the occasion in a satin suit, we may
at least regret that such cunning was resorted
to by him who, advocating the high cause of

* Hollis' Memoirs, 179.

civil freedom, stamped on its face the ugly
features of a conspiracy, and degraded acts
which should spring from a nobler source, to
vulgar trickery.   On these Irish impeachments
Hume has truly observed, that " this step,
which was an exact counterpart to the proceedings in England, served also the same purposes." We trace the same management in
the Scottish affairs.

The ministers of Charles at Edinburgh
were held out to public odium as " incendiaries ;" this new art of calumny seems to have
afforded a hint to the English party to apply
political nicknames.   An early invention of
this kind about this very time was the term
" Delinquents." The Commons who were then
usurping a power far more extensive than a
Star-chamber tyranny, spread a general terror
by this expedient.   They declared any persons
to be delinquents on the slightest petition, and
as such they were to be prosecuted.   Many
were so stigmatised, of whom afterwards nothing
more was heard, but the dreadful sentence was
always suspended over their heads.   They who
would have opposed their more violent measures were silenced, and they who were thus
branded knew that their fate depended on 'their
acquiescence.   In this novel tyranny no one

could be brought forward as a witness in any
case the Commons disliked to hear. On one
occasion we find Sir Walter Earle, the creature
of Pym, giving information of some dangerous
words spoken by persons whom he did not
name; on which the Speaker was directed to
issue a warrant to apprehend such persons as
Sir Walter shall nominate. The whole kingdom seemed at the mercy of Sir Walter Earle,
or any other whisperer in the Speaker's ear.
The Catholic Lords were so appalled, that Clarendon tells us they early withdrew themselves
from the House of Peers, which was the drift
of the powerful party. The reign of Pym was
a reign of terror. Judges in open court were
dragged from their bench, and hurried to
prison, and a troop of horse struck a panic
through the learned brotherhood of Westminster-Hall. " The barbarous curiosity of opening
letters" was also revived. We hardly can for-
give these rapid demolishers of Star-chambers
and High Commission Courts for reviving
them in a more fearful shape, and advocating
the cause of civil freedom by the very means
which annihilated it. To whom but to one
great organizing head can we ascribe such a
systematic conduct, and such an unity of design? The purity of the patriotism of Pym,

however plausible its pretexts, and however
able his talents, it must at least be confessed
was directed against Strafford with every appearance of personal malignity.

When the King addressed the Houses from
the throne supplicating for the life of Strafford
and pleading for his own conscience, the party
enraged at discovering that they had not yet,
as they had imagined, sufficiently intimidated
the Sovereign, now took the more certain
means. The King's address was on Saturday.
On Sunday the pulpiteers in the city were
thundering with " the necessity of justice upon
some great delinquents ;" and on Monday morning a rabble of six thousand streamed forth
from the city, armed and accoutred with all
the hasty weapons they could snatch up;* these

---

* There is a curious instance of party-paragraphs in " the
Diurnal Occurrences," May 3d. We are there told of this
very mob that they were " a great number of citizens, five
thousand or thereabouts, being for the most part men of
good fashion," who having stopped the Lords, &c. complained
that " they were undone for the want of execution on Strafford ; trading was so decayed thereby." The writer in his
notice that these citizens " for the most part were men of
good fashion," and no doubt they wore their holiday array
which they had not put off since the preceding " Sabbath"
Lectures—has entirely omitted the more material information, that they were all armed men with rapiers, dags, and
clubs.

thronging down to the Palace-yard, hideously clamoured for "justice and execution!" The King spoke to them from a balcony, and desired they would go home and mind their business. The life of the Sovereign was menaced under his own windows, and Charles the First was more degraded as a Monarch at that moment than when on the same spot a few years after he ascended the scaffold.

Whose hand behind the curtain played the strings which gave such regulated motions to these wooden actors of insurgency? This rabble of themselves might, as they did, find some sign-painter to hang by the heels certain rude figures to represent members who had voted against the bill of attainder, but it required more intelligence and a deeper malignity to post up a correct list of fifty-nine Commoners, branding them with the odious title of " Straffordians, or betrayers of their country." This was indeed a violation of the privileges of the House, greater than any they complained of, and to a vindictive populace it was writing their names in characters of blood. We shortly after find a petition of Sir John Strangeways in behalf of himself and the fifty-nine members, declaring that though he had been absent at his house in Dorsetshire, during the voting of the bill of Attainder, yet by having his name inserted in that black list his person had been rendered odious and his life was in danger.*

All the while these commotions were going on, the Commons were proceeding uninterruptedly with their own designs. The King sent down a message for the prevention of these tumults, but the Commons could only see "the City petitioning." The King complained that no Court of Judicature had been left the power to punish tumults, for they suddenly seemed to have lost the skill to define "what tumults are!"† The Lords affrighted — we are told they were " fearful of having their brains knocked out"—were no longer free to act; — the Commons, however, were — and were silent — for they required tumults. Several members of the House of Commons resorted to clubs of apprentices, who being distributed into fraternities, vast bodies of all the crafts, shoemakers, tailors, porters, watermen, and others, were ever at hand " to petition," or do any other job,

* Rushworth, iv. 279.

† A jury in Southwark impanelled to examine one of these tumults were superseded, and the Sheriff enjoined not to proceed, by an order of the House of Commons. Husband's Collections, 251.

by the order of some unknown master. This exhibits a parallel scene to revolutionary France, when the hired mobs were ruling the city of Paris—afterwards the parallel may extend, when the meanest classes were legislators and executioners! The petitions were now echoing the resolutions of " Master Pym," and the organized rabble were put over to the care of an approved ringleader the Puritan divine Cornelius Burgess, who called them out at his beck, or dispersed them by the motion of his hand. Exultingly pointing at his rabble-patriots, he would exclaim " These be my band-dogs! I can set them on, and take them off again as I please."* When the Lords were slow and reluctant in passing the bill of Attainder, the mobs were let loose, and the terrified Peers immediately declared that they were drawing to a conclusion, and to manifest their passive obedience subscribed the famous " Protestation" of the Commons which at first they had declined. At the same time they declared that they were so encompassed with multitudes of people that it was the only hindrance to the dispatch of the bill.† The Commons ordered

* This anecdote is well known, though I cannot recover the original authority. It is mentioned by Echard.

† Rushworth, viii. 743.

Dr. Burgess to read this " Protestation" to the
people, and tell them they might return home.
At the voice of this political Neptune, the
waves of this rabble of rebellion rolled away.

When the cry against the Bishops was to be
given, we find Dr. Burgess still more active;
a tumultuous mob even broke into Westminster Abbey, threatening to return in greater
numbers to pull down not only Prelacy, but
the Abbey itself. They clamoured to deface the
monuments of the kings; the dilapidations of
St. Denis had nearly occurred among our own
sepulchres of royalty; those venerable and glorious remains of antiquity escaped, but by a
moment, from becoming a heap of ruins. The
Abbey endured a sort of siege for some hours.
The Dean beat the populace off with stones
thrown from the leads. We know what these
Puritanic barbarians afterwards did with all
the cathedrals through the kingdom. At this
moment the mob met by day and even at
night, summoned by the sound of a bell, or
other signal, in the fields or some other spot of
assignation, in order to concert their measures
and to be directed by their conductors. At
this Parisian scene of revolutionary terror, Pym
said "God forbid that the people should be

disheartened from obtaining their just desires !"
This violent scene was concerted at the alarm
of Pym's party on the King's return from
Scotland, when the warm loyalty of Sir Robert
Gournay, the Lord Mayor, had received the
King in great splendour at the Guildhall.

How timidly truth shows herself to him
who first ventures to lift her veil! In the days
of honest Rapin it was little short of treason to
breathe a suspicion on the cruel arts practised
by the popular party. Our historian apologises
for having discovered the truth! " I am very
sensible some will take it ill that I positively
affirm the tumults I am going to speak of were
the effect of the practices of the party against
the King, and that several pretend it was all
owing to accident and the discontents of the
people." * The same defence is still reiterated,
but truth is now not only bold but strong.

By such artifices as these the industrious
party of Pym and his colleagues, not only
struck a panic in the Court, and among the
Lords, but, what they did not consider of inferior consequence, they impressed on the public mind a strong sense of their own power.
It was from this time that the people began to

* Rapin, xi. 293.

be more regardful of Parliament; and as Baxter, an impartial contemporary, tells us in the curious folio of his life, "sided with them not only for their cause, and their own interest, but also supposing them the stronger side, which the vulgar are still apt to follow."

CHAPTER VII.

THE DEATH OF STRAFFORD.

AT this crisis two important events hastened the catastrophe of Strafford's story — the army-plot and the sudden death of the Earl of Bedford.

The discovery of a plot in the army, who were however distant in the north, to march direct to Westminster to over-awe the Parliament, whatever the plot was, now was opportunely revealed by Pym. Instantly he struck through all parties the terror he delighted in, and probably he was himself alarmed. The petitions of an army are a mutiny, and too well resembled his own — they were the commands of those who knew how to be obeyed. Were the army to form the mob, instead of the mob the army, even Pym had found a master.

The secret history of the army-plot, as it was called, is obscure in many parts, but sufficiently clear in others. Its detail, and its important results, shall be the subject of our following chapter. By the adroit management of Pym, whose vigorous conceptions could create mighty consequences from slight events, and on whose bold designs now revolved the fate of an empire, the army-plot gave rise to that famous " Protestation" of the Commons which was ordered by themselves to be subscribed by the whole nation. The tumults still paraded Westminster crying out for "justice" in the blood of Strafford.

At this critical moment too, the unlooked-for death of the Earl of Bedford, had broken off that new administration of the leaders of the Opposition which had nearly been formed. Lord Say had already dislodged Lord Cottington from the Mastership of the Wards; Bishop Juxon had resigned the Treasurer's staff; St. John was made Solicitor-general, the sullen enemy of his master; and Pym was prepared to be the Chancellor of the Exchequer, where formerly he had been one of the clerks. In full view of the places before them, the Patriots, now the place-hunters, had bribed the King, with a pledge to spare the life of Strafford, and to settle the royal revenues as amply as any which his predecessors had enjoyed. So compliant, so meek is Faction, when in changing its position, it would wish to lose its name.

These halcyon politics were now removed for-.ever from the hapless Monarch by the death of the Earl of Bedford, who, though he had been the opposer of Strafford, lamented the passions of his party, and looking into futurity, predicted on his death-bed, that their violence would bring greater mischief on the kingdom than it had ever sustained by the long intermissions of the Parliaments. The Earl of Bedford, though a wise and moderate man, would not, however, desert his party, as Strafford had done, and devote himself to the Court; it is therefore uncertain, as Warburton acutely observes, whether this proceeded from a point of honour to his party, or a point of duty to his country — unhappy times! when the wise and the moderate are constrained to act with those whose principles they would willingly disavow!

The death of the Minister of Charles had been irrevocably decided on by the prevalent party in the Commons. Whitelocke was certainly well informed of the state of the politics of his day; he ascribes the more than violent proceedings of some of "the great men" to a most humiliating cause. As the change of Ministers, which had been accepted by the King, had only partially occurred, being interrupted by the death of the Earl of Bedford, and as Charles afterwards found no inclination to receive Hampden, Pym, and others, though he had received full as evil counsellors in Lord Say and St. John his Solicitor-general, those who were left out were " baffled and became the more incensed and violent against the Earl joining with the Scotch Commissioners who were implacable against him."* Could we have imagined that our Patriots had been thus actuated by personal malignity, and that their ruthless ambition could only be appeased by the blood of a great man? It is too sad an apology for the rancour of their persecution to allege that supreme of human motives—self-preservation, conscious as they were that Strafford must fall, or that they must perish. Were the Minister suffered to live, there could be no safety for them; for it was known at least to themselves, that Strafford could attach acts of treason to some of their leaders, less dubious than any of those "constructive or accumulative treasons" by which they had now succeeded in attainting him; nor could they trust the life

* Whitelocke's Memorials, 40.

of their victim in the hands of the King, who
from his throne had so humbly supplicated
for it.   And, however Charles the First had
pledged the dismission of his ill-fated servant,
no degradation of the man could lessen the
wisdom of the statesman; and perhaps they
dreaded more than ever the influence of councils, whose sagacity had been schooled by recent experience, and whose haughty impetuosity had been tempered by adversity.   All
that can be alleged to palliate the guilt of
Strafford's execution by this party is, that he
perished from expediency and not by justice.
This at once separates politics from morality,
a violation too often practised by the Achitophels of all parties.

The bill of Attainder even in the Commons
did not pass without the opposition of nearly
a fourth part of the House; and with the
Lords, Strafford was condemned only by the
majority of seven votes.   Of eighty Peers who
had constantly attended, only forty-five had
the courage to assemble when the bill passed,
so intimidated was the noble Aristocracy amidst
the yellings of a menacing Mobocracy.   The
Bishops had been deprived of their votes; the
old canon being urged, which prohibited them
from deciding *in causa sanguinis;* a piece of

Ecclesiastical mockery which never spared the life of a victim from the grasp of the ecclesiastical talons.* It is evident that a full and free House, would have saved the head of Strafford at that moment; but what excesses of the party the rejection of their bill would have led to, in that terrifying hour of commotion, was a question they dared not ask themselves.

The Bill of Attainder passed the Lords on a Saturday, the 8th of May, with its memorable accompaniment, of a bill for not dissolving the Parliament without their own consent; hence called " the perpetual Parliament." Both Houses immediately waited on the King to move his assent. Monday was fixed on to receive his Majesty's resolution.

That hour was more than painful when the Peers retiring from their audience abandoned the Sovereign to himself! The agony of Charles was more poignant than perhaps he ever experienced on any other occasion. His conscience —his policy— his affections— were opposed to

---

* The Inquisition condemned their living victims to the flames—on the plea that by this means they shed no blood! Bishop Williams prepared a speech to assert the rights of the Bishops to vote on cases of life and death, replete with the most curious erudition. It has been preserved by his faithful biographer Hacket. (ii. 152.)

the tyrannical necessity of dragging a great Minister to the scaffold which the hands of his enemies had prepared. Through this awful Sunday the King struggled with himself: he might still listen to the cries of the populace scattered under the windows at Whitehall, in the palace-yard, and in Westminster Hall. And five days only had elapsed since his barge was waiting at the Privy stairs to carry him to the House of Lords, when the tumult raged, and it was considered that his life was insecure had he left the palace. At times his natural magnanimity, the promise " on the word of a King," which he had within the last fortnight renewed to Strafford that " he should not suffer in life, honour, or fortune,"* seemed to prevail over his great facility of yielding up his own judgment to that of others. His Privy Council, sitting in the midst of a general commotion, urged an entire submission to the will of the Parliament to preserve himself and his posterity ; it was a principle of State that the safety of the kingdom was to be preferred before the life of an innocent man. They laid some stress on the generous letter of Strafford himself,

---

* The letter Charles the First addressed to Strafford, by its peculiar orthography, evidently by his own hand, is in Strafford's Letters, ii. 416.

which had absolved the King from all his scruples, and released him from the inviolability of
his promise. This trivial Council, which showed that their argument did not exceed their
courage, would have satisfied a colder heart
and a meaner understanding, than those of
Charles, and eagerly would it have been embraced by the terror of a trembling despot, or
the selfishness of the weak prince who flies
from all the cares of royalty—but it could not
enter into the restless emotions of Charles the
First. When the King consulted the Bishops,
they referred him to the Judges to satisfy him
of the legality; but in this extremity, the solemn bench was deserted by the lofty magistracy of Justice. They had already withdrawn
their first opinions, and had given way to the
popular cry; terror had laid down a new com-
mentary fitted to the novel doctrines of constructive or accumulative treasons, where no
one particular act being treasonable, yet collec-
tively the whole amounted to treason. They
delivered their opinions with a vague unanimity; and the King complained that such dubious answers and critical distinctions served
to confuse his thoughts without allaying his
scruples. The Judges finally advised the King
to confer with the Bishops, to tranquillize that

compunction and remorse, where no law-cases could afford even the authority of a poor precedent; and which a juggle of words, the offuscating jargon of sophistical lawyers, could never appease.

On this occasion again appears in the scene that subtile politician Bishop Williams. This eminent man had been recently liberated by his Peers from the petty persecutions of Laud, after having been more than three years immured in the Tower. Williams had slided once more into the royal favour; and not long after was inaugurated into the See of York. It is said that his political foresight had predicted his own restoration to the royal councils; but Williams in this second sight, hardly contemplated among its phantoms, the shade of his rival Laud fixed in the prison-chamber where he himself had been barred.

The capacity of this learned man was equal to his time-serving spirit. He had prodigally wasted a genius of the first order in political life, in complicate intrigues, and expedients of the day, with a versatility of principles betraying that subtile wisdom of the serpent, which is scarcely compatible with the harmlessness of the dove. This politic and refining Statesman, with a Machiavelian casuistry now distinguish-

ed betwixt a PRIVATE and a PUBLIC conscience. He told Charles that the public conscience of a King must dispense with his private
conscience as a man. The conscience of a
King to preserve his kingdom was greater than
that of a master or a friend for the preservation of a servant or a friend. The question
was not whether he should serve Strafford, but
whether he should perish with him — and therefore the corollary of this logic of politics being
deduced, the astute Archbishop, between his
greater and his lesser consciences, counselled
even for conscience-sake, to act against conscience.*

* Clarendon indignantly brands the argument as " un-
prelatical and ignominious. Such was this Bishop's prodi-
gious boldness and impiety!" The argument is odious to our
moral sense. As Clarendon appears to have had a rooted
dislike to Bishop Williams, and as the great adversary of
Laud is rather a favourite with the Republican party, pains
have been taken to palliate what offends in its morality, and
to explain what is enlightened in its policy. Mrs. Macaulay
at once calls it " a sensible state of the question"— she resolves the condemnation of death of Strafford by Charles
into " a point of honour with the King, and not of conscience. A King of England is never to interpose his private
opinion against the Legislature. Laws of honour are only
laudable among a licentious banditti." We may perceive
that Mrs. Macaulay wrote at the era of that new morality of
which we afterwards witnessed such marvellous results. I

The conduct of the Prelates in this tortur-
ing hour has been sharply arraigned by those
who are inveterately hostile to the order of
Episcopacy, and it has even been lamented by
Lord Clarendon. The misery of these learned
men must have equalled the conviction of their
impotence. A remedy was asked for the re-
mediless. They sadly knew their weakness.
Already they were degraded in the eyes of their
country—they were about to be rejected from
the rights of free men, to give an equal vote
with their fellow-citizens; nor could they be
insensible, while their chief lay in the dungeons
of the Tower, and the screams of a maddened
populace were echoing, " No Bishops !" that

will abandon to her all " the Laws of Honour," for what
they are worth ; but not the King's *veto*. How far the King
of England is bound to submit his private opinion to that of
the Legislature, on a point on which the oracles of law differ
among themselves, is a nice and delicate question.

Mr. Brodie insists that Clarendon, while he so strongly
condemns Williams here, has done it unjustly, since the
other Bishops acquiesced. But it does not appear that they
acquiesced in the principles of the casuistical Bishop, as the
reader will shortly find in a note or two farther. The argument is so perfectly characteristic of the subtilizing manner
of this extraordinary personage, that Clarendon cannot be
accused of purposely rendering the sophistry more odious
than it is — he has certainly stated it with a malicious per-
spicacity.

heads more able to contrive mischief than their
own, and hands more skilful in the arts of destruction, were fast undermining the foundations of their own Hierarchy. In that day of
dereliction and terror, could the Bishops be
more exempt from the common infirmities of
our nature than were all the Right Honourable Privy Councillors? These already had
bowed with " hat in hand giving them good
words" to the insolent citizens, as these Lords
going to their House, tremblingly passed
through their sullen lines, promising, provided
they would be quiet, the blood of Strafford!
Or were the Bishops to be less terrified than
those oracles of the law, who in the sanctuary
of justice, sitting at the tribunal of life and
death, had revoked their decrees, and vacillated,
till they echoed the cry of the populace around
them ?

Two Prelates, at least, of the five consulted
by Charles, should not participate in the odium,
if it be an odium, cast on their brothers. The
learned Usher, indeed, as all the Bishops did,
referred the King to the opinions of the Judges,
who by their office and their oath were to ex-
pound the law ; but Usher still referred to the
Monarch himself the more delicate and more
difficult conclusion, whether after all that had

passed during the trial, he considered that
Strafford was a guilty man. Archbishop Usher
was not less perplexed than he who in his
perplexity had consulted the resolver of his
doubts—but there are sufficient testimonies to
show that Usher never persuaded Charles, as
has been said, to consent to the execution of
the State victim.* Juxon, the good Bishop
of London, exhorted the King to do nothing
against his conscience, but more particularly
reprobated the extraordinary piece of political
casuistry of Bishop Williams. On the second
meeting in the evening, Juxon seems to have
stood in silence; a silence not unintelligible
to the feelings of the desponding Monarch.†

* The circumstance of Usher's attendance on the Earl in
his last minutes is a strong confirmation of the nature of his
advice to the King; but the authorities which are stated in
the Biog. Brit. p. 4075, are conclusive.

† I have spared no pains to combine my researches relative to Juxon, because his conduct has been strangely
misrepresented. Oldmixon reproaches Juxon for " having
acted cunningly and said nothing at all;" and ridicules
Echard for telling us what I have written above. Saunder-
son is referred to for the authority that " on the last meeting" (for there were two on that Sunday, a circumstance not
noticed by our writer) " the Bishop of London spoke not a
syllable." Mr. Brodie quotes Nalson, who says that Juxon
dissuaded his master from passing the Bill, " but other authorities," adds Mr. Brodie, " do not support the statement.'
(iii. 181.)   We

Thus the day was wearing away in debates and council, and the King still remained irresolute and miserable. In the evening Charles called for a second meeting of the Bishops. His councillors had offered no council to which his heart could assent. Every one seemed to suppress his own thoughts by appealing to others for that fatal decision, which by being made together in a body, seemed to save the individual from its responsibility or its injustice.*

We may accord these opposite accounts of his speech and of his silence; and it is rather a curious instance of what sometimes happens in historical researches, that contradictory facts may both at the same time be equally true.

That Juxon spoke what I have said is amply confirmed by Sir Edward Walker, who had it direct from the King. At the evening meeting he was silent, having already spoken and having nothing more to say.

The passage from Sir Edward Walker the reader may like to see. Having ascribed the opinion that the King had a double capacity, of a public and a private man, &c. to Usher, who he understood had made that distinction, " the King replied, ' No, I assure you it was not he !' whence I infer it was either York, or Durham, for at the same time the King fully justified the Bishop of London for his stout opinion against it." (360.) This, with the recollection that there were two meetings in one day, prove that all the accounts, however they differ, are correct.

* Whether from a loyalist, or a parliamentary partisan, as a warning, or a derision, a paper was this night fixed on the

Charles stood as it were alone in the universe, about to do an act, which the universe itself would wonder at, or would condemn. It was a tale which his elevated spirit felt was to be reserved for posterity, and which posterity alone could decide on. At this moment, it would seem, the Queen came in dismay, supplicating for her children, in tears and grief, and with her sad voice importuning the King to avert the momentous danger, urged on as she was by the councils of all around them.* Clarendon has feelingly observed that "the part which the King had to act was not only harder than any Prince, but than any private gentleman had been exposed to." It is said that no man doubted that the King without any scruple of conscience might have granted the Earl his pardon; had not other reasons of

gates at Whitehall, announcing that on the morrow there would be acted in the House of Peers, a famous Tragy-Comedy, called " A King and no King."—Observations on L'Estrange, 244.

* It is probably true that the Queen might, late in the day; have joined in the intreaty of so many others for the death of Strafford as a means of appeasing the popular cry. Many writers have repeated the fact, but how greatly they have erred in assigning to her certain motives, is shown in our inquiry of Henrietta's influence over Charles the First.

state hindered him.*   In truth Charles was no longer himself free.

Importunity and Necessity, were the two evil geniuses which stood by the side of Charles till he could no longer wrestle with them.   After the second interview in the evening with the Bishops, still wavering, the King seems to have delayed the last act till the morning.†   With one pen full of ink we are told he hastily signed the Commission granted to three noblemen for passing the two fateful Bills, which had been extorted from him.   It was imagined that they offered some miserable comfort to the desponding Monarch when they told him that as his will had not consented to the deed, so neither by the medium of this Commission had his own hand signed the warrant for death.   But even this heartless subterfuge was denied for his consolation when Archbishop Usher, after the Commission was signed, bursting into tears, lamented the fatal signature, praying that the King might not suffer from a wounded conscience !

---

* This is said in Abp. Usher's Life by Parr.

† Hamond L'Estrange, 258.   On this contemporary authority, I have fixed on the morning of Tuesday, but it may have been late in the preceding night, as Echard gives it.

Charles who had more than once left the trial of Strafford, which he had constantly attended, with tears in his eyes, in signing the Commission bitterly wept, exclaiming that " Lord Strafford was more happy than he!" The various and contending feelings in his breast Charles himself showed when he charged Archbishop Usher, on the next morning, to assure Strafford that " If the King's own life only were hazarded by saving his, he would never have consented to his death."*

But the disturbed state of his mind and the utter recklessness of his own existence Charles surely betrayed when he allowed that bill to pass, which had been violently carried in the course of a single day through the two Houses, and by which the Parliament deprived the King of that last remaining authority of the Sovereign — the power of dissolving them. This Bill was of far greater importance to himself than the Earl of Strafford's life; it was virtually signing his own dethronement, as in conclusion it proved to be his own execution. So completely overpowered was Charles the

* From the notes of Archbishop Usher found in his alma-nack, containing the heads, or memorandums of what the King desired him to communicate to Strafford. Strafford's Letters, ii. 418.

First by the fate of Strafford, that he cared no longer for his own.

To the last moment it was doubtful whether Charles would consent to issue the Commission. Whitelocke gives us a report that the King was at length brought to it by a promise before he had signed, that the life of Strafford should be spared. If the King had been practised on by some such artifice, we are not furnished with the knowledge. In the manuscript letter to the Queen which I have quoted, written at a distant day, Charles says himself, that " He was surprised with it, instantly after he made that base sinful concession." Did the mystifying casuistry of the double Royal consciences of Bishop Williams prove so unanswerable, at the moment, as to have silenced the compunctions which Charles never ceased to feel all the rest of his days? " That he should ever have been brought to it," observes Whitelocke, " was admired by most of his subjects as well as by foreigners." The world indeed wondered, and none more than the great master of plots and counter-plots, Pym himself. After all his industrious ingenuity, his fertility of invention, the arduous conduct of that awful trial; after all the terror he had spread through the country, all the artifices

he had practised in an insurrectionary metropolis; all the breathless labours his Epicurean
habits had endured* — still the demagogue
doubted of his own success, and to the last
dreaded to be foiled by the magnanimity of
Charles. When Pym first learned that the
commission was signed, he lifted his hands in
ecstasy, exclaiming, " Has he given us the head
of Strafford ! then he will refuse us nothing !"

On Monday, Maxwell, the Gentleman Usher
to the Lords, hurried to acquaint the Commons
with the good news of the Royal assent by
Commission to the two bills, bearing also a
message from the Lords that they were waiting for the Speaker and the House of Com-

---

* We know so little of the private characters and habits
of our early patriots, that we despair ever of forming a more
intimate acquaintance with these great and able men.
Hacket has characterised Pym, in his curious though often
pedantic manner, *Homo ex argillâ, et luto factus Epicuræo,*
as Tully said of Piso, that is in Christian English " a painted sepulchre, *a belly-god.*" (ii. 149.) His translation is a comment. It is evident that he does not refer to the last image,
to merely philosophical doctrines, but to the more vulgar
Epicurean habits. The wooden cut, which authenticates his
speeches, to which I have before alluded, conveys to us the
jollity of a votary to Bacchus and Ceres. All accounts
agree that his anxious labours exhausted him and produced
his death.

mons to join them. So transported was this
officer by the amazing intelligence, that he precipitated himself at once into the House, without the usual form of first demanding entrance,
and he appeared without that insignia of
office, his black rod. Exceptions were made
at this unofficial and abrupt violation of the
dignity of the House, but as most of the members soon shared in the wild joy of the informal
and hasty Usher, he was favoured by escaping
from a committal.

But the struggle in the Royal breast had
not passed away with the agony of the horrible
concession. Still Charles ruminated in the solitude of his own conscience, and still he seemed to be hanging on some frail hope that yet
one more attempt remained, at least, to save
shedding the blood of the condemned victim.

On the following morning, Tuesday, the
King addressed a letter written with his own
hand to the Lords, and which was delivered
with unusual solemnity by the hand of the
Prince of Wales; as solemnly and as mourn-
fully was it received. Twice it was read
amidst the deepest silence. " After serious
and SAD consideration," says Rushworth, twelve
Peers were deputed as messengers to the King,
humbly to signify that his intentions could

not be advised by them, without danger to himself, his Queen, and his children. So dreaded was the alarm at that moment of the popular fury, by the Lords as well as the King, that even Charles had only proposed to spare the blood of Strafford, as the King himself now observed to the Lords by an If—" If it may be done without discontenting my people"— more he cared not to say, and was retiring, when the Lords observed that they were suitors for his Royal favour to the innocent children of Strafford. This last mark of attention bestowed on the unhappy man, touched the sorrowful Monarch, who seemed grateful. The Lords then offered to return into his own hands the letter which he himself had written; this Charles waived, observing, " My Lords, what I have written to you, I shall be content if it be registered by you in your House. In it you may see my mind; I hope you will use it to my honour."

The pathetic letter of Charles the First, written on this trying occasion, betrays his deep emotions with the simplicity of nature. It implores, as the humblest suitor might implore, to have the liberty of extending the Royal prerogative of mercy; mercy which the King as much required for himself, from the hands of

Parliament as the victim on whom he wished
to bestow it.   In the history of his life it de-
serves to be perpetuated for posterity.   Charles
evidently designed it to stand on the Records
of the House of Lords, if not in the form of a
protest, at least as a perpetual testimony that
however they had obtained a forced acquiescence, he had no otherwise consented to the
execution of Strafford.

" My Lords,

" I did yesterday satisfy the justice of the
kingdom by passing the Bill of Attainder
against the Earl of Strafford.   But mercy being
as inherent and inseparable to a King as justice, I desire in some measure to show that
likewise, by suffering that unfortunate man to
fulfil the natural course of his life in close imprisonment; yet so, that if ever he make the
least offer to escape, or offer directly or indi-
rectly to meddle in any sort of public business,
especially with me, either by message or letter,
it shall cost him his life, without farther process.   This, if it may be done without the dis-
contentment of my people, will be an unspeak-
able contentment to me.

" To which end, as in the first place, I by
this letter do earnestly desire your approbation,

and to endear it the more, have chosen him to carry it, who is of all your house most dear unto me; so I desire that by conference you will endeavour to give the House of Commons contentment likewise, assuring you that the exercise of mercy is no more pleasing to me, than to see both Houses of Parliament consent, for my sake, that I should moderate the severity of the law in so important a case.

"I will not say that your complying with me in this my intended mercy, shall make me more willing, but certainly it will make me more cheerful in granting your just grievances. But if no less than his life can satisfy my people, I must say *Fiat Justitia.* Thus again recommending the consideration of my intentions to you, I rest,

"Your unalterable and affectionate friend,

"CHARLES R."

"If he must die, it were charity to reprieve him till Saturday."

At this day, removed from the prejudices and the passions of the contemporaries of Charles the First, will the unadorned simplicity of this letter be passed over without emotion? Not a sentence but is impressed by the deep feeling which dictated it. The unusual form of the letter, as well as the infant messenger who presented it—gave it the air of a domestic, rather than a royal communication, and betrayed all the tenderness of a sorrowing friend seeking for an equal affection.

Yet at the time, this letter was censured with severity by the ultra-royalists. In their eyes royalty was degraded by becoming a suppliant to the people by the mediation of the Peers. For what purpose should the King write to annul, or to alter, that sentence, which he had himself just passed, and which they had gained with so much danger and many artifices? Could he rationally expect that they would undo, what he himself had failed in the courage not to have done? Could the King expect aught but a second repulse? And to have sent on this forlorn hope the young Prince, was it to accustom the heir of the Crown from his very childhood to the denials of his subjects? And to desire the respite of two or three days for the condemned prisoner, was begging for a power and authority with which he had not parted by conceding the act of attainder. Even the form of the letter was objected to; it was not Kingly. A court-missive to the Peers bears the King's signature at its head, and is never subscribed, with the equality of private friendship.

Such were some of the discourses of the day. Unhappy monarchs! who so often when they act in conformity to state-interests are condemned as heartless men; and when they descend from the throne are scorned at for the strong sympathies inspired by the devotion and despondency of friendship.

The pitiable postscript of this letter, " *cette froide prière*," as the vivacious M. Guizot exclaims, is remarkable, as it has been said that this graceless addition was the suggestion of the Queen, for a very sinister design. Burnet relates an anecdote which he had from Lord Hollis himself, whose sister Strafford had married. The King sent for Hollis to consult on means to save his relative's life. Hollis observed that the King might legally reprieve this condemned prisoner, but this he would not advise. Hollis drew up a petition for Strafford for a short respite to settle his affairs, and a speech for the King, who was to come down to the House holding the petition in his hand. Hollis had persuaded many, by a sort of political logic, of the expediency of saving Strafford's life, who, as he assured them, in that case reverting to his former principles would become wholly theirs. His preservation thus would be more serviceable than if made an example

on such new and doubtful points. In the
mean while it had been intimated to the Queen
that Hollis had engaged Strafford to accuse
her; of what we are not told. On this the
Queen not only hindered the King from going
to the House, changing the speech into a message writ with the King's own hand and carried
by the Prince of Wales, which Hollis observed
would "perhaps have done as well, the King
being apt to spoil things by an unacceptable
manner." "But to the wonder of the whole
world," continues Burnet, "the Queen prevailed with him to add that mean postscript, 'If
he must die, it were charity to reprieve him
till Saturday,' which was a very unhandsome
giving up of the whole message. When it
was communicated to both Houses, the whole
Court-party was plainly against it; and so he
fell truly by the Queen's means."

This is one of those anecdotes which are
sometimes cited as historical; and even Mr.
Hallam has recently repeated it. Burnet, long
after he had heard it in the looseness of conversation, records the reminiscence in his lively
manner. Let us take the story as we find it.
The secret anecdote concerning the postscript
Hollis could hardly have known but from

another. Had the Queen dreaded every hour an accuser in this State-prisoner, and for what crime we are never told, she would not have been urgent to impede the course of law, even for a day. She would not have exerted her fascinating influence to add the postscript, but rather to have suppressed the letter. What Hollis related of himself may be deemed correct; what he told after another can be only supposititious. The mystery in which some have involved this humble postscript, and Burnet's malicious intention, were designed to cast a fresh odium on an unpopular Queen. Henrietta, after all, never suggested this postscript which has attracted so much criticism. The King in his audience with the Lords assigned the simple and natural motive. Charles said " my other intention proceeding out of charity for a few days' respite was upon *certain information*, that his estate was so distracted that it necessarily required some few days for settlement."* And this fact is even confirmed by Hollis himself, who in his proposed petition, which had been submitted to the King, urged this very motive as its plea ; the real suggester of this humble intreaty was Strafford himself,

* Rushworth, iv. 266.

merely for a domestic purpose, as we find in Laud's Diary.*

The extraordinary letter which Strafford addressed to the King to free him from his promise of saving his life, and to relieve the agony of his conscience in consenting to his death, accords not with that surprise and disappointment which he showed on learning his fate. It is said that the Earl on hearing of his fate, suddenly rising from his seat, and looking up to Heaven, exclaimed, " Put not your trust in Princes nor in the sons of men, for in them there is no salvation." There is a mystery in this conduct now perhaps too late to clear away ; and more than one reason has been assigned. Carte has even questioned the authenticity of the printed letter. To have reproached Charles with the sentence of death which Strafford knew was inevitable, is so utterly inconsistent with the magnanimity which had dictated the noble letter, that we must believe we know the story too imperfectly to comprehend it.

I do not like to leave the reader without preserving some particulars, which exhibit the magnanimity of this great minister.

The death of Strafford was as dignified as his

* Laud's history of his Troubles, 177.

life. Unsubdued by the stroke of Fortune, he
was yet overcome by the tenderness of domestic life—his friends and his family occupied
his last thoughts.

On the night before the execution, the Earl
sent for the Lieutenant of the Tower to ask,
whether it were possible for him to speak with
the Archbishop now in the Tower. " Master
Lieutenant," said Strafford, " you shall hear
what passes betwixt us; it is not a time either
for him to plot heresy, or me to plot treason."
This seems to have been said with playful
irony. The Lieutenant desired his Lordship
would petition Parliament for that favour.
" No," replied Strafford, " I have gotten my
dispatch from them, and will trouble them no
more; I am now petitioning a Higher Court,
where neither partiality can be expected, nor
error feared." A sharp and indignant reprimand of them—he deigned not to be queru-
lous. Strafford then requested Archbishop
Usher to desire Laud " to be at his window,
when I shall go abroad to-morrow, for a last
farewell."

Not seeing Laud, he begged to approach
nearer to his apartment, but the old man was
now hastening to the window of his cell. Thus
met the two great Ministers of Charles, and the

scene was ominous of the fate of their master !
The aged Laud lifted his feeble hands to
bestow the blessing which he could not speak,
fainting in the arms of his attendant. Laud
who could not suffer the sight of his great
friend led to the scaffold, yet himself soon
mounted that scaffold with no disturbance of
mind. When Laud was reproached by the
Puritans for that womanly softness, he said
that when he should come to his own execution they would see that he was more sensible
of the death of the great Earl than of his
own.

The Lieutenant desired Strafford to take
coach for fear the people should rush in upon
him and tear him to pieces. The Scotch Balfour imagined that he was at Edinburgh.
Strafford firmly replied, " No! Master Lieutenant, I dare look death in the face and the
people too." He pleasantly added, " Have
you a care that I do not escape— I care not
how I die, whether by the stroke of the
executioner, or the madness of the people, if
that may give them better content; it is all one
to me!" Not less than a hundred thousand
persons, for many had arrived from all parts,
were viewed in a long perspective on Tower-
hill. They witnessed his death in silence,

offering neither insults nor reproaches. Whether many sympathised with the fate of the
great statesman may be doubtful, certainly
many rejoiced at it. It was not the criminality of the man, which the populace might
have misconceived but could never have comprehended, which probably touched them, but
it was a Minister of State submitted to a criminal's fate; it was the first public execution
of the kind which the populace had ever beheld. At first their awe chastised their joy —
but the secret satisfaction betrayed itself when
the head of Strafford fell from the block.
Most who returned home waving their hats,
shouted through the towns they passed, " His
head is off! His head is off!" and bonfires
blazed, or windows were broken, for all did
not join in the popular acclamations. Some
departed in silence and musing, and as Monsieur Guizot has happily expressed it, full of
doubts and uneasiness as to the justice of that
wish which they came from witnessing accomplished.

Strafford in walking from the Tower, took
off his hat frequently, saluting the people.
His firm step and lofty air are described by
a contemporary account, to have been like that
of a General marching in triumph, rather than

to a scaffold.*   This self-possession in the grace
of his motions, and the ease of his language to
the last moment of life on the scaffold, evinced
the undaunted spirit of the man.   The pang
of bidding a last farewell to some friends on
the scaffold softened his accustomed severity;
but when Strafford beheld his brother Sir
George Wentworth weeping excessively, " Brother," said the Earl with a vivacious cheerfulness, "what do you see in me to cause these
tears?   Does any indecent fear betray in me
guilt,—or my innocent boldness, Atheism?
Think that you are now accompanying me the
third time to my marriage-bed.   That block
must be my pillow,—and here shall I rest from
all my labours.   No thoughts of envy, no

* Echard repeated this simile, as he did some others in
his compilation — on which Oldmixon, not at all aware that
they are not the property of the laborious compiler, attacks
them with ferocious criticism.   " Mr. Echard's similies are
extremely natural; nothing in the world is so like a triumph
as to have one's head cut off."   The Archdeacon had stolen
another on Laud's fainting in taking leave of Strafford, " as
if his soul would have forced its way to have joined the
Earl's in its passage to eternity."   Oldmixon exclaims, " He
plays with eternity as flies do with the flame."   I give
these not so much for the amusement of the reader, but to
show how our English history has sometimes been written
for a party-purpose.

dreams of treason, nor jealousies nor cares for the King, the State, or myself, shall interrupt this easy sleep."* While undressing himself and winding his hair under the cap, looking on the block, he said, " I do as cheerfully put off my doublet at this time, as ever I did when 1 went to bed." This sentiment may to some appear unnatural; but if we reflect what of late he had undergone, and what, had he lived, he could not escape from, Death offered a relief to such a man which life could no longer afford.

There are some remarkable passages in his speech. Strafford doubtless had meditated in his imprisonment, on the fate of other illustrious men — and some too Ministers of State, who like him had been cast forth as a sacrifice to the people, and not always more criminal than himself. To these he seems to have alluded. " Although it be my ill-hap to be misconstrued, I am not the first man that hath suffered in this kind; it is a common portion that befalls men in this life. Righteous judgments shall be hereafter. Here we are subject to error, and misjudging one another. I was so far from being against Parliaments, that I did always think Parliaments in England to

* Nalson, ii. 195.

be the happy constitution of the kingdom, and
the best means to make the King and his people happy." Strafford kneeling down, made a
solemn protestation—" I am now in the very
door, going out, and my next step must be
from time to eternity, either of peace or pain—
I solemnly call God to witness I am not guilty,
so far as I can understand, of the great crime
laid to my charge, nor ever had the least
inclination to injure the King, the State, the
Laws, or the Religion of this kingdom." This
solemn acknowledgment, this address to the
God whom he feared, at the moment of death,
seems intolerable to some; yet there may be
much more truth in the confession than they
choose to allow, or with their prejudices are
capable to conceive. Strafford in the legacy
of his words to the people, paid a tribute to
the Constitution :*—that " he was ignorant of

* Mr. Brodie informs us that certain draughts of speeches
of the Earl are not genuine. Certainly those are not which
are full of contrition for his past conduct. Mr. Brodie perceived that they were at variance with that which Rushworth
took from his lips on the scaffold —" though charity," continues Mr. Brodie, " would induce all who are acquainted
with his correspondence, &c. to wish that it had been otherwise, or at all events that that portion at least of the speech
actually delivered on the scaffold, in which he declares himself to have been always a friend to Parliaments were not

the nature of that Constitution," as Mrs. Macaulay asserts, was no ignorance peculiar to Strafford.

With the prescience of a statesman, Strafford professed his apprehension of future evils, recommending to every man to lay his hand on his heart, and seriously consider whether the beginning of the people's happiness should be written in letters of blood ? " I fear," he added, " they are in a wrong way !" Strafford foresaw the approaching ruin of the Church, and solemnly forbade his son, from a religious motive, ever to purchase Church-lands. It was Strafford's notion that the revenues of the Church would be seized on by the nobility and the gentry. He was not far from the truth in the result; but he could not yet have imagined that a baser class of adventurers were to become Lords over Lords, and masters over gentlemen.

He passed half an hour at prayers. In rising

authentic, for it is deplorable to believe that his last moments were polluted with an untruth." Brodie, Brit. Empire, iii. 124.

Who is polluted with an untruth ? Those passages which Mr. Brodie might point out as inimical to Parliaments, the Earl would probably have defended as being only hostile, not to Parliaments, for which he was an advocate, but to Eliot, to Pym, to Prynne, to Hampden, to Vane and their friends, whom he marked out as a faction.

to approach the block he gave his last reminiscences to his family—naming them endear-
ingly to his brother. He concluded " Now I
have nigh done ; one stroke will make my wife
husbandless, my dear children fatherless, and
my poor servants masterless, and separate me
from my dear brother, and all my friends ; but
let God be to you and them all in all." He
took his solemn leave of the noblemen and
others about him, offering his hand.

There was a copy of the heads of notes for
his speech written by his own hand, and found
on the scaffold, among them were these—" Submit to what is voted justice, but my intentions
innocent from subverting, &c. ; acquit the King
constrained—strange way to write the beginning of Reformation and settlement of a Kingdom in blood."

When Archbishop Usher gave an account
to the King of the calm majesty of Strafford's
death, adding that he had seen many die, but
never so white a soul return to its maker,
Charles, turning aside, could not forbear those
emotions of tenderness, of grief, and of remorse,
which his tears could not efface, and which
haunted his memory, and embittered his last
hour.

In the whole compass of English history, no

incident offers more critical difficulties in its
narrative, than the trial of Strafford, and no
character seems more tender to touch on than
that of this able minister. Even among his
own contemporaries the opinions of men were
strongly opposed, and more particularly on the
mortal sentence. The passions of those days
being involved in the principles of a free constitution, have been transferred to our own, and
Strafford remains still a name which kindles
the vindictive spirit of those who view nothing
but undeviating despotism on one side, and
nothing but the holiest devotion of patriotism
on the other. One of the most acute investi-
gators of legal evidence, in his elaborate review
of the present subject, after the keenest scrutiny, to bring Strafford within the letter of the
law, has ingenuously confessed that these legal
points may be still open to every sort of legal
objection. In truth those writers who have
denounced this minister, hardly pretend that
he was amenable to any existing law; it was
for this reason that the baffled Commons desist-
ed from the trial of a man, whose presumed
and undefinable crime of an intention to sub-
vert the fundamental laws of the realm, had
yet never entered into the code of our juris-
prudence. Yet the philosophical historian to

whom we have referred, has not hesitated to
pronounce that " He died justly before God
and man ;" but Mr. Hallam adds, so strong is
his love of truth, and so firm is his attachment
to party, " In condemning the bill of Attainder
we cannot look upon it as a crime." Such was
the hard fate of Strafford! He was tried for a
supposititious crime, and stands condemned by
a paradox! This is in the nature of things
where party is prevalent and justice is violated.

Were it possible to discover a philosopher so
ignorant and so innocent of traditional prejudices and vulgar opinions as first to have learnt
the tale of Strafford only by his trial, he would
hardly hesitate to acquit the illustrious prisoner ; but surely he would be confirmed in his
sentiments, or his suspicions, when he had further meditated on the voluminous discussions
of those who advocate the justness of the bill
of Attainder. He might wonder at that anxiety and that perplexity which they betray by
their legal subtilties ; he would find himself
involved in the most abstruse arguments, as if
the crimes of Strafford were rather of a meta-
physical nature, than overt acts of treason
which even some dormant law might be ima-
giued to reach ; he might smile at the prelimi-
nary questions they have sometimes been com-

pelled to resort to before they venture to deduce their inferences ; he might be startled at the monstrous ingenuity of the incomprehensible charges of constructive or accumulative treason, and at the solution of that enigma which. explains that, however there was no established law for Strafford's condemnation to death, yet was he justly condemned by the Legislature, though he would have been unjustly condemned by any ordinary Court of Law.* And finally, after all the tedious sophistry of lawyers, he might be surprised that these writers have usually wound up their vindication of the anomalous proceedings and the violation of public justice, by pleas of necessity, and apologies to palliate, what they found had been so troublesome to explain.† Yet let us not forget

* Brodie, iii. 99.

† Brodie, iii. 104. Here is a notable instance. After having occupied several pages in controverting the enlightened opinion of a great statesman himself, Charles Fox, on the Commons' " departure in the case of Strafford from the sacred principles of justice," Mr. Brodie closes thus, " There seemed every reason to conclude that the fate of the Empire depended in a great measure upon his; a view which even brings the matter within Mr. Fox's idea in regard to self-defence." The ingenuity, if not the ingenuousness, is here admirable ; as if not quite confident of all his previous legal distinctions, this historical controversialist, in his last distress

the illustrious names at the bar who opposed
the heartless St. John, and the inveterate advocates, Glynn and Maynard—the bar at least
was honourably divided.

We escape from the intricate and tenebrous
labyrinth of the lawyers, emerging from their
cloudy arguments to the open day-light of human nature. We will consider Strafford as the
minister of Charles the First. We may not
flatter ourselves that we can penetrate into the
secret recesses of his comprehensive mind, but
it is the privilege of the passionless historian,
with a wider scope of information than contemporaries possess, to form juster views of the
man. We have to offer neither invectives nor
apologies.

The poet May, who still retained some courtly reminiscences, even in his character as the
historian and the Secretary of the Parliament,
struck by the genius of the great Minister,
compared Strafford with the Roman Curio of
his own Lucan.

Haud alium tanta civem tulit indole Roma,
Aut cui plus leges deberent recta sequenti.

---

of argument, offers to rest his cause by accepting the very
opinion which he had been all along contending with !

Perdita tunc Urbi nocuerunt secula, postquam
Ambitus, et luxus, et opum metuenda facultas,
Transverso mentem dubiam torrente tulerunt,
Momentumque fuit mutatus Curio rerum.

·In all our pregnant mother's tribes before,
A son of nobler hope she never bore ;
A soul more bright, more great, she never knew,
While to thy country's interest thou wert true.
But thy bad fate o'er-ruled thy native worth,
And in an age abandon'd brought thee forth ;
When Vice in triumph through the city pass'd,
And dreadful wrath and power laid all things waste.
The sweeping stream thy better purpose cross'd,
And in the headlong torrent wert thou lost.
Much to the ruin of the State was done
When Curio by " Ambition's bribe " was won ;
Curio, the hope of Rome, and her most worthy Son.
                                                    ROWE.

A modern historian to whom every respect
is due, for his discernment and impartiality on
the general subjects of our history, has pronounced of Strafford that " He was the most
active and formidable enemy to the liberties of
the people.   He laboured, his own letters prove
it, to exalt the power of the throne on the ruin
of those rights of which he once had been the
most strenuous advocate."*   Such a popular
opinion well merits that closer scrutiny which
gratifies the love of truth.

* Dr. Lingard, x. 136.

Was it then ambition reckless of its means,
which so wholly contaminated this great spirit
as basely to work in enslaving his fellow-coun-
trymen to the tyranny of a despot? Was an
Earldom weighed against a Baronetcy? Few
Statesmen, it is suspected, reject the seduction
of political ambition, even in the private station
occupied by independent Strafford; but it may
yet be a question whether Strafford ever considered that his Sovereign was this absolute
tyrant? Even May confesses that " He understood the right way, and the liberty of his
country as well as any man; for which in former Parliaments he stood up stiffly, and seemed
an excellent patriot." At his trial, Strafford
declared that his opinions had suffered no
change, whatever they might deem, or miscon-
ceive of his conduct. Alluding to the Commons, he said, " I am the same man in opinion
that I was when I was one of them." And
some days after, with deeper emotions " I confess I am charged with treason by the honourable House of Commons, and that it is my
greatest grief; for if it were not an arrow sent
out of that quiver, it would not be so heavy as
it is; but as it comes from them, it pierces my
heart, though not with guilt, yet with grief,
that in my grey hairs I should be misunder-

stood by the companions of my youth with
whom I have formerly spent so much time."

Let us take Strafford at a moment less unguarded than when he stood at the bar of his
Peers, an impeached Minister — let us seek him
in the secret confession of his privacy, and in
the day of his glory. Strafford flattered himself that he had triumphed over his great adversary Pym, and that party.

"Now I can say the King is as absolute here
(Ireland) as any Prince in the whole world can
be ; and may be still, if it be not spoiled on
that side (the Commons.) For so long as his
Majesty shall have here a deputy of faith and
understanding, and that he be preserved in credit, and independent upon any but the King
himself, let it be laid as a ground, it is the deputy's fault if the King be denied any reasonable claim."

We may assume this as the secret principle
of Strafford's political conduct. He considered
that the King was to be invested with " absolute power," but he explains the ambiguous
phrase, and he restricts this mighty power by
any " reasonable claims." Arbitrary power
therefore when unreasonable, would be illegal.
Strafford had a peculiar expression to describe
the right of the King, amidst his difficulties to

raise supplies.   It was to be done "candide
et caste"—this appears by the evidence of Lord
Cottington and others on the trial.   In a curious paper addressed to the King on the subject
of "war with Austria," he employs the same
expression; he impresses on the King to exercise "the power only for public and necessary uses; to spare the people as much and
often as it is possible; this being the only
means to preserve, as may be said, *the chastity*
of these levies."*   In another place, alluding
to the Ship-money, he says, "I am satisfied that
monies raised for setting forth a fleet was
chastely bestowed that way."   It is evident that
by the *chastity* of levies of money he meant an
entire application to the necessary purpose for
which they were proposed.   Had Strafford had
none but arbitrary notions in his head, he had
never troubled himself with such nice distinctions.   But the obnoxious phrase of "absolute
power" would be construed by a Commonwealth-man odiously, passing over the fact
that Strafford in his style, however high, seems
always to have subdued its worst construction.
Had Charles been the Nero, which has been
so artfully impressed on us, would Strafford

* Strafford's Letters, ii. 62.

have laboured to render the tyrant, as he did the King, absolute?

Strafford, like most men of that day, could not have entertained those correct notions of a popular constitution which required such a length of time after his own age for their establishment. The principles of our political freedom were in his day fluctuating, depending on precedents, and always involved in controversy. He himself has more than once lamented this cruel uncertainty, and earnestly prayed for the time when " the prerogative and the liberty of the subject should be determined." So doubtful and obscure were then the conflicting sentiments even in the capacious mind of this great statesman! Candour requires that we should credit what his intimate friend Sir George Radcliffe assures us; we have no reason to suppose that he has ascribed supposititious sentiments to his great friend. He asserts that Strafford " disliked the abuse of regal authority, but it appeard to him most hard and difficult to keep the interests of the King and the people from encroaching one upon another," that " Experience had taught him that there was less danger to increase the regal power than that the people

should gain advantage over the King ; the one
may turn to the prejudice of some particular
sufferer, the other draws on the ruin of the
whole."

This opinion betrays more the dread of a
Democracy than an assent to the passive obedience of arbitrary power. On the scaffold
Strafford himself declared that " he had the
ill hap to be misconstrued, for that he had ever
considered that the Parliament of England
were the happiest constitution that any kingdom lived under." Strafford, so late as in
1639, advised Charles to call a Parliament ; and
Whitelocke observes, that " Strafford had the
honour of the people's good opinion, for pro-
moting this resolution." In the style of his
correspondence with the King we observe the
most complete personal devotion ; but we must
recollect that he had to engage the affections
of a distant master, and that confident in his
own ability as a minister, which the result of
his Irish administration had shown, in the im-
provement of the revenue and the quieting of
that unhappy kingdom, he was desirous to in-
spire the King by the confidence he himself
possessed. However ambitious of office, with
his noble spirit and his statesman-like views
and his independence of fortune, he would not

tamely stand by as the obsequious deputy of a capricious tyrant. The phrase " The King of absolute power," however odious in the popular sense, would not be so in constitutional usage; it may imply only the obedience due to the Sovereign; a King of England, the English lawyers have said, is the most absolute Prince in Europe, for the executive branch of the Constitution is itself absolute power.

Abstract propositions in the science of politics mislead, because opposite parties in adopting identical terms, affix different associations of ideas. It is the timely, shall we say the fortunate, application of such propositions, either in favour of the liberty of the subject, or the maintenance of the Sovereign's power, which alone preserves the variable unity of our Constitution. The Sovereign sometimes requires protection from the people, as well as the people from the King. Even Pym in his speech against Strafford, observed, " If the prerogative of the King overwhelm the liberty of the people, it will be turned into tyranny; if liberty undermine the prerogative, it will grow into anarchy."* To such an abstract proposition we may believe that Strafford would

* Rushworth, viii. 662.

have willingly subscribed—yet the conduct of
the patriot Pym and the minister Strafford was
in diametrical opposition—the one in agreeing
with the identical proposition would have had
" the prerogative of the King" more strongly
impressed on his mind as being " undermined;"
the other " the liberty of the subject" as being
" overwhelmed." And should we further allow,.for the sake of argument, that neither
were stimulated by personal hostility, or acted
from party motives, the one would have been
alarmed at anarchy, while the other would have
abhorred tyranny. Each perhaps by false associations of ideas was governing the public
mind—and the unhappy nation in that critical
period of the Constitution, was doomed to feel
the successive evils of that tyranny, and that
anarchy, of which their leaders had formed
such unsettled notions.

Mr. Brodie has said that " It cannot be
disputed that the generous tear which has
been shed for Strafford might well have been
spared." And as Mr. Brodie provokingly found
in the sage and temperate Whitelocke a glow-
ing eulogy on the magnanimous .Strafford, he
at once hastily suspects that the text has been
interpolated. This noble character of Strafford,

which Hume has transcribed into his text however, is genuine.*

At this day when the sentence of Strafford becomes but " a problem in political ethics," and as an Æsopian fable with its instructive moral, truth should be dearer to us than the memories of Strafford and of Pym—or the orgasm of a female demagogue in Mrs. Macaulay, the cavils of a Scotch advocate in Mr. Brodie, or even the liberal views of a philosophic historian in Mr. Hallam. It is good to be jealous in the maintenance of freedom, but in the silence of seclusion not less dear to the good and the wise, is the sanctity of truth!

Strafford suffered execution by the decision of the Judges, whose judicial opinion may still raise a blush in their successors on the bench : it was a huddled opinion extorted from their

---

* Brodie, iii. 94. This writer refers to the *first* edition of Whitelocke's Memorials, (16,) edited by the Earl of Anglesey, who took great liberties with the text and made important castrations. The *second* edition of 1732, published by subscription, was printed entire from the original manuscript. This valuable edition appears without a new preface, or the name of an Editor, and which after frequent inquiries I could never learn. The entire passage, which raised Mr. Brodie's suspicions so unjustly, appears *ad verbum* in the genuine edition.

personal fears, where particularising no act, they
condemned a man on the generality.*   A philosophical lawyer of our own times, who himself would have voted for the death of Strafford,
is compelled to offer an apology for this judicial opinion, observing that the two articles —
one of which was quartering troops on the people of Ireland, which however " had been enforced so seldom, that it could not be brought
within the act of treason," and another article
in which the Peers had voted him guilty, but'
" not on the whole matter"—may be said, to
use the words of this able writer, " at least to'
approach very nearly to a substantive treason,
within the statute of Edward III."†   So difficult it was to determine the character of the
crime—and so unconsciously might it have
been committed, at a period, when, as Mr.
Hallam observes, " the rules of evidence were

---

* Sir George Radcliffe has stated the fact concerning the
Judges with remarkable simplicity.   " The Judges were asked upon what grounds they had delivered their opinion to
the Lords ; to which they would give no answer, but that as
the case was put to them it was treason."   One of the articles voted was for having quartered a serjeant and four soldiers on a person, for refusing to obey his orders as Deputy
of Ireland, and this was deemed " levying war against the
King !"—*Strafford's Letters*, ii. 432.

† Hallam, i. 568.

very imperfectly recognised or continually transgressed."

Mr. Hallam rejoices at the condemnation of Strafford, but he acknowledges that "He should rather found his conviction of Strafford's systematic hostility to our fundamental laws, on his correspondence since brought to light, as well as his general conduct in Administration, than on any overt acts proved on his impeachment.* What now becomes of the justice of the Peers, and the Judges? since to have rendered justifiable the death-condemnation of this Minister, on clear and positive evidence, we are told that it required that his Judges, to save their consciences, ought to have lived one hundred and fifty years later than they did; that is, to the time of the publication of Strafford's private correspondence.

In regard to this private correspondence, and some unconstitutional language, held in Council, no one has yet thought necessary to ascertain what might be the true meaning this Minister attached to these ambiguous expressions; no one yet has placed himself in the situation of the Minister to comprehend his motives, or to penetrate into his design.

* Hallam, i. 567.

What meant Strafford by recurring to " extraordinary ways" should the Parliament refuse supplies? What when he told the King that " having tried the affections of his people, and being refused, he was absolved from all rule of government?" Why did he exult that he had conferred on the King in Ireland " absolute power?"

This high style may on its face admit of the most odious construction. But it is harmless, if " the extraordinary ways" was no grievance, but the suggestion of some " chaste" system of Finance. " An absolved King" is a phrase which seems in separating the executive power from the legislative, to make the monarch independent of the laws; the phrase was thrown out in the heat and collision of opinions amidst a Privy Council, and with a view of the peculiar circumstances into which the King was then cast. It might mean as much as his enemies could wish, or as little as his Advocate might choose. " Absolute power" does not necessarily include " arbitrary power;" absolute power may be only an efficient power for a defined object, and on this principle every English monarch becomes a most absolute Sovereign in his executive capacity; arbitrary power, depending only on the caprice of the individual, is indefinite

and unlimited. Who can ascertain the extent
of Strafford's devotion to the King? Would
he have crouched as the vile creature of a bru-
tal despot? Would he, whatever might be his
ambition, have sacrificed the nation to the arbitrary rule of a capricious Sovereign? Would
he have stood by the side of Charles the First
had he believed the King that tyrant, which is
still the hollow echo of partisans? This is the
question which should be resolved.

The style of the Minister, indeed, is often an
evidence of his resolution to support the King
against that superior force under which Charles
the First had of late succumbed. Strafford,
confident in his own powers, could fearlessly
have grappled with what he fatally deemed
a chimerical Faction.

If we look into some parts of Strafford's conduct, we may be convinced that at least he was
sensible of the value of the Constitution; he
solemnly swore this as he laid his head on
the block. He had felt as a Briton, and had
been ranked among our Patriots. But at times
to Strafford the power of the Commons seemed
more evident than their authority. We know
that Charles the First in his early manhood,
after the ungenerous treatment he had received
from his first Parliament, and repeated trials

to gain their favour, abhorred, or perhaps dreaded the very name; and since that long-past day he had gained nothing by concessions but a sense of his own weakness. But his Minister, was not hostile to Parliaments; it was by his persuasion that they were assembled; and he iterated his prayers that the King and his Parliament should meet in mutual confidence.* This fact of itself would be sufficient to discover the limits the Minister seems in his mind to have set to his devotion to the King; this fact is not denied by his enemies, but they have neutralised its merit; one, by maliciously assuring us he only meant dependant Parliaments,† another by maintaining that he merely

* I shall transcribe a passage on the Irish Parliament which will at least convey some notion of Strafford's opinion of all the Parliaments in Charles' reign.

" The Parliament is ended here; the King, I trust, well satisfied in the service done him, and if I be not much mistaken his subjects infinitely satisfied in particular regards towards them, which indeed is the happy effects of Parliaments. And yet *this is the only ripe Parliament that hath been gathered in my time, all the rest have been a green fruit broken from the bough,* which as you know, are never so kindly or pleasant. Happy it were if we might see the like in England; every thing in its season — this time it becomes us to pray for, and when God sends it to make the right use of it." Strafford's Letters, i. 420.

† Macaulay, ii. 461.

prudentially referred to Parliaments at times, in order to save himself from the very fate he met with.* Strafford was perhaps a superior Minister who anticipated a happier era when the Monarch might find in his Parliament a source of strength, and the Parliament in the Sovereign a source of honour.

It was at one of those awful and opposite crises which approximate to Revolution, that the Minister Strafford stood forth, the champion of his Sovereign. Strafford had ruled that land of Ire—as Fuller quaintly but expressively calls that unhappy country long conquered by its neighbour, and ever in war with its own children—with firmness and wisdom. The acts for which he was impeached chiefly relate to his Irish administration; but we know that that government has always been irregular from obvious causes, and too often compelled to resort to martial law. Mrs. Macaulay replying to those who asserted that the sentence by which Strafford fell was not according to Statute law, plausibly insisted that "circumstances may arise of so peculiar and urgent a nature as to render it necessary for the legislative power to exceed the strict letter of the law."† Abstract positions like these are

* Brodie, iii. 82.　　　† Macaulay, ii. 463.

equally strong on either side; Strafford might
have defended his own troubled administration in Ireland by adopting the very argument
which was pointed for his destruction. Strafford himself was so unconscious of criminality,
in the government of Ireland, that he appealed
to it as the evidence of his able administration;
nor was this entirely denied by his adversaries.
Never was this Minister taken more by surprise than when Pym having opened his introduction to the trial, a sealed paper was produced which appeared to be sent from the
Irish Parliament, purporting that the Commons
there had voted the Earl guilty of high-treason.
Strafford was startled; at once he saw through
the long scene which was opening on him—
exclaiming that "There was a conspiracy
against him to take his life!"* Pym and his
Committee remonstrated with the Lords that
he who stood impeached of treason had dared
to accuse the Parliament of a conspiracy against
him. The Earl was compelled on his knees to
retract his words. Strafford, however, here betrayed no deficient sagacity. It was indeed
one of the preliminaries of a conspiracy, by
getting up an impeachment among the Commons at Dublin to prepare the minds, and

* Whitelocke's Memorials, 40.

prejudice the passions of the Parliament at London.

The situation of the minister was surrounded by the most thorny difficulties — he felt them—and he pleaded for them. " Do not, my Lords," cried the oppressed statesman when before the tribunal of the nation—" do not put greater difficulties upon the ministers of State than that with cheerfulness they may serve the King and the State, for if you will examine them by every grain, or every little weight, it will be so heavy that the public affairs of the kingdom will be left waste, and no man will meddle with them that hath wisdom and honour and fortune to lose."

A strong administration is not a popular one, and it has never been difficult to render the commanding genius of a great minister odious to the people. In the case of Strafford, unparalleled artifices were directed to this single purpose. " The brutish multitude," as Sir Philip Warwick indignantly calls them, at the decapitation of Strafford, exulted that " his head was off!" they had been persuaded that that was the cure for all their grievances; but the great statesman of France, when he heard of the event, which in some measure he had himself promoted, sarcastically remarked that " the

English nation were so foolish that they would
not let the wisest head among them stand on
its own shoulders." The people and the minister seem to be placed in an opposite position
to each other, whenever the safety of the State
demands a severe administration; such a hapless minister is converting into enemies at least
one portion of that kingdom whose stability
costs him so many vigils, and whose very prosperity may gather strength to rise up against
him. Some of the greatest ministers who have
guided the fortunes of Europe would not have
proved to be less criminal than Strafford, had
they encountered Judges and enemies as terrible. As Richelieu in France, Pombal in Portugal, and Pitt in England. Nothing is less
difficult than to make a minister who has been
long in office a criminal, if his enemies are his
accusers. But in comparing Strafford with
other great ministers, his situation had this peculiarity: the party opposed to the minister
had an army in their pay ; the reverse has been
more usual.

If ever a great minister could have saved a
sinking State, the mind of Strafford was competent to that awful labour ; but his lofty spirit
was to be mortified by his own personal defects,
and to succumb beneath the rising genius of

the age, which was developing its mighty
limbs in the darkness of intrigue and revolution.   His imperturbable courage would have
wrestled with the daring aspirations and tumultuous force of popular ambition; but the
crisis of a kingdom had come, and he could
not give stability to what was passing away,
nor have dispersed what was soon to overwhelm; nor could he repair the incapacity, the
supineness, and the treachery of so many others.
Imperious, vindictive, confident in his own
energy, and above all devoted to the Sovereign
—yet could his implacable enemies only triumph by counting up the infirmities of fourteen years!

Whatever has been alleged in diminution
of the odium which the leaders of the patriotic
party incur for the condemnation of death passed on this minister, it must remain a perpetual
example of the passions of Parliament.   If we
consult the journals of the House of Commons,
we may find how even a noble cause may terminate in an ignoble effect, whenever the end
is made to sanctify the means, and the wisdom
to disguise the error.   At those moments and
at such a crisis, justice may be forced down by
the ardour of numbers, and truth may vanish
amidst the illusions of the passions.   It was

quite evident that the party of Pym had
meditated on a government of Terror, and
to cement the popular cause by the blood of
their Governors. Laud was immured, and this
greater Victim lay in their hands — they had triumphed, and the public cause which they had
adopted had consecrated that triumph. Had
the parliamentary leaders, with ordinary humanity and higher wisdom, shown themselves
to have been honourable in their means, and
dignified in their end, they would have been
the great moral masters of the nation — and of
Europe. They could have degraded the unhappy minister, despoiled him of his power and
his honours, reduced him as Charles offered,
" to be not fit to serve even the office of a
constable," and exiled him from his father-land;
but they practised the meanest artifices, and
closed by that astonishing act of injustice, when
to condemn the minister, his prosecutors submitted to become themselves criminal. He
whom they despaired to make guilty, they at
once convicted.

But it is the result of evil measures which
ought to teach us to dread them. Evil measures, when they are suffered to become popular, create " a taste for evil;" then it is that
the wicked rejoice, and the iniquitous are never

satiated with triumphs. The undisguised dereliction of legal justice in the case of Strafford, was but a prelude to the many which
were to follow. An English Marat of that
day, as an apology for the present and for
future " legal murders," tells us their secret.
" There is," says this barbarous politician, " a
necessitated policy that my Lord of Strafford and
some others should be given up, as a just sacrifice to appease the people." * The French Revolution is abundant in facts which confirm
" the necessitated policy" of the demagogues.

The most illustrious of foreigners, on these
odious proscriptions of individuals, which open
such a wide field for intrigues and personal
hatreds, has noticed our Bill of Attainder.
He classes it with those laws of Athens and of
Rome, by which an individual was condemned
by the suffrages of thousands of the people.
The various ostracisms which have been practised by some States, seem more akin to it ;
but the people who could not tolerate eminent
virtue or eminent genius, only betrayed their
own weakness, yet were not the less unjust and
cruel — but these ostracisms were bloodless !
Cicero would have such laws abolished, for this

* A pamphlet of the day entitled " The Earl of Strafford
characterised." 1641.

admirable reason, because the force of law con-
sists in being made for the whole community.
When Montesquieu delivered his own opinion,
he was awed by the great reputation of the
English nation — he conceived our Constitution
perfect, and us, as men without passions.   The
foreigner has done us more honour than in the
example of Strafford we have merited.   He
concludes his chapter thus, " I must own notwithstanding that the practice of the free'st
nation that ever existed induces me to think
that there are cases in which we must cast a
veil over liberty, as formerly they concealed
the statues of the gods."   The brilliant Montesquieu, as if he were composing his Temple
de Gnide instead of L'Esprit des Loix, gives
the fancies of a poet for the severe truths of
a legislator.   Beccaria is not of the opinion of
Montesquieu.

The tragical history of the Earl of Strafford
is among those crimes in our history, which
are only chastised by the philosophical historian.   The passions of contemporaries, and
the prejudices of posterity are marshalled
against the magnanimous minister, immolated
to the mysterious purposes of a powerful party,
who remorselessly pleaded, to cover their shame,
in the style of Caiaphas, " It is expedient for

us, that one man should die for the people."
Strafford perished for a crime which no law
recognized, and which Pym himself, when confounded by the indignant glance of the noble
prisoner at the bar, rendered inexplicable, by
calling it " Treason far beyond the power of
words !" Strafford might have left the bar
of his Peers as a guilty man ; as it was, he left
it only as a persecuted one. The ferocious
triumph could only be satiated by an inglorious homicide !

CHAPTER VIII.

THE ARMY PLOT—HISTORY OF COLONEL GOR-
ING—PYM'S MANAGEMENT OF THE PLOT—
DEFENCE OF LORD CLARENDON AND HUME.

THE Army-plot, as it is called, spread a consternation through the kingdom, and is still
more remarkable for its immense consequences,
not only as it hastened the catastrophe of Strafford's execution, but as, at no distant day, it
instigated Parliament, from their jealous fears
of the military, to demand the militia; an
usurpation which fell little short of dethroning
the King, and which terminated in the civil
war. So important an incident has given rise
to opposite opinions and statements, between
the great parties who now divide our English
history : the aim of one is to substantiate the
reality of the plot, and criminate the King;
the other deny it altogether, and insist that
it was a mere artifice of faction.

The history of this plot is involved in great obscurity—it changed its face more than once —and a contradictory tale has been shaped by opposite parties, suiting it to their own purpose. To unravel the perplexed skein of these intrigues—to analyze the contending elements of this confused compound—has been the labour of some of our contemporaries, and still remains to exercise our curiosity and our candour.

All parties have agreed that the origin of this Army-plot was a rising jealousy of the Scottish army. The arrears of the English army had remained undischarged, and in other respects they had of late suffered a studied neglect.* An English military force, in truth, was no longer required by Englishmen who had

---

* Mrs. Macaulay, the perpetual advocate for the Parliament, pleads for her party: "The English army, without attending to circumstances, or comprehending the difficulties the Commons lay under, showed symptoms of great displeasure." (ii. 446.) It is lamentable for the cause of truth, that these political advocates whenever reduced to frame apologies, never for once look to "the difficulties" which the unfortunate Monarch "lay under." But what were "these difficulties of the Commons?" They had involved themselves in a dark labyrinth of intrigues, and they were compelled to sacrifice even themselves, to the idol which their own hands had made.

adopted a foreign policy, had invited invaders, and for the benefits already conferred, chorused that cheering burthen to their street-ballads, which the honest Covenanter Baillie exultingly gives—" the binding word ever," as he calls it, was,

" Gramercy, good Scot !"

The English officers had witnessed convoys of monies pass by their quarters to their northern brethren. Officers unpaid would mutually communicate their dissatisfaction, and there was no difficulty in agreeing that the Parliament, and not the King, neglected them. Many of these officers were Members of the House and young men ; Wilmot, then commissary, had boldly told the Speaker, when passing a vote of money, on the urgent demands of the Scots, that if the Scots could get money by sending up a piece of paper, he did not see why the English should not use the same easy messenger. Hence seems to have originated in those petitioning days, the first idea of a military petition. It is evident that the strong partialities of the ruling party in the Commons were wholly bent towards the " dear brethren," whom they would consider as an army far deeper engaged in their interests than their own English, among whom doubtless were many friends of the King. A petition was drawn up by Percy, the brother of the Earl of Northumberland, subscribed by Wilmot, Ashburnham, O'Neal, and a few others — the professed object was to settle the King's revenue, which would include their own ; without infringing on the liberties of the subject, or on the sacredness of the laws. This paper was shown in a secret conference with some of the confidential servants of the royal party. The present subscribers were desirous of procuring the King's approval by some testimony which might serve to engage others. More than one draught of the petition was made, ere Charles put his initials C. R. to one, as a mark that he had perused and approved of it.

Percy addressed a letter to his brother, which some have thought was concocted to exculpate himself and the King towards the Parliament,* by criminating some of his associates. Percy tells us that on his first interview with the King he discovered that others had been treat-

* The Parliamentarians, not satisfied with Percy's letter, insinuate that he suppressed much which he knew, while Echard, a writer on the opposite side, asserts that Percy was induced by Pym to send this letter that his companions might be criminated, and thus furnish " a double evidence " preparatory to " a complete discovery."

ing before him; and, as he asserts, on principles contrary to those originally proposed, "inclining a way more high and sharp, not having limits either of honour or law." Already the Army-plot was assuming an altered countenance.

Colonel Goring, afterwards Lord Goring, who became distinguished during the civil war by his active intrigues, was now by the King's earnest desire admitted of the party, as also was Jermyn, the favourite of the Queen. Goring proposed the most daring designs, which Percy declares were positively rejected by all present, and in his interviews with the King, more than once forbidden by the King himself. Goring was anxious to learn who was to be the Commander-in-chief, while he himself refused any subordinate place. Several noblemen were mentioned by different persons, but no one proposed the Colonel himself. After a great debate nothing was concluded. The conspirators, if these petitioners can be so called, now discovered that they consisted at least of two opposed parties; the one restricting themselves to moderate measures, while the other seemed intent on nothing less than maintaining the King's absolute power.

According to Percy's narrative, in consequence of the disagreement of the parties, the whole project was laid aside — it had vanished! Goring seems to confirm this account of their inconclusive debates, in his pretended confession to the Parliament. "Certainly if they had stayed where I left them, there was no conclusion at all. It appears there were two several intentions digested by others (he avoids to say by whom) before they were communicated to me; and I know not whether my hearkening to them was a fault, but I am sure it was no misfortune."* According to Percy, Goring was the spokesman of the party who proposed "the violent courses"— the rescue of Strafford, and the march of the army to London. Goring on this point contrived an artful evasion. He told the Parliament, "I endeavoured to show them that as the design would be impious if the most desperate counsels had been followed, so it would be the weakest that ever was undertaken if they were omitted." By this ingenious turn Goring would screen himself by concealing the fact. of himself having proposed "these desperate counsels." Probably not one of the party could have recollected the Colonel's mention of the warm condemning epithet, "impious."

* Nalson, ii. 275.

Some time after—the precise interval which would be material to fix on, has not however been ascertained,—Goring reveals the Army-plot, which no longer existed, and whose object appears never to have been determined, to his friend the Earl of Newport, the Governor of the Tower, who having conducted him to the Earl of Bedford and Lord Mandeville, they, to relieve themselves from the weight of this dangerous communication, hastened to inform the other leaders of the Parliamentary party. Percy, Jermyn, and others of the Army-cabal received private notice that they were betrayed, though it was not known by whom; for Goring required that his name at present should be concealed. They instantly took flight; so suddenly that Jermyn had not time to change his dress, and went off " in his black satin suit, and white boots," which circumstance was adduced as evidence by the Parliament that the courtly beau had not intended to leave England on that day which the King's warrant he carried with him pretended. The flight of nearly all the party tended to confirm the deposition of Goring, and their guilt, and struck an universal panic which greatly served the purposes of the anti-Straffordians.

The moment which Goring chose to di-

vulge this Army-plot was most favourable to
the views of that party who were in great
want of some fresh collateral aid to lay the
head of Strafford on the block; and Goring
was quite certain of thus recommending himself to their high favour. He seems to have
watched for the lucky hour.

Lord Mandeville, afterwards Lord Kimbolton, and finally Earl of Manchester, who was
so perfectly acquainted with the history of his
times, and a chief actor in them, is an authority
as unquestionable as impartial. His Lordship
has in explicit terms declared the motives of
Goring's treachery, and the dexterity and artifice with which he chose this particular moment for his discovery. " Col. Goring whose
ambition was not answered in being promised
the place of Lieutenant-General of the army,
and finding others employed whose persons he
disliked, he having a full information from Mr.
Percy and Mr. Jermyn of all the design, thought
it would tend most to his security and advantage to reveal the conspiracy, and being versed
in all the methods of falsehood, he chose the
time and means which he thought would be
most acceptable to the Parliament." *

* Nalson, ii. 273, from the MS. Memoirs of the Earl of
Manchester.

The causes which Lord Mandeville has assigned for the conduct of Goring we can confirm from other sources. We have the remark
which Jermyn privately made to Goring, on
Goring's objecting, as Goring pretends in his
deposition, to marching the army to London.
" You do not," said Jermyn, " dislike the design ; for you are as ready for any wild mad
undertaking as any man I know ; but you dislike the temper of those persons who are engaged in the business." *

But we have another authority which Lord
Mandeville could not have seen, which confirms the motive assigned for Goring's aban-
donment of the party which he had evidently
joined—it is that of the Queen herself, who
informed Madame de Motteville that Goring
was enraged at the disappointment of not having been chosen General in chief. However
strenuously Goring denied before Parliament
that he had ever contemplated on the desperate
designs so dexterously ascribed by him to
others, the Queen's story proves quite the contrary, and confirms the narrative of Percy.†

* Rushworth, iv. 254.

† Percy charges Goring with proposing " the violent
courses,' while Goring asserts that he knew nothing of the
plot, till it was communicated to him by Percy. Here is a

Goring had proposed to rescue Strafford ; but Wilmot had entertained a similar project; each unknown to the other. The ambition, if not the zeal of both these military adventurers, was equal. The King and the Queen, to whom these officers had separately, in confidence, communicated their design, dared not give a preference to either, certain by their choice of converting into a dangerous enemy the other, and dreading at that critical moment a discovery of this secret intercourse with the army. The perplexed Monarch inclined to give the command to Goring, and to satisfy Wilmot by the equivalent of another splendid appointment. The courtly Jermyn, Master of the Horse to the Queen, the suavity of whose manners was imagined could not fail to reconcile these contending interests, and who valued himself on the impossible faculty of pleasing all and displeasing none, was dispatched to persuade either of these officers to relinquish the chief com-

palpable contradiction by the parties themselves. But the veracity of Percy may be trusted. Goring swore to Sir Philip Warwick, which oath, observes Warwick, " was no great assurance," that he never revealed the plot till he knew that the chief members of both Houses were before acquainted with it. The Earl of Manchester's and the Queen's account agree with Percy's narrative.

mand to the other; but Jermyn found that his flatteries and cajoleries were quite inefficient with these sturdy and secret rivals.

It may perhaps be deemed a most uncertain thing to assign the motives of a person of the character of Goring. Bold in enterprise, and scornful of danger, with considerable abilities, he was, however, utterly profligate in his principles. If this volatile man were impatient at the vacillating and timid conduct of the King and the Queen; if he did not much like some of his associates, and perhaps suspected the fidelity of others; if he were too proud to play a subordinate part; all this might account for his desertion of that party, but will hardly for his avowed perjury, and his reckless treachery. The truth is, that Goring, versatile in his conduct, was apparently of no party, but dexterously profiting by both. His whole life was a series of such acts. He would have been willing to have obliged both parties, would both have been satisfied to have been betrayed. He gave a remarkable instance of this duplicity on the present occasion. Jermyn, on his flight, ran off to Portsmouth to his friend Goring, who was the Governor, and who at that moment he knew not was his betrayer. Jermyn had a royal warrant to procure a frigate;

Goring had just received an order from Parliament to arrest Jermyn. He hurried his friend a-board, and pocketed the order from the Parliament, pretending afterwards that it had reached him an hour too late. When Governor of Portsmouth, he took large supplies of money from the Parliament for fortifying the place, and at the same time, from the King, to admit the Royalists on some favourable opportunity. He declared that he held the place faithful to the King and Parliament for their use, and not to be delivered up but by both their consents.

Goring seems always to have relied on the ingenuity of his own duplicity, on the gracefulness of his person, and his consummate address; these resources he could command at all times; to be deceived by him was sometimes to love him, for he showed himself to be an excellent actor on the most critical exigencies. Accused, he had the art of persuading others of his integrity. Lord Digby, having listened to his tale of the Army-plot, where Goring on his own unavoidable confession, was guilty of a wilful perjury in consorting with persons under the most solemn oath of secrecy, with a reserved intention to betray them, his Lordship indignantly exclaimed, that " He was a perjured man!" Goring, pathetically appealing to the Commons for having broken all former ties of amity for his present duty as a subject, cunningly professed that the military were to submit themselves to Parliament in passive obedience, which he did not weakly express thus, " It belongs to an army to maintain, not to contrive the acts of State." The Commons, gratified by this profession of unlimited obedience, not only voted that Colonel Goring had done nothing contrary to justice or honour, but also voted the expulsion of Lord Digby from the House as unworthy to continue any longer a member!

Insincerity was the habit of the man who could be at once a favourite with the Parliament, and at all times could ingratiate himself with the King. Clarendon has given one of his finest touches to the portrait, " He would appear with a bashfulness so like innocence, when in truth it was a formed impudence to deceive; and with a disorder so like reverence, when he had the highest contempt of them." Goring was a man whom no oath of secrecy could bind, and whose oath on any occasion, even by his friends, was not deemed as any proof of evidence.* Of such a

* Sir Philip Warwick's Memoirs.

man it is as vain to conjecture the motives, as it is difficult to comprehend the views, when we examine his mutuable actions. When he first met the army-confederacy, proposed the most desperate schemes and aspired to the command, his ardent ambition might vouch for his sincerity; but when he disliked to act with some of his new associates, he cared not how soon he broke with them, and courting the Parliament by a very timely service, in divulging a plot, which seems to have no longer existed, he secured his own safety, and his own good fortune,—reckless of a soldier's honour, with a dispensation granted by the House of Commons from all moral obligation.

In this little comedy of a confused plot, there was an under one. Mrs. Macaulay tells us that " The Queen, who without the requisite talents had more than a female propensity to intrigue, entered with greater violence than judgment into the extreme of the King's proposition of bringing the army up to London, to surprise the Tower and overawe the Parliament." In this great conspiracy Henrietta's confidential agents were Davenant and Suckling, and she adds " a Mr. Jermyn." Why " a Mr. ?" Our historian must have been as familiar with that name as any other in Cla-

rendon's History; she here betrays that feminine disposition which she has herself so singu-
larly confessed.   Our lady democrat, indulging
not only her sexual but her political "propensity," delighted thus to spurn at the silken
favourite of the Queen ; the future Earl of
St. Alban's, and afterward the secret consort of
Henrietta.   In love affairs can a female historian grow malicious in imagination, and tinge
with the gall of jealousy or envy, the page of
obsolete amours ?

The agents assigned to the Queen were certainly the sort of counsellors quite suitable to
Henrietta's profound politics of which she has
been so gravely accused.   It may be easily
imagined that the plots of these gentlemen
were romantic, well adapted for one of the
Queen's pastorals ; they were more expert in
such denouements than they ever showed themselves in political ones.

Pym wound up the public to the highest
pitch of dismay and curiosity, by rumours, and
afterwards by gradual disclosures, for partial
revelations produced more effect than would
the whole had it been at once revealed.   He
first broke the alarming, though yet obscure intelligence, to the House, of " desperate designs
both at home and abroad."   They were in a

mood to imagine more than was told. They sate from seven in the morning to eight at night. Indignant as much as terrified, the Commons resolved instantly on " a Protestation," not only to be signed by all the members, but shortly after ordered by themselves, for the Lords first threw out the Bill, though they afterwards subscribed it—that the Protestation should be subscribed by the whole nation !" *

This was in fact the Scottish Covenant—so closely they copied in all their proceedings that model, which so long admired, was now delightful to imitate. It had rested in their thoughts, and, as we shall find, it now crept into their parliamentary style. A short time previous, that honest Covenanter Baillie had hinted to the Presbytery of Irvine, that " the lower House is more united than ever; and they say *not far from a Covenant.*" He was no fallible prophet, for he was in all their secrets, and a short time after, writing on this fierce debate he exclaims, " Blessed be the name of the Lord ! They all swore and sub-

---

* Two Lords refused their signatures, alleging that they knew of no law that enjoined it, and that the consequence of such voluntary engagements might produce effects that were not intended.

scribed the Writ. I hope in substance our
Scottish Covenant." And the politic Covenanter remarks, "We see now that it hath
been in a happy time that so much time hath
been lost about Strafford's head." This humane man maddened by his presbyterial notions, loses even in his language any decent
sympathy, and notices "the head of Strafford"
as the slayer would his stalled ox. But the
zealot was right enough in his notion of the
Scottish Covenant of the English Parliament!
Sir John Wray in his anti-papistical, anti-epis-
copal, and choicely puritanic speech, this day
took care to remind them of that Israelitish
term, and he seems to have had the merit of
introducing that biblical oratory which so long
after illumined this new style of the British
Senate. " Let us endeavour to become holy
pilgrims (not papists) and to endeavour to be
LOYAL COVENANTERS with God and the King;
first binding ourselves by a Parliamentary or
NATIONAL OATH (not Straffordian nor a Prelatical one) to preserve our religion entire and
pure without the least compound of superstition and idolatry, Mr. Speaker! making Je-
rusalem our chiefest joy, we shall be a blessed
nation. But if we shall let go our Christian
hold and lose our Parliament-proof, and old

English well-tempered mettle, let us take heed that our buckler break not, our Parliament melt not, and our golden candlestick be not removed." Matters must have advanced very far-when such a speech in the English Parliament was not only listened to, but seemed worthy of being recorded.*

Hume has said of this famous " Protestation," that " in itself it was very inoffensive, even insignificant, containing nothing but general declarations." The passionless historian in the calm of his study, saw little more in this extraordinary act of the Commons but an incident to be recorded. The Covenanter of that day, however, grimly rejoiced; and Father Philips the Queen's confessor, with tremulous nerves, wrote " The Protestation is much like, but much worse, than the Scottish Covenant."

If we now look at this state-document, we may consider it as conveying to us a singular

---

* In the true spirit of party-writing, the wretched Oldmixon calls this " a true English speech — how piquant and pleasing is the blunt honesty of this Lincolnshire knight!" and contrasts it with " the long sentences, the sophistry, and affectation in the Lord Clarendon's florid discourses." All that we can add of " this honest Lincolnshire knight" is, that his sagacity lay as much in his nose, as in his brains, when he smelt gunpowder in the House, and spread a panic by land and water as we have already noticed. See p.153.

mixture of the two distinct parties in the
House, who were then acting for different
ends, though acting in unity—the Puritanic
and the political. Hence we find the party
who had chiefly in view " the true reformed
religion" inveighing against " Papistry," while
the Politicians—they had hardly yet earned
the distinction of Republicans—whose theme
was " tyrannical Government," did not fail to
lay great stress on " Illegal taxes." This famous Protestation was drawn up in heat and
haste, and by an expression which none complained of at the moment, offended their friends
out of the House, and flurried the Covenanters.
The Commons had declared in their Protestation that they were " to protect and defend the
true reformed Protestant religion expressed in
the doctrine of the Church of England." This
phrase doubtless had long been parliamentary,
and they had been so accustomed to it, that it
naturally occurred in their eagerness to draw
up their national " Covenant." But the doctrine of the Church of England included Epis-
copal government which they were fast overturning, and rites and ceremonies which they
had formally denounced as Romish. Many
pretended they could not subscribe to maintain
an establishment they had resolved to destroy,

and doctrines which they were perpetually disavowing. The Commons were reduced to the
humiliating necessity of sending after their
Protestation, an explanation of their meaning,
which was that by the doctrines of the Church
of England, they meant nothing more than
whatever it held contrary to Popery, and Popish
innovations, without extending to its government and ceremonies. In a word they meant
nothing more by the Church of England but
what the Kirk of Scotland, in its spiritual illu-
mination, allowed to all Christians—viz. all
they enjoined and nothing they disliked. This
is a striking instance of the passions of Parliament! When Charles the First found himself
compelled to publish an Explanation of the
famous " Petition of Right" to prevent the
country from misconceiving its purport and his
assent, the King heard only the scream of insurgency, but in the present case, where the
Commons were fixed in the same dilemma,
their time-serving and factious Explanation
was embraced by their Covenanting friends
with Hallelujahs!

Clarendon's account of the Army-plot, Mr.
Brodie, with more than the severity of a partisan, has charged as " exceedingly disingenuous, and even inconsistent," and convicts

Clarendon of having on this particular occasion as well as on another, in both of which he (Clarendon) is mistaken,* fabricated a spurious document. With a freedom which exceeds even that of historical inquiry, Mr. Brodie, in more than one place, repeats his condemnation of the noble writer as " a dextrous forger of speeches and letters," from an ingenuous story told of himself in his own life of his adroitness in adopting the peculiarities of the style of others. Clarendon once displayed this faculty in two political *jeux d'esprit*, in the shape of the speeches of the eccentric Earl of Pembroke, for an accommodation with the King; and the Puritan Lord Brooke, for utterly rooting out all courtiers. The contrast was amusing, and the speeches were inserted in some of the Diurnals. The sullen gravity of our contemporary heavily criminates these pleasantries of the day. Charles the First, who had flattered himself that he could never fail in discovering Cla-

---

* See Brodie, iii. 306, where in a note alluding to " the Porters' Petition," which Clarendon has given, and which Mr. Brodie, ashamed even of his ridiculous " Radicals," has " no hesitation in pronouncing a forgery by that author." Mr. Hallam has chastised this precipitate and passionate historian, by referring to the Journals where this very petition is fully noticed.

rendon by his impressive style, and who backed
his critical discernment by wagering an angel
with Lord Falkland, had only the merit of
being deceived and charmed by the adroitness
of the mimetic genius of the immortal writer.*

But Lord Clarendon must be judged by our
candour as well as by the passions of party.
We must adjust our views to that point of
sight whence he contemplated the scene.

Clarendon, as far as the King stood implicated in marching the army to London, which
he says "was the chief matter alleged," calls

---

* Political fictions are dangerous; for we historians, who
are always grave, are not always sagacious. Such extem-
porary pleasantries, and sometimes lampoons, as these of
Clarendon, were practised by others — it was a fashion with
the wits, who were chiefly Loyalists. Butler forged, as Mr.
Brodie, a sound advocate, could prove. Sir John Birken-
head was a clever fellow at these spurious speeches and
letters. President Bradshaw on his death-bed was made to
recant what he never recanted; Henderson, the polemic,
was thrown into the same state. This was practised as well
on the other side. Two speeches are printed of Strafford's,
full of contrition for his past conduct, which he never could
have spoken; we have the authentic speech taken by Rushworth himself when on the scaffold. A series of " Familiar
Epistles from Col. Harry Martin to his Miss," paints to the
life the loose habits and *espiègleries* of this witty profligate,
and I think they have been referred to by some inconsiderate writer as a genuine correspondence.

the plot " an imposture," and he was even warranted to infer by the letter of Percy to his
brother the Earl of Northumberland, that " it
is evident there was no plot at all!"

But to turn the Army-plot into a *ruse* of
the party, and to show the little danger which
they had attached to it, Clarendon charges
Pym and others with agitating the public
mind and raising terrifying tumults, while they
never divulged the plot till three months after
the presumed discovery. Here the noble writer
supposes that the discovery was made nearly as
early as the plot was concerted; the confederacy occurring in March, while the plot was
only publicly denounced in May. Mr. Brodie
detects, as he concludes, the inaccuracy of
Clarendon. But he should have acknowledged
that the incident was obscure; its correctness
depended on the precise date of Goring's first
communication to the party. This has not
been satisfactorily ascertained. If the Queen's
account be correct, Clarendon may not have
widely erred, for the Queen said, that on the
very night of the interview with Jermyn, when
Goring found that he was disappointed of the
chief command, stung with anger, he hurried
to discover the whole design. Mr. Brodie acknowledges that the plot was imperfectly

known to Pym about twelve days before the
public disclosure. It was let out by parcels—
which answered the purpose better than had
the whole been known at once. Mr. Brodie
concedes something still more, when he does
not deny that during this very period, while
the nature of the plot remained vague and unknown, it was however carefully noised about
the city, and had stirred up the tumults. The
party therefore, in conformity with their new
system of policy, had been providently spread-
ing the infection of a panic though they were
yet ignorant, whether the causes of their terror
were at all adequate to the immense couse-
quences they were producing,

Clarendon has given " the Petition of the
Officers," which has not elsewhere been preserved ; and it has excited surprise how the
noble writer obtained the copy of a petition,
which is acknowledged to have been destroyed.
This " petition," Mr. Brodie shows, " carries on
its face the most unequivocal marks of fabrica-
tion"—indeed it alludes to events which did
not happen till after the time assigned to it.
This strange discordance Rapin had already
detected, and justly inferred that the petition
inserted in Clarendon's history could not be the
real one, which Mr. Brodie amply confirms.

Yet must not the more recent historian be indulged in the gratuitous triumph of his self-complacency, when he exclaims, that " he has set Lord Clarendon's veracity at rest." Clarendon, after all, was not a forger as Mr. Brodie from too warm prepossessions hastily imagines. The fact is, that the petition is what it professes to be, but it has been erroneously assigned to a period to which it does not belong. To such a mistake the collectors of historical documents, undated, are liable to. Had his Lordship attentively examined it at the moment of its insertion into his history, he too might have discovered the error; but such papers were probably collected at distant periods, and further, it appears that an Amanuensis usually transcribed these state-papers into the manuscript of the noble writer. This petition of the officers was drawn up several months after the time assigned to it in Clarendon's history, by Captain O'Neale, and other of the army royalists.* This is a curious instance where an historian has been condemned during

---

* We owe this detection to the acuteness of Mr. Hallam, who by the very documents which Mr. Brodie has printed was enabled to discover the fact, which Mr. Brodie had overlooked — at the very moment he was so bitterly criminating Clarendon for having fallen into a similar mischance.

half a century for an imposture on apparently the most obvious evidence, till the sagacity of the later historian has detected the accidental inadvertence, and vindicated the honour of the elder.

Mr. Brodie's observation on Hume is a specimen of unphilosophical taste. He scolds that illustrious philosopher for ridiculing the idea of marching the army to London ; but "ridicule," adds the graver Scotsman, "which is a species of argument that he always uses, will never rebut the most decisive proofs that the thing was contemplated; and Hume overlooks the circumstance of military assistance being expected from France — assistance from Catholics, &c. while the metropolis would be in the power of the army." *

The argument of Hume however is perfectly serious and to me conclusive. "The King rejected the idea as foolish, because the Scots who were in arms, and lying in their neighbourhood, must be at London as soon as the English army. This reason is so solid and convincing that it leaves no room to doubt of the veracity of Percy's evidence, and consequently acquits the King of this terrible plot of bringing up the army, which made such

* Brodie, iii. 115.

a noise at the time, and was a pretence for so many violences." " This terrible plot " seemed to Mr. Brodie the most exquisite ridicule!*

What " military assistance was to be ex-

---

* The judicious Malcolm Laing indulges an odd fancy which Mr. Brodie has no difficulty in adopting. He says that " a part of the army would have sufficed to march against the Parliament, while the main body remained to oppose the Scots." This might have happened, had the Scots been less shrewd than they showed themselves to be at all times during this reign. But supposing that the English army had marched to London from York and taken the whole Parliament prisoners, and this is supposing an impossibility, they would still have to fight with an enemy of undiminished strength and flushed even by a triumphant invasion. But a circumstance more important has been overlooked by these writers. The communications between the Scots and their paymasters the Parliament, were so closely kept up, and each so entirely depended on the other, that had any part of the English army moved towards the metropolis, it would inevitably have produced a battle — or a pursuit. When Malcolm Laing refers to the petition in Clarendon " where the officers say," to secure the King and Parliament from such future insolencies, &c. they would wait upon him, "that is to march directly to London :" Mr. Brodie eagerly repeats this confirmation of Malcolm Laing's idea. But neither of these writers was aware that the petition they were referring to had been drawn up at a subsequent period, and by another party. Their premises therefore being false, their argument can be no otherwise.

pected from France?" Pym indeed declared
that " the French were drawing down their
army in all ' haste to the sea side.' " This must
have been one of his chimeras to alarm the
mob. We discover no such movements in
French history. Richelieu still was in the
vigour of his administration, and we are acquainted with the vindictive policy which the
great Cardinal had successfully adopted to depress the English Monarch ; Richelieu was at
that moment the secret ally of the Scots, and,
had circumstances admitted, would not have
scrupled being the ally of the English Parliament. Charles had already sternly refused to
submit to his aid. The idea of a French invasion, particularly that Portsmouth was to be
given up to them, could only have originated
in the false rumours which were perpetually
renewed by the encourager of political panics,
and which are gravely recorded by their historian, as secrets of state.

The Army-plot seems to be a jumble of incidents and cross-purposes. The first malcontents, consisting of young officers of distinction,
had confined their attempts to the prevalent
mode of redress, so freely exercised at that
moment — a petition to Parliament. Unquestionably when those eminent officers, who were

all Royalists, consulted the King on the form
of their proposed petition, it renewed the hope
of Charles of recovering his regal influence
over the military. The King however proceeded so cautiously in the style of the petition,
that more than one was destroyed before he
confidentially ventured to affix his initials.

A distinguished military adventurer, Colonel Goring, who seems to have contemplated
making his fortune in one day, proposed the
daring measure of the march of the army to
the metropolis. We are told by Percy, that
this mad project was instantly rejected by the
first petitioners, and twice by the King himself
for its folly and impracticability. It was indeed a scheme suitable to the romantic notions of the Queen and the heated fancies of
her pair of poets, and her courtly Master of
the Horse, who however ridiculed it in private.
The parties who formed the confederacy could
no longer agree—the whole project was given
up—the petition was destroyed and the confederacy was dissolved. Thus the Army-plot,
as it is called, ceased to exist, if indeed it can
be said that it ever commenced.

This was however a crisis, and the fate of
Strafford was in suspense. Charles may have
willingly listened to many a scheme for the

abstraction of this victim of state. To what last effort would not Charles have submitted in order to hold himself guiltless of the murder of a great minister, and a faithful servant? The King had bowed down to his personal enemies, as he conceived some of them to be, in the new administration of the Earl of Bedford,—who pledged the life of Strafford for their admission into power. In his despair he probably listened to those adventurous spirits, who were projecting the rescue of the noble prisoner from the Tower. A passage in Strafford's farewell letter to his secretary Sir Henry Slingsby bears a dark indication of some uncertain project. * Sir John Suckling had procured a resolute captain with a hundred picked men, to be admitted into the Tower, but Sir William Bal-

---

* After the bill of Attainder had passed, Strafford in his farewell letter mysteriously writes---" God may yet, if it please him, deliver me—the person you were last withal at Court, sent to move that business we resolved upon, which if rightly handled, might perchance do something; but you know my opinion in all, and what my belief is in all these things—I advise you to absent yourself till you see what becomes of me. *If I live* there will be no danger for you to stay, but otherwise keep out of the way till I be forgotten." —Rushworth, viii. 774. It is quite evident that in his cup of adversity even its dregs were tinctured with some faint hopes.

four, the Governor, was Scottish in heart, and afterwards showed himself a hero in the Parliament's service. Balfour refused the bribe of twenty-two thousand pounds, and the marriage of the daughter of Strafford with his son — the condition of his connivance at the meditated escape.

Pym on the earliest communications of the army-plot, was unquestionably frightened — but not out of his wits—for from the first intimations, however they may have reached him, to the deposition of Goring, and the subsequent ones which gradually came out, this industrious master of intrigues never turned a plot to his own advantage with more dexterity, or ever invented one more successfully for its important results. The conspiracy of Catiline did not shake Rome with a more general panic, than that which now disturbed the metropolis, and rapidly spread through the kingdom. The terror, that the King had still the military at command, dismayed the hearts of the Commons, who seem to have felt themselves in the condition of Belshazzar when he beheld the hand-writing on the wall—" the joints of my loins were loosed, and my knees smote one against the other." And they manifested their terror by soon dispatching to the English army

"four cart-loads of money, and more was ordered suddenly to follow."* So that the first
petitioners who had concerted a petition, which
was never presented, and who now were all in
flight, are proved by the subsequent conduct
of the Commons themselves not to have been
quite so unreasonable in raising a mutiny—for
their defrauded arrears!

As the evidence is in the King's favour, that
he was not privy to "the wild mad undertaking," it has been insinuated by those who think
it makes for their cause to implicate Charles
the First, that the evidence was given by all
parties in a manner not to lose the royal favour.
It is remarkable that the greater number of
those implicated in the Army-plot were Royalists, for they afterwards showed their personal
attachment to the King. There had been nothing very strange, had Charles, considering
the miserable condition to which he was now
reduced, attempted to conciliate the favour of
the army—the Commons themselves in their
fright lost no time in doing it.

Such is the history of a plot, which never
occurred, but which was contrived by the arts
of Faction, and the skill of Pym, to produce
the same results as if it had. It is the history

* Rushworth, iv. 292.

of a confederacy, or a conspiracy where people
were not all of one mind, and where oaths
were probably taken with different intentions.
The evidence is contradictory; for every one
in criminating another, was very cautious to
spare himself. An oath of secrecy, said to
have been taken, is denied by others on their
oath; and a petition bearing the royal initials,
no one could produce. He, who publicly perjured himself, furnished most of the details;
others probably as carefully suppressed what
has never reached us. And to make the end
as obscure as the beginning, the Commons,
having issued proclamations for apprehending
the conspirators, and having taken them, never
proceeded against one of these persons; every
one seemed ready to vindicate himself and to
criminate others.

But Pym was astute; he saw enough and
imagined more; the plot which had been given
up by the plotters, to such a politic partisan
was as serviceable as the plot which was going
on. Clarendon might conscientiously affirm
that "it was no plot at all," and believed too
little of what had passed away; Brodie and
Macaulay may maintain with Pym, that it was
a most desperate plot, and describe that which
yet never existed. Had the army received

their pay, we should have had no plot. And
had Goring not perjured himself at the moment Pym eagerly grasped at all the benefits
he knew how to derive from a Royalist-plot,
in the pending trial of Strafford, this affair
would never have entered into our history —
nor led to those mighty results which were
soon to occur.

CHAPTER IX.

THE MARQUIS OF HAMILTON.

IN political life an honourable character, however it may design an honourable purpose, by an ambiguous conduct, and by pursuing indirect measures, through dark and crooked ways — whatever may be the result—will inevitably incur the suspicions and the reproaches of both parties. No subsequent explanations can ever clear up this double-dealing; not even should this man by his last decided actions, and at the cost of life itself, confirm his adherence to that cause which apparently he had first adopted. Evil actions, however accompanied by good intentions, will always retain their nature.

The extraordinary history of the Marquis, afterwards the Duke of Hamilton, will illustrate this reflection. Mixed characters when

pourtrayed through all the shades of truth are
not drawn.without difficulty ; but the motives
of subdolous and artificial men, belonging as
it were to two opposite parties, yet governed
by no other principle than their own preservation, may be as mutable as the events of
their lives. Such at times, may be as zealous
in the cause they adopt, as at other times they
may be equally prompt to betray it. To both
parties the integrity of these characters becomes
alike problematical. Of the Duke of Hamilton and his brother the Earl of Lanerick, Warburton has not hesitated to declare that they
were " both Knaves," notwithstanding the apologies and the eulogies of Burnet ; while Hume,
as if his penetrating acuteness were at fault,
could only decide that " the numerous accusations against Hamilton have neither been
proved, nor refuted."

The history of the Marquis of Hamilton
affords a striking illustration of the true character of Charles the First—of its better and
its infirm qualities : of that warmth in his personal attachments to which this Monarch was
so frequently a victim, having adopted for a
principle of conduct, " never to suspect nor desert his friends," and of that deficient discern-

ment in human character which seems to have operated such a disastrous influence over his affairs.

What indeed is more endearing to a feeling heart than an inherited friendship? The constitutional temper of Charles was susceptible of this profound impression; and when the day came that Charles required a partner of his regal cares, he could only view in the son of the friend of his father, that devoted being who is not to be found among the casualties of life.

The father of the present Marquis had distinguished himself in the service of the late King, by his skilful conduct in the Scottish affairs, which had required great prudence and management. James the First had conferred on him a title which had never before been borne but by the royal blood—that of the Earl of Cambridge. Hamilton indeed was the nearest kinsman to the royal house of Scotland. Both the fathers had encouraged the mutual affections of the Sons; and they had grown together in their prime. When Charles was Prince, young Hamilton was his frequent companion in " the hard chases of the stag and in the toilsome pleasures of a racket;"* and Hamilton

---

* Sir Philip Warwick sarcastically adds, " by which last he often filled his own and emptied his master's purse," 105.

was one of the young noblemen who hastened
to wait on the Prince in Spain.   Charles placed
Hamilton on the same equality as Buckingham ; the Prince called him by the endearing
familiarity of his baptismal name, and " James "
was as usual with the Prince, and afterwards
the King, as " George."   On the death of
Buckingham, the Marquis enjoyed more of the
royal favour than was even shared by his other
kinsman, the Duke of Lenox, whose devotion
to the King was shown, not only during the
life, but after the death of Charles.

On the decease of his father, who died early,
the Marquis of Hamilton withdrew into privacy ; a remarkable step for a young nobleman,
and those who have attempted to inquire into
the cause of this secession have only clouded it
over with mystery.   Burnet has always ready a
favourable motive for the conduct of the Hamiltons.   The munificence of the father had so
heavily incumbered the family estates that the
son could not maintain the same eminence at
Court, and the pensive youth delighted in the
retired life he led in the isle of Arran.

So early then did the Marquis's cool conduct betray his love
of self-preservation ? or may not the sarcasm be rather the
result of an opinion which Warwick, as Warburton did,
had formed of the Marquis's character ?

We may infer that the personal affection of Hamilton for the King was not of that nature which rendered his voluntary exile very painful. Charles, however, never forgot the companion of his youth, but often solicited his hermit-friend to return to Court, and accept the favours and the honours which he designed for him; even Buckingham offered his prodigal friendship. On the unexpected death of the favourite, the high office of Master of the Horse was pressed on him; Hamilton could no longer refuse; and from this day the Marquis possessed the boundless confidence of his Royal master.

A beautiful instance of that generous, if not that wise principle, which Charles had adopted in the intercourse of friendship, was shown to Hamilton. The Marquis, in his absence in Sweden, as General of the Scottish troops, which by the secret orders of Charles had joined Gustavus Adolphus, was accused of treasonable designs; it was hinted that even the life of the King was not safe in his hands. The Lord Treasurer Weston gave weight to the accusation, cautioning the King not to admit Hamilton to his bed-chamber. Charles rejected the calumnious insinuation, and on the return of the Marquis, privately communicated the infamous charge. The confusion of Hamilton was remarkable—Charles relieved him from the surprise by not suffering him to speak in his own vindication, but to put an end to the vile calumny, the King commanded the Marquis that very night to sleep in his bed-chamber! Hamilton often declared that he looked on this noble confidence, and the remembrance of that night, as having obliged him more than all the honours and bounties which he had received.*

When the troubles in Scotland broke out, it was a natural choice in Charles the First, among the numerous Scotchmen who formed so strong a party in his Court, to fix on the Marquis of Hamilton for the confidential office of his High Commissioner in Scotland. Not only was the King led to this by the strong affection which he bore the Marquis from his early days, but because in some respect, Hamilton might be said to have an hereditary claim to be the representative of Majesty. The late Marquis had served as High Commissioner in Scotland, and had prudently contrived a settlement, not however without violent opposition; this difficult adjustment of affairs had endeared him to the Monarch, but it had provoked the

* Burnet's Memoirs of the Dukes of Hamilton, 13.

sullen Presbyters and democratic Knoxites.
When Charles had decided to carry matters
farther than his father had ventured, he consulted Hamilton, and when the universal explosion burst forth as it were at a single moment, over mitred heads, and Episcopacy was
about to be abolished, at that disastrous moment did Charles appeal to the friendship and
confide to the fidelity of the Marquis of Hamilton, to be his sole adviser in the affairs of Scotland, and to allay, or to chastise the perturbed
spirits of his countrymen.

It must be confessed that this appeal of his
Royal master to the zeal of his friend was as
painful as it was critical. The Marquis was
conscious that his name was unpopular among
his Scottish compatriots; nor was he more es-
teemed in England.

The liberal bounties of his Sovereign and
his friend, had raised up to him enemies both
in the Court and the country; the Marquis
possessed certain monopolies of wine and iron,
by which he had pressed harder on the people
than any other man durst; all which profits
reverted to Hamilton and to his pensioners.
This accusation, which had cast some odium
on his name, we receive from Clarendon, who
could not have known what Burnet informs us,

that these monopolies, according to the custom
of the times, were only assignments of the revenue derived from certain taxations for re-
payment of debts which Hamilton had contracted by the King's secret command, when he
joined Gustavus Adolphus with six thousand
Scots, for the recovery of the Palatinate.
Hamilton, too, was as little a favourite at Court
as with the people. The contrivances by
which he eluded intermeddling further in any
business than suited his ease or his interest,
were considered as a perpetual evidence of his
dexterity in self-preservation. There was an
imperturbable calmness about Hamilton which
no zeal could kindle, and which gave the appearance that he was never in earnest. The
truth is, that the Marquis was a person of great
reflection and foresight, one of a melancholy
turn, who raised objections more easily than he
could frame resolutions, and foresaw danger
much more clearly than he could predict success.
He was ever in that comfortless state of reserve,
though not perhaps of indifference, to which the
crooked politician is doomed who dares not entirely trust himself to any one, knowing that his
friend may become his enemy, and his enemy
his friend. His eulogist, Burnet, acknowledges
that " Had not his mind been of a great and

undaunted stayedness and calmness, the shocks
he met with had dashed him to pieces." And
what was still more fatal to the great affairs in
which Hamilton was to be so eminently engaged, was the melancholy cast in his character. This was frequently observable even in
his countenance. It induced him to think that
he was destined to be unfortunate in all his
enterprises. At times he believed that he was
acting under the blasting influence of some in-
auspicious star, which was thwarting all his
attempts. This sad feeling appears by his frequent requests and determination to retire from
public affairs. This singular state might have
been the result of the extraordinary exigencies in which this politic Marquis was so often
placed. There was a painful and secret conflict in his mind, when sometimes pursuing a
conduct quite opposite to his principles, he
wavered between his allegiance to his Royal
friend—his attachment to his country and his
countrymen—and his regard to self-preservation. Hamilton had therefore to manage with
perpetual anxiety the oppositionists he found
in both countries; but his views of the future
were of so melancholy a cast, that when he
advised Strafford and Laud to retire, he also

seems to have anticipated both their fall, and
his own.

In the rising troubles of Scotland the un-
ceasing torment in the heart of Hamilton was
to decide whether, to employ his own language,
" the madness of the people was to be indulged," or " the Kingly way was to be enforced ?"
He had the melancholy sagacity to foresee from
the first the future scenes which were preparing. It was the sad and solemn second sight
of his countrymen, contemplating on the phantoms of his despair amid the clouds and storms.

When the King communicated his determination to invest the Marquis with the character of the High Commissioner for Scotland,
it was unfeignedly protested against by the
Marquis, who declared it to be an employment
full of danger, and the success always doubtful.
Afterwards when it became necessary to renew
a second time the Commission, the same repugnance was even more forcibly testified. He
dwelt on the hatred which the chief Covenanters bore him — on the rage and malice of
the common people against him, so that his
life was in hourly peril, which indeed he valued
not for his Majesty's service, but that his violent death, knowing his Majesty's keen sense

of such an act, would hinder the business from ending quietly. " The work, too, is of a nature," he added, " which must certainly make me lose your Royal favour, for it is so odious, that the actor of it must be disliked by your Majesty, for though I should do all things by your Royal command, yet your Royal honour would oblige your Majesty not to seem to care for me. I am now perfectly hated by all your subjects who have withstood your Majesty, I shall hereafter be by all who wish prosperity to your affairs in both Kingdoms."

After this ænigmatical style, the Marquis suggested a very extraordinary mode for his own self-preservation. " Where, or how, I may be called to an account for this undertaking I know not, it is a business of that nature that a pardon ought humbly to be begged before it be meddled in, since it is an act so derogatory to kingly authority.

" Is it fit for an honest man and a gentleman to be made the instrument of doing that which he hath so often in public and private condemned in so high a degree, and withstood to the certain loss of most of my country, and many of your Majesty's court and Kingdom of England? Nor can I ever hope to live without perpetual accusations of such who will find

themselves grieved by that which will be done,
for not dissuading your Majesty from this
course, or at least for accepting that employment and proving your instrument therein."

These were the confused and hesitating emotions, the melancholy prescience, and the uncertain results, which perplexed the mind and
tormented the heart of the Marquis of Hamilton, on his acceptance of the critical office
of the High Commissioner for Scotland. It
was distressful to his feelings — disastrous to
his quiet. But amidst these conflicting sentiments, we discover that extraordinary caution
for self-preservation which constitutes the
marking feature of his character. Hamilton
had much fear, through all the doublings of
his winding ways, that he should be forced into
many an equivocal position, and while his ambiguous character should raise suspicions in all
men, " he could not hope to live without perpetual accusations." The Marquis suggests a
mode of self-preservation as extraordinary as
the exigence itself—that a pardon as he calls
it, or rather a private warrant from the King
should be granted to him before he opens his
dark negotiations. This was the Royal Amu-
let to preserve him from the noxious influence
of his own witchcraft.

And this singular warrant, extorted from the entire confidence and personal affection of Charles, was actually granted. Burnet, in his Memoirs of the Hamiltons, alludes to it; he found it among the Hamilton papers, but as he probably did not consider it as very honourable to his hero, he dropped it, among other important suppressions which that partial, though entertaining, biographer acknowledged, at an after-day, when from a servile Tory, Burnet turned into a furious Whig. This private warrant has, however, been recovered by the zealous industry of Lord Hardwicke: it is granted to the Marquis " to converse with the Covenanters," and runs thus, " for which end you will be necessitated to speak that language which if you were called to an account for by us, you might suffer for it. These are, therefore, to assure you, and if need be hereafter to testify to others, that whatsoever you shall say to them, to discover their intentions, you shall neither be called in question for the same, nor yet it prove any way prejudicial to you; nay, though you should be accused by any thereupon."

We must now notice a very curious anecdote of a private interview of Charles the First with the Marquis of Hamilton, told by Cla-

rendon with all the charm and warmth of his
narrative genius. It is no gracious task to tell
a story after Clarendon, but I will not content
myself with a cold reference.

His Lordship describes the Marquis's conduct
on this occasion. " It was as great a piece of
art, if it were art, as I believe will be found
amongst the modern politicians." " The Marquis came to the King, and with some cloudiness, which was not unnatural, and trouble in
his countenance,* desired his Majesty to give
him leave to travel." The King was surprised
and troubled. The Marquis declared he fore-

---

* It is delightful to compare contemporary writers who
could have no knowledge of each other's writings, which
only posterity can possess — at distant intervals, and when
their authors are no more. Confronting these writers together, who never before had met, often furnishes an indis-
putable confirmation of that truth in history, which it has
been too much the fashion to depreciate. The cloudiness
in the countenance of Hamilton, so expressive of his character, is also noticed by one who well knew him — Sir
Philip Warwick. " I wondered much" — when Hamilton
was a young man and an early favourite at Court under
James — " that all present who usually at a Court put the
best characters upon a rising man, generally agreed in this,
that the air of his countenance had such a cloud on it, that
Nature seems to have impressed aliquid insigne, which I
often reflected on when his future actions led him first to be
suspected, then to be declaimed against." p. 103.

saw a storm — and by his own unskilfulness he
might be more obnoxious than other men.
The King assured him of his protection, and
bade him be confident. The Marquis with some
quickness replied, " I know your Majesty's
goodness would interpose for me to your own
prejudice — and I will rather run any fortune
from whence I may again return to serve you."
He had communicated with the Archbishop
and with the Earl of Strafford, at whom the
same fatal arrows were aimed, but he added,
" the Earl was too great-hearted to fear, and
the Archbishop was too bold to fly."

Charles at that critical moment, was disturbed by his own fears — and was silent. The
Marquis resumed. " There is one way by
which I might secure myself without leaving
the kingdom, and by which your Majesty, as
these times are like to go, might receive some
advantage; but it is so contrary to my nature,
and will be so scandalous to my honour, in the
opinion of men, that for my own part I had
rather run any fortune." The King impatient-
ly asked what that way was? The Marquis
replied, " that he might endear himself to the
other party by promising his service to them,
and concurring with them in opinions and designs — that his supposed interest in his Majes-

ty's favour, might induce the principal persons
to hope he might have the influence they desired. But he knew this would be looked on
with so much jealousy by other men, and
shortly with that reproach, that he might by
degrees be lessened even in his Majesty's own
trust; and therefore it was a province he had
no mind to undertake," and concluded by renewing his suit for leave to travel.

The King saw nothing in this political expedient, but what might tend to procure him
important information. With boundless confidence in the integrity of the friend, and the
companion of his youth, Charles was delighted
to retain Hamilton in his active service, and
again assured the Marquis that " it should not
be in any body's power to infuse the least jealousy of him into his royal breast."

Clarendon commenting on this secret anecdote, observes that Charles was so constant in
this resolution, that Hamilton enjoyed the
liberty of doing whatever he found necessary
for his own purposes; with wonderful craft and
low condescensions and seasonable insinuations
to several leading men, advancing their distinct
and contrary interests; so that he grew in no
less credit with the English Parliament than
with the Scotch Commissioners, and with great

dexterity was preserved from any public reproach which would have ruined any other man,
nor for a long time did he incur the jealousy
of the King, to whom he continued to give the
most important information, which, adds Clarendon, if there had been persons enough who
would have concurred in prevention might
have proved of great use.   This confession of
Clarendon, whose prejudices strongly lie against
Hamilton, we shall find essential, as we advance in the investigation of this extraordinary
character.

The piece of secret history which we have
from Clarendon requires a critical examination.
The drift of the conversation as given by the
noble writer, accords with the ideas of Hamilton as we find in the Hamilton papers published by Burnet; and that extraordinary
scheme of communicating with the Covenanters is authentic.   Yet to invest this remarkable
conversation with authenticity is not easy.
Lord Clarendon prefaces the conversation by
assuring us that he received it " from a very
good hand."   Was it from the King himself?
We know it was not from the Marquis, for
at no time would he plead this justification,
even at the urgent moment of his trial, so tender in this Machiavelian intrigue was he of the

credit both of the King and himself. A scep-
tic might reasonably object to the full details
of a conversation between two great personages
at which no one was present. He might admire the description even of their gestures.

Clarendon, though indistinctly, has fixed the
time of its occurrence. It was " after the calling of the Council of the Peers at York was
resolved upon, and a little before the time of
their appearance." Now the Peers, after a
summons of twenty days' notice, met on the
24th of September, 1640; so that the conversation as given by Clarendon must have taken
place in July or August of that year.

We can ascertain that on the 5th and 8th
of July, 1639, Hamilton delivered to the King
his two papers of Advices and of Reasons which
we have noticed ;* and that Hamilton, having
succeeded in obtaining a licence to protect him
in the subdolous part he was about to act, this
extraordinary private warrant is dated at Berwick nine days after, the 17th July, 1639.

The conversation reported by Clarendon as
having occurred in 1640 could never have taken
place, since its object had already been long obtained. Hamilton at that period is represented

* Burnet's Memoirs of the Hamiltons, p. 144 — who furnishes the respective dates of these papers.

as breaking his scheme for the first time to the King, and as suggesting with a mixture of diffidence and aversion that ample and singular licence which he already possessed.

Here then is a conversation which could not have taken place at the time assigned, and yet one that on the whole exhibits a true account of a strange and secret incident between the parties. The whole tenour of the conversation indeed accords with the sentiments of Hamilton as they appear in the papers of advice he laid before the King, and the important political secret of his double-dealing, as given by Clarendon, is indisputably ascertained.

How are we to resolve this paradoxical case? Were the papers of Hamilton, among other papers of the King, inspected by, or reported to Clarendon? It is evident he knew nothing of the warrant, for he would not have passed over in silence this political curiosity. The great historian was right in his conclusions of the unlimited confidence of the King, and the exemption of his Minister from all responsibility in his ambiguous course.

The delicacy of Lord Clarendon's situation may have been this: he could not publish these arcana of state, as he would any public document; but in the dramatic form of a con-

versation, which could never have occurred at
the period assigned, he followed up the train
of ideas which we actually discover in Hamilton's papers ; and to impress on the reader the
authenticity of the secret history, his Lordship
assures him that he received it " from a good
hand." But with all the felicity of his ingenuity Clarendon could not conceal the impossibility of giving a secret conversation between the King and the Marquis. Whose was
"the good hand" which could furnish those
fine individualising touches of the two great
personages, in secrecy and privacy ? Who
heard his Lordship's wish to be permitted to
travel ? Who marked "the cloudiness on his
Lordship's countenance ?" Who observed when
" the Marquis with some quickness replied "—
or when " the King was much disturbed," or
when " much delighted with the expedient ?"
These are the creative, yet veracious, touches of
a great genius, who from his familiarity with
the temper, the habits, the language of the
personages themselves, could speak their very
thoughts, and paint their very gestures — and
thus endow the men he well knew, with the
immortality of his own genius ; Lord Clarendon was the Shakespeare of history.

And thus I think we may infer that should

the conversation of Clarendon prove to be in some respects an invention, it cannot be denied that it revealed to the world an important truth.

Hamilton once possessed of this secret warrant, proceeded to act with extraordinary zeal; and when it happened, as it frequently did, that his conduct and his language afforded sufficient reason to alarm the friends of the King, and to set on watchful informers who were thus enabled to convey certain evidence of the prejudice to the King's service done by Hamilton, to the amazement and incomprehensibility of the best friends of Charles, whenever Hamilton was admitted to the King's presence, all the charges against him, however positive, were thrown aside in silence. A private interview — a whisper in the King's ear, — the plea of the secret warrant — reinstated the Marquis in the Royal confidence, which we shall show, if he were sometimes startled, he never lost. We should not therefore be surprised at the strong conviction of many, who have denounced Hamilton as a traitor, since even his perpetual eulogist Burnet does acknowledge that, " he (Burnet) often stumbled," as he phrases it, " at some of his speeches, which were hard to be understood," but when he discovered the secret warrant, "it reconciled the truth of these (unfavourable) reports with the innocence of the Marquis." *

There seems to be no reason to suspect the sincerity of Hamilton on his first entrance into the office of High Commissioner in the Scottish affairs. He warned the King of the real intentions of the Covenanters. "It is more than probable that these people have somewhat else in their thoughts than religion. But that must serve for a cloak to rebellion, wherein for a time they may prevail; but to bring them again to a dutiful obedience, I am confident your Majesty will not find it a work of long time, nor of great difficulty, as they have foolishly fancied to themselves." He put the King on his guard that his agents abroad might prevent any arms being bought up by Scotchmen. He counselled Charles to hasten with his fleet and his army, or he must yield to all the demands of the Covenanters; but he leaves the King to decide how far in his justice he should punish the folly of the people, or how far he should connive at their madness. Hamilton ever viewed the two opposite sides of a question, dubious of both.

Something of vacillation appears in the Mar-

* Burnet's Memoirs of the Hamiltons, 148.

quis's closing hint. Hamilton on his entrance into Edinburgh was certainly awed by having been met by the greatest number of the people which had assembled together for many years; sixty thousand persons in the small city of Edinburgh formed an army, unarmed. This concourse was headed by five hundred Ministers. When the Royal Commissioner attempted to elude their oratory in public, they pursued their victim of State to his privacy; there with tears in their eyes, they came to inform him of the danger in which their religion stood.

When the King first received the encouraging news that the reduction of the Covenanters would not be a work of difficulty, he wrote to Hamilton a letter of which I shall transcribe the important passages—they conduce greatly to let us into the character of this active, however unfortunate Sovereign.

" HAMILTON :

" Though I answered not yours of the fourth, yet I assure you that I have not been idle, so that I hope by the next week, I shall send you some good assurance of the advancing of our preparations. This I say· not to make

you precipitate any thing, for I like of all you
have hitherto done, and even of that which I
find you mind to do—but to show you that I
mean to stick to my grounds, and that I expect
not any thing can reduce that people to their
obedience, but only force. In the mean-time
your care must be how to dissolve the multitude, and to this end I give you leave to flatter
them with what hopes you please, so you engage not me against my grounds, consenting to
the calling of Parliament, until the Covenant
be disavowed and given up.

" Your chief end being now to win time that
they may not commit public follies until I be
ready to suppress them; and since it is, as you
well observe, my own people, which by this
means will be for a time ruined, so that the
loss must be inevitably mine, and this if I
could eschew, were it not with a greater, were
well. But when I consider, that not only now
my crown, but my reputation for ever, lies at
stake, I must rather suffer the first, that time
will help, than this last, which is irreparable.

" This I have written to no other end than
to show you I will rather die than yield to
those impertinent and damnable demands, as
you rightly call them, for it is all one as to

yield to be no King in a very short time. So wishing you better success than I can expect, I rest

" Your assured constant friend,

" CHARLES R."

The first instructions of Hamilton were to proclaim the Covenanters traitors — he ventured to transgress his instructions, as he then observed, at the hazard of his head. At that moment the Marquis had not yet obtained the private warrant of the King, which was subsequently granted. His sole care now was to disperse this enormous multitude; to soothe and to wheedle, not to menace and condemn. Now he writes to the King not to hasten his warlike preparations.

Charles on these opposite counsels was entirely compliant : with unabated confidence in his Minister the King replies with great sense and patience.

" HAMILTON :

" The dealing with multitudes makes diversity of advertisement no way strange, and certainly the alteration from worse to less ill, cannot be displeasing; wherefore you may be confident I cannot but approve your proceedings hitherto, for certainly you have gained a very considerable point, in making the heavy multi-tude begin to disperse, without having engaged me in any unfitting thing. I shall take your advice in staying the public preparations for force; but in a silent way (by your leave) I will not leave to prepare, that I may be ready upon the least advertisement.

" Your assured constant friend,

" CHARLES R."

Now Hamilton discovers that the Covenant is not illegal, and the bond of mutual defence which they had subscribed, and which Charles insisted should be given up to him, would admit of explanations. The King's Advocate in Scotland, Sir Thomas Hope, was himself a warm Covenanter, who appears to have silently directed their movements. The Marquis now alarms the King with the state of his affairs, both in England and in Scotland, where a close alliance was formed between the two parties, both equally adverse to him. On the first rupture the Covenanters would march into England, confident as they were of having many good friends there: nor had France ever forgotten the Isle of Rhé, for her secret hand was cherishing the malcontents of Scotland. In

spite of these critical difficulties, Hamilton
craves his Majesty's pleasure, to whose service
he would willingly sacrifice his life.

At this conflicting state of affairs Charles
expresses no wonder, no alarm ; he only regrets
the spirit of the dispatch, while he informs
Hamilton of the strength of his army, the
goodness of his artillery, the arms which he
had procured from Holland, his fleet ready.
The King adds, " and last of all, which is indeed
most of all, the Chancellor of the Exchequer
assures me of £200,000. for this expedition.
Thus you may see that I intend not to yield
to the demands of those traitors the Covenanters."

The Marquis continues disheartening the
King—many of the Council in Scotland were
secret Covenanters—and certainly he did not
communicate any false intelligence when he
feared that his Majesty would be faintly followed by the English.   Charles wrote—

" HAMILTON :

" I must needs thank you that you stand so
close and constantly to my grounds, and you
deserve the more since your fellow Counsellors
do rather dishearten than help you in this business, for which I swear I pity you much.   As

long as this damnable Covenant* is in force,
whether it be with, or without explanation, I
have no more power in Scotland than as a
Duke of Venice, which I will rather die than
suffer. If they call a Parliament without me,
it would the more loudly declare them traitors
and the more justify my actions. My resolution is to come myself in person, accompanied
like myself; sea-forces, nor Ireland shall not be
forgotten."

The Marquis now attempted to menace the
Covenanters, who not being yet ready for an
open rupture, affected to talk only of " their
innocent intentions." The Marquis now asks
leave to return to Court that he may personally
explain the emergent difficulties to the King.
There were at least three of these " speedy

---

* This term " damnable Covenant" doubtless appeared to
Rushworth, who copied part of the King's letter from Burnet, excessively offensive, and strongly indicative of the
tyrannical character of Charles; for Rushworth has distinguished the words in the printing. The expression, however,
had been first used by Hamilton, as we learn from Charles
himself, who, however, would not have hesitated to have
employed the term had it occurred to him. Doubtless, however, this style inflamed the prejudices against the King with
the many, who looked on this " Covenant" as sacred as the
one in holy writ.

journeys." At every return of the Marquis
from Court, he found affairs more embroiled,
and the " Tables," or Committees of the four
classes of the nation, more frequently summoned. Whenever the Marquis, published a Royal
declaration at the Market-cross, right opposite,
on the same day, was suspended their Protest.

The King is more perplexed—in one letter
Charles tells the Marquis, " I confess this last
dispatch does more put one to seek how to
judge of the affairs of that Kingdom than any
that I have yet received." In another, Charles
sensibly observes, " Why I should go further I
see no reason ; for certainly those who will not
be contented with what I have done already
will be less contented if I should do more."
The style of Charles is evidently changed ; the
regal tone is lowered, and as was usual with
him, those lofty pretensions of Royalty which
resulted from the theoretical politics of ancient
days are laid asleep. Even that more than
tender point — Episcopacy, is surrendered !
Charles yields all ! " The Buke," as the Liturgy was called, and the Church discipline of
the five articles of Perth. The King only
changes an ambiguous expression in the paper
which Hamilton was to offer the Assembly at

Glasgow, by which instrument the humiliated Monarch had given way to all their demands.

The Assembly at Glasgow met, their Presbyters with their Lay-elders, and as Hamilton describes it, " not a gown among them, but many had swords and daggers." In this curious dispatch the Marquis delineates the Scottish Counsellors,—personalities which Burnet could not venture to publish;* but it was a gallery of portraits and full-lengths of contemporaries, which struck Charles with great admiration of the skill of the artist.

Our baffled statesman desponds—" So unfortunate have I been in this unlucky country, that though I did prefer your service before all worldly considerations, *nay even strained my conscience in some points*, yet all hath been to small purpose; for I have missed my end in not being able to make your Majesty so considerable a party as will be able to curb the insolency of this rebellious nation, without assistance from England, and greater charge to your Majesty than this miserable country is worth. As I shall answer to God at the last day, I have done my best, though the success has proven so bad as I think myself of all men

* It is in Lord Hardwicke's State-papers, ii. 113.

living most miserable. And seeing this may perhaps be the last letter that ever I shall have the happiness to write to your Majesty, I shall, therefore, in it discharge my duty so far, as freely to express my thoughts in such things as I do conceive concerneth your service. I have sent this by a faithful servant of your Majesty's, whom I have found to be so trusty, as he may be employed by you, even to go against his nearest friends and dearest kindred."

If this "faithful servant" were a Scotchman, he did not find his like among the closest intimates of Charles. The warmth of the style, we must infer, denotes the earnestness of Hamilton. " If I keep my life (though next hell I hate this place) if you think me worthy of any employment I shall not weary till the Government be again set right, and then I will forswear this country." And he closes this most desponding dispatch by a solemn request to the King —

" I have only this one suit to your Majesty, that if my sons live, they may be bred in England — I wish my daughters be never married in Scotland — I humbly recommend my brother to your favour. May all your intentions be crowned with a wished success, which I

hope to live to see, notwithstanding of all the
threats that is used to

" Your Majesty's, &c.

" HAMILTON."

The King must have been affected by the
pathos ; perhaps never before had a disappointed minister composed a cabinet dispatch so
much in the style of a last will and testament.

But while the Marquis desponds from his
own personal disappointments, he plans the
future operations of the King ; advises what
places should be secured, where the fleet was
to lie in the Frith, where the Royal army was
to enter Scotland. He has not omitted noticing that the ambition of the Bishops had
been great, and their folly greater. It is evident that Hamilton, though ministerially he
protected the Bishops, and even supported
them in their personal distresses, was no better
friend to the Episcopalians than other Scotchmen.

Charles was struck by the important communication of this elaborate dispatch, and returned an answer by the same trusty messenger.

" HAMILTON:

" I have sent back this honest bearer both

for safety of my letters, and to ease me from length of writing; therefore in a word I thank you for your full and clear dispatch, totally agreeing with you in every point, as well in the characters of men, as in the way you have set down to reduce them to obedience; only the time when to begin to act is considerable: to this end I have fully instructed the bearer with the state of my preparations, that you may govern my business accordingly. You have given me such good satisfaction, that I mean not to put any other in the chief trust in these affairs but yourself."

It was now the close of the year 1638. The King now allowed of the Convention, or Assembly, as it was called, of Glasgow, but it was carried on in such a disorderly way that the Marquis resolved to dissolve it. The Bishops had been insolently cited to appear; their lay-elders and their ruling-elders were in fact a cover for these democratic conventions, exacting unlimited freedom. Hamilton, in dissolving the Assembly of Glasgow, betrayed such visible marks of grief as affected its members. The Assembly, though declared traitorous, if they continued their sittings, would not disperse, but proceeded with increased rapidity and violence. Having deposed the Bishops and excommunicated eight, the Assembly closed by addressing a letter to the King, justifying their proceedings, and complaining of the usage they had endured from the Royal Commissioner. The Marquis flew back to Court, leaving the country in confusion and revolt.

Charles, incensed at his affronted authority, resolved, though reluctantly, for he could hardly depend on an army which had more of the parade than the force of one, to reduce the Covenanters to obedience. The saddened spirit of Hamilton we may conceive to have been in torture; for now his duty to his Sovereign and his friend was to compete with his love for his country—his affections for his relatives —and his intercourse with his most intimate connections. One of the charges afterwards raised against Hamilton, is, that many of his friends and followers passed over to the Covenanters.

We may infer, in justice to Hamilton, that having evidently reluctantly accepted the office of High Commissioner, he had flattered himself that he should have restored tranquillity to his unhappy country, without coming to the last extremities. In his heart he was Scottish, and could have little sympathised with the fatal predilection of Charles for Episcopacy in an unepiscopal land; and to this perhaps he alludes when he declared that " his duty or his love of the King, had made him digest some things which otherwise he had not borne so well. On the other hand he perceived the re-bellious spirits of some of his countrymen, kindling through the people whom they had lured on and inflamed by the cry of religion. Hamilton might have rejoiced to chastise the insolence of some of the leaders of the Cove-nanters, but when he turned to them, could he strike at his dearest connections, the followers who were to fortify his influence, the fellow-citizens who looked up for their protector in a Hamilton? Doubtless the patriot confessed the real sentiment of his heart, when he owned that " the thing in the world at which he had the greatest horror, was the engaging in a civil war with his countrymen."

There was still at that day an irascible na-tional jealousy; the Scottish man at times seemed to imagine that Scotia had sunk into a province of Britain; and there had been art-ful rumours, and even accusations, that Hamil-ton aimed at the sovereignty and independence of his father-land. This ambition, however, no action of his life had betrayed, and those who had so confidently rested their surmises on the little army Hamilton had led to Germany, and on the intention of the Marquis, as they conceived by his mysterious conduct, to plunge the nation into universal confusion that he might fish in such troubled waters, these persons knew not what is now known, that the army of Hamilton had been raised by the secret command of Charles, for the possible recovery of the Palatinate.

Hamilton, however the affection for his native land might prevail, could still conscientiously have acted against Scotland; for when accused as " an incendiary " he distinguished between the conquest of a kingdom and the suppression of a rebellion. He declared that " he had never advised his Majesty to conquer that kingdom, for he takes the suppressing of a party in arms against the King, or who were rejecting his authority, to be very different from conquering the kingdom." *

The Marquis was now to command an army and a fleet against his countrymen. When he received orders to open hostilities, he again urged that the issue of a battle, always dubi-

* Burnet's Memoirs of the Hamiltons, 255.

ous, was much more so when the one side was desperate and the other but half cordial.* The event justified the prediction.

The Marquis, General by land and sea, and always in his military capacity remarkably inefficient, anchored his fleet in the Frith. He had promised by frequent incursions to harass the coasts, and by perpetual alarms to create diversions and scatter their collected forces. The only exploit he performed was possessing himself of an island which had been left unprotected, and landing five thousand soldiers to air and exercise themselves, from the close confinement of the ships. The Marquis himself appears to have been more actively employed than his army. The lady his mother,† a zealous Presbyterian and a flaming Covenanter, and whose two daughters were the wives of Covenanters, came down to visit her dutiful son, and her hurtless enemy ; the Scots on shore laughed, observing that "they knew the son of so gude a mither could ne'er harm them."

* Burnet's Memoirs of the Hamiltons, 132 and 139. Confront the opinion of the Marquis with Clarendon, i. 214. They are similar. Burnet's work was published many years preceding Clarendon's.

† Lady Anne Cunningham, daughter to the Earl of Glencairn.

Hamilton never attempted to interrupt the fortifications of Leith, where all hands were at work, and even all ranks.   It appears that Hamilton was in communication with several of the chiefs of the Covenant: one interview is attested in the presence of witnesses; but others were under more suspicious circumstances: we are told of a conference at night with Lord Loudon on the birks of Barnbougal.

Yet the Marquis could defend his own conduct in having never betrayed the King's service, avowing that such secret conferences were designed for the best purposes; and it has farther been alleged in his favour, that his troops were raw and undisciplined, incompetent to act against Leith.

It is certain, however, that the total inactivity of the Marquis in his military operations, and the rumours of his apparent confederacy, had raised strong suspicions among the King's party; Charles himself had none; and the Royal correspondence continued almost daily with Hamilton.

Again the King's resolution was to be shaken by the account the Marquis gave of the numerous force of the Scots, and a treaty was suggested in preference to a battle.   Thus affairs languished, till Charles acknowledged the mortifying truth of which the Marquis had formerly apprised him. We gather this from a letter of Secretary Vane.

" His Majesty now doth clearly see and is fully satisfied in his own judgment that what passed in the gallery bewixt his Majesty and your Lordship and myself, hath been but too much verified on this occasion. And therefore his Majesty would not have you begin with them, but settle things in a safe and good posture." Such doubts on the Royal side of its own strength, and such resolution on that of the Insurgents, terminated in the hasty pacification of Berwick.

After that event, when the Earl of Loudon, then at London as a deputy of the Scottish Covenanters, was committed to the Tower, for having subscribed a letter to the French King, soliciting his aid against England, the dextrous management of Hamilton on that occasion is remarkably displayed. The alarming situation of Loudon, imprisoned on no doubtful act of treason, embarrassed his Scottish friends, who, it is certain, dreaded the result. The King had designed to bring Loudon to his trial, but a rumour seems to have spread among the Scots, that Charles had given orders for beheading

him without a trial ; that story, such as it is,
we shall shortly more critically examine. Hamilton had frequent interviews with Loudon
in the Tower ; he obtained his enlargement in
that spacious state-prison, and found no difficulty in convincing the King that Loudon was
not formed of that hard Scotch temper which
no art could render malleable, he would spread
out and soften at the stroke of court-favour.
The man, whom some have told us the King
had commanded to lose his head, was now seen
at the King's levee —and

     " Kiss'd the hand just raised to shed his blood."

Loudon, in fact, was gained over by the King
and made Chancellor ; and we are told that
Hamilton in a private conference at Whitehall was locked up with Loudon from two in
the morning till four in the afternoon.* Such
was the influence and the mysterious conduct
of the Marquis of Hamilton : the present was a

---

* Nalson's Collection, i. 376. Nalson, in preserving the
information delivered to the Secretary of State by a physi-
cian " who suspected the Marquis to be an arch traitor,"
leaves the reader to exercise his own judgment. Nalson did
not know, what we know. The information given to the
Secretary is without doubt genuine and correct.

great *coup . d'état ;* the crafty politician not
only appeared to have abstracted a friend for
the King from his enemies, but he had secured
his own reputation with the Covenanters, by
saving the Earl of Loudon, whose head they
well knew was in jeopardy.

It is evident that Hamilton remarkably studied the interests of the opposing parties, but
in being serviceable to both, whatever good
was effected by him, was always neutralized.
If ever there were a politician who had sagacity to dive into the secrets of the man with
whom he came in contact, we surely may fix
on Bishop Williams. When this Statesman
had resolved to be serviceable to Charles the
First at that critical moment when the Scottish intrigues and the Scottish army were
equally advancing in England, Williams, who
had always declined the acquaintance of the
Marquis, now sought his intimacy. This
shrewd observer of human nature acknowledged that he was at a loss to decide whether Hamilton were a good or an evil genius. "I have
found him to be very opposite to the vulgar
opinion formed of him, which considers him
cunning and false; I believe him not to be
false to the King, nor do I find any great cunning in him, but rather that he wants a head-

piece."* It is possible that the mystery which involves the character of Hamilton may have originated in the single circumstance that he had designed great matters, without the capacity of conducting them.

Knowing, as we now do, that Hamilton carried about him the secret warrant which held him irresponsible for his double-dealings, it is hard for us to decide at once on his guilt or his innocence, on his sincerity or his duplicity. Was he with the King, or with the Covenanter? The Searcher of all human hearts alone can detect the silent motives of man. The intelligence Hamilton gave the King was always true; his warnings were predictions, and his counsels, as Lord Clarendon himself acknowledges, were always useful.

But he is accused at the same time of having revealed the King's plans; of having told the Covenanting Lords that he had no commission to fight, which intimation rendered them more hardy; and it is even said, that he advised the Covenanters not to trust the King. At York, such was his dextrous conduct with the Scotch Commissioners in his promises of future service, that he secured his own indemnity with them; and on a later occasion he equally secured

* Hacket's Life of Williams, pt. ii. 143.

the favour of the English Parliamentarians, from the recommendation of their allies the Scotch, who declared that Hamilton had always been true to them. Once, after an elaborate address from his chair as High Commissioner, when he had earnestly impressed on his auditors the severity of his duty in delivering the Royal commands, he descended from that chair of State, and familiarly mingling with some of the noble leaders of the Covenant, he took them into another apartment; there he observed, " Before the Lords of the Council I spoke to you as the King's Commissioner, but now I am come among you like a kindly Scotchman :" And it is added that he advised them to persevere, by which they would carry every thing before them, but if they fainted, or gave way, they were undone.*

It was therefore not only with many suspicious actions, but with many loose speeches

---

* This remarkable conversation is given by Bishop Guthry, who at the same time furnishes his authorities. The same story had reached Montrose in the same words. It must have staggered those who considered the Marquis of Hamilton as the King's Commissioner. The language is so strong, that one may doubt its correctness — it was instigating the Insurrectionary spirit, and can hardly be excused on the plea that Hamilton was covertly attempting to wind himself into their secrets.

caught up by listeners—and with private conferences with the leaders of the Scottish and
of the Parliamentary parties, observed by watchful eyes, that Hamilton was repeatedly charged
by the Court-party. The unfavourable result
of all his negotiations seemed to confirm the
whole tenor of his conduct in the minds of
those who did not hesitate to condemn Hamilton as an arch-traitor. The Royal confidence
was hardly ever shaken—yet once, it seems to
have been startled—for even Charles could not
avoid remarking that " Hamilton had been very
active in his own preservation."

The Earl of Lanerick, the brother of Hamilton, the King had commended for the frank-
ness of his speech, and the openness of his
nature, and even Clarendon distinguishes him
both for his ability and his honour; yet by
others the Earl is considered to have adopted
the same line of conduct as the Marquis.
Lanerick was selected to supply the place of
his " unfortunate brother;" and matters were
now reduced to this point, that one brother
was to be answerable for the other! We learn
this from a communication of the Earl to some
confidential friend to whom he sent a dark
account of that mysterious affair which in the
Scottish history took the name of " The Inci-

dent,"—an extraordinary story, of an "Incident" which never occurred, and which shall form the subject of the following chapter.

The mysterious conduct of the brothers still continued. Two years after the affair of "The Incident," when in 1643 the Scots had resolved to raise an army to maintain their "cause," the Marquis sate among them, and seemed only a looker-on; while his brother Lanerick, who had the custody of the King's signet, put it to a proclamation to raise this very Scottish army. This extraordinary act done, the ambiguous brothers hastened to Charles, at Oxford, to justify their proceedings, and to explain that inevitable crisis which affairs had taken. They had however been anticipated by the zealous friends of the Monarch, and the ever-watchful and vindictive Montrose had again denounced the Hamiltons for their infidelity. Yet even in the present alarming event, Charles seems to have seen no treachery, but only misfortune in the brothers. Had they been criminal, would they have returned to Court—they who could have framed apologies for their absence? The charges against Hamilton were however of so high a nature, and took so wide a view of all his proceedings, and were so positively asserted by the Marquis

of Montrose, that to satisfy the friends about
him, the King was compelled to put both brothers under arrest. The Marquis had of late
been created Duke of Hamilton, and he who
had so long deprived Charles of the zealous
services of Montrose, and whose rankling jealousies of that aspiring genius had induced him
to pursue the meanest artifices to accomplish
Montrose's ruin, now drank himself from the
poisoned chalice, returned to his own lips.

The imprisonment of the Hamiltons was
however not commanded without reluctance.
The Duke received the assurances of his Majesty's favour, from the first moment of his
confinement by Secretary Nicholas, and William Murray, of the bed-chamber, the confidential agent of the King, brought repeated
messages of the King's unchangeable amity.
The charges never came to a trial; but the imprisonment of the Duke lasted two years. His
brother Lanerick escaped from his confinement
to London, and finally returned to Scotland.
When some advised the King to hang Lord
Lanerick's page at the window of the apartment, for aiding his master's flight, Charles
declared that "no servant should suffer for his
fidelity to his master."

Lanerick, pursuing the same principle of

conduct, whatever was that principle, appeared'
in Scotland loyal to the King in raising a party
against the proud and fierce Argyle, and at
the same time friendly to the Covenanters; for
even his eulogist Burnet acknowledges that he
was forced to comply in many things with the
public counsels.

The few at Court who pretended a semblance
of friendship for the Duke of Hamilton suggested to him that to clear himself from the
heavy imputations attached to his name, it
would be necessary to concur vigorously in his
Majesty's service in Scotland; but Hamilton
declared that till he was legally exonerated by
a public trial, it was not fitting for him to act;
nor had he any longer any hopes to recover
Scotland, where his presence had so often failed.
When he was lying under the imputation of
having betrayed the King's service, he was at
the same time receiving letters from Scotland
upbraiding him for his services to the King,
and in the style of the Covenant, assuring him
that " had he been as faithful in serving the
King of Kings, he would have been rewarded,
but that now he was well served for prefer-
ring the one to the other." Such is the catastrophe of a worn-out politician,— or as Frede-
rick the Great once sarcastically likened such to

" squeezed oranges," which having used are thrown away.

The Duke of Hamilton at length was relieved from his imprisonment in the castle of St. Michael's Mount, in Cornwall, when it surren-dered to the Parliamentary forces. This mysterious man had long kept up an interest with some of the leaders of the Parliament. At the time of Strafford's trial and Laud's fall, when a dark cloud was hanging over his head, he found a shelter in the favour of the Scottish Covenanters, for many personal obligations he had conferred on some of that party. At that critical moment he pressed the Scots to intercede for him with their English allies, which they not only did, but bound themselves for his future good behaviour to the English Parliament. We are told from good authority, that Hamilton became a confident in all their private designs against one another, and at times obtained many concessions from the King.

The last great act of his life closes this involved scene of human passions, and it will leave the enigma of his life unsolved. Hapless and hopeless, as his fortune had been, at the sight of the imminent danger of the imprisoned Monarch, Hamilton seemed to rouse within him a mightier spirit. He raised a Scottish army to restore his unfortunate Sovereign. But even in this last expedition to England, at the head of a considerable army, his melancholy weighed down the heart that now beat with more generous emotions. The night before he marched, in taking leave of a friend, Hamilton not only expressed his sense of the danger, but the conviction of its destruction to himself. He had, however, determined to stake his life on this last cast. The conduct of this army betrayed a fatal secret, that the Duke of Hamilton was the most inefficient of Generals. He had formerly shown this in Germany, where a fine army had mouldered away under his hands—in the Frith, where in spiritless inactivity he had not risked a single military movement. And now his persecuting genius rose before him in that very army whose precipitated march had entered England, greater in number than in strength. The Duke, as if conscious of his own deficiency, had been persuaded to submit the conduct to the Earl of Calander as Lieutenant-General; yet neither were cordial to each other, and the friends of the General divided from the friends of the Lieutenant. Some veteran Irish troops disdained to serve under the Scotch commander,

who was a punctilious old soldier trained up in
the German wars. The army marched without
unison, and often in separate divisions. The
Scots did not combat so resolutely for the King
as they had fought earnestly against him. The
Kirk had not blessed Duke Hamilton's army.
Their greatest disaster was, that they had to
encounter Cromwell. Five weeks the Scots
had been suffered to advance, though perpetually harassed, till at length they were defeated.
Scorning to retreat homewards with ignominy,
a mutiny broke out, when the Earl of Calander
escaped to Holland, and the Duke of Hamilton
was carried a prisoner to Derby. Hamilton
was now so sincere, that he cared not to preserve himself, if he could not preserve his
army.

The Duke of Hamilton now had no enemy
to deceive, and no friend to confide in. He
entered his prison and he maintained his honour, which now no promises could seduce, and
no persecution could menace. In the second
evening of his imprisonment, when a stern
serjeant peremptorily commanded him to leave
the court-yard where he was sauntering, the
Duke was struck by this first mark of that
great change in the condition of him who not
a few days before had commanded so many

thousands; but he knew that his master in solitude had long borne, as a Monarch should
bear, the indignities of his ill-fortune — and
never more did Hamilton imagine that he
should view that countenance of Majesty and
of friendship. Yet this happened! At the
close of the following year the Duke was removed to Windsor Castle, where also was the
King. When Charles was leaving Windsor
to hasten to his trial or execution, Hamilton
prevailed on his keepers to be allowed to speak
to the King, as he passed by, but for a minute!
The interview was hardly suffered to last that
single minute which had been so hardly begged.
As Charles was passing, the Duke hurried to
meet him, and kneeling down, had only time
to say, with that powerful emotion which is
beyond all feigning — " My dear Master!"—
Charles embraced the old companion of his
youth — the minister whose counsels had occupied him so many years—the confident of
his secret thoughts, and now the sharer of his
adversities—shortly too to be the participator
of his fate. The King embraced Hamilton,
and had only time to reply—" I have been so
indeed to you!"

The confidence of Charles in the Duke of
Hamilton remained to the last uninterrupted,

though the enemies of Hamilton were ever in-
stilling into the King's mind the darkest suspicions, and what to a Monarch, and more particularly to Charles, was most likely to excite
his jealousy, insinuating against Hamilton the
most treasonable aspirations. When the King
was confined in the Isle of Wight, and the
governor informed him of the defeat of the
Scotch army under the Duke of Hamilton,
Charles observed that "It was the worst news
that ever came to England." The governor
thought that " his Majesty had no reason to
be of that opinion, for had Hamilton beaten
the English, he would certainly have possessed
himself of the thrones of England and Scotland." It had long been a popular notion that
such was the concealed ambition of the Duke
of Hamilton.

The King, however, was not of the opinion
of the governor; for after a short pause, his
noble confidence in Hamilton was such, that
Charles replied "You are mistaken; I could
have commanded him back with the motion
of my hand."*

* Ludlow.

CHAPTER X.

THE INCIDENT.

" THE Incident," as it was called, is a presumed event in the history of the Hamiltons
which occurred on the second visit of Charles
to Scotland, and which no one could comprehend at the time. It baffled the inquisitive
Clarendon, though the King gave him all the
benefit of his knowledge.

In the mysterious intrigues at this period,
the more we labour the darker grows our work.
These plotting and counter-plotting politicians,
like the silk-worm, cloud themselves over with
their own opaque web, till at length they
perish by their own ingenuity. Some recently
acquired information will throw a partial light
in these dark passages.

Montrose, who had long been in the secrets
of the Covenanters, and had watched the ambiguous conduct of the Hamiltons with some

of that party, and was convinced in his own mind that the brothers were both traitors—Montrose was himself engaged with the Covenanters, much against his will, in consequence of the King's first ungracious reception of him, which had been contrived by the artifice of Hamilton.

When the King was at Edinburgh in 1641, William Murray of the bed-chamber, at that moment an avowed enemy of the Marquis of Hamilton, and attached to the Earl of Montrose, became the medium of communication between Charles and his future hero. Montrose, since his personal interview with the King at the pacification of Berwick, was supposed, though unconquered in arms, to have been vanquished by words; a paper had been attached to the door of his apartment even at that time, inscribed

Invictus armis, verbis vincitur.

He was now under restraint in the castle by order of the Covenanters. Montrose assured Murray that the proofs of treason were ample, and sufficient to bring them home to the Hamiltons, who had confederated with Argyle to betray the King through the whole of the Scottish transactions. Montrose offered to maintain his proofs in Parliament; the offer was nearly

tantamount to a proof—as Clarendon in a suppressed passage informs us that by the law of
Scotland the delator who wrongfully accused
of high-treason was himself condemned to the
same punishment the convicted traitor would
have suffered. We are informed of another
fact by Clarendon. The offer of impeaching
the three noblemen to break their factions, was
accompanied by a more extraordinary one—
that of getting rid of them altogether by assassination! which, says Clarendon, Montrose
frankly undertook to do. Events of this nature the still barbarous customs of the age had
not rendered so singular and repulsive as they
appear to our more subdued manners; the
Court of France, where Montrose had some
time resided, offers several remarkable instances, even under the eyes of Louis XIII.
called " the Just."

At this moment the King seemed embarrassed and fluctuating in his own opinion of
the fidelity of the brothers; other obscure suspicions of a confederacy which we shall have
shortly to show, also developed themselves.
Forbidding with abhorrence the horrid expedient of the military adventurer, Charles, however, consented that the proofs of treason should
be laid before Parliament.

So far we have proceeded with Clarendon's account, who knowing nothing more, describes on a Sunday morning the sudden flight of the Hamiltons and Argyle—the city of Edinburgh under arms—and the reports the three Lords gave out of dreadful conspiracies against them. The Hamiltons sent letters to the King and the Parliament, " not without some reflections on his Majesty." *

This remarkable passage, which long implicated Charles in the rumour of the assassination, has been cleared up by the letters of Secretary Nicholas, to which we shall shortly refer.

Lord Lanerick has addressed to some confidential friend " A relation of the Incident." It is an episode in the history of the Hamiltons; it betrays their distracted feelings. Such was the peculiar situation of the brothers, that both had acted in a manner to become equally suspected even by their partial master.

" You should blush when you remember to have owned so much friendship for one branded with the black name of a traitor; or to have loved a person that was capable of ingratitude to a deserving master, for though I should have forgot his Majesty as a subject, I could never

* Clarendon, i. 576.

have forgot his Majesty's particular favours to me, who from nothing hath heaped both fortune and honours on me. I must beg of you the trouble of reading this paper, and shall not desire a more favourable construction of my actions than you would of his, you never saw.

" It is true *the opinion I found his Majesty had of my brother* I conceived made him in some measure *jealous of me,* which upon divers occasions I strove to clear myself, and professed to him that my affection to his service was such, *as if I believed my brother were not so dutiful to him as he ought to be, no man should more willingly contribute to bring him to his deserved punishment than myself.* His Majesty then, and upon divers occasions, was pleased to say, he believed me to be an honest man, and that he had never heard any thing to the contrary ; but that he thought my brother *had been very active in his own preservation.*

" This expression of his Majesty's made me look more strictly unto my brother's actions, to see if I could find that in any particular whereby he strove to preserve himself, he had prejudiced the King's just designs. Possibly my blood might claim such an interest in his as to procure a partial construction of his actions from me ; but truly, the nearer I looked into his thoughts, the greater affection and fidelity I found in him to his Master; and if in this judgment I have erred, it was the brain's fault, not the blood's, for all interest I laid aside.

" I must confess his Majesty found great opposition in this country, yet (as I hope for mercy, though I found myself suspected by him,) I strove to do him the best service I could; and when all differences were coming to some accommodation, and I in hopes his Majesty might have returned with satisfaction to England; all those hopes were destroyed, by this unfortunate accident which now forceth this distance betwixt his Majesty and us."

After an account of this presumed plot, Lord Lanerick declares, and the confession may be true, of the miserable days of these plotting intriguers, " *I was not so much troubled with the hazard of losing a life, wherein God knows these many years I have not taken great pleasure,* as with the great prejudice I saw this would bring to his Majesty's affairs and the peace and quiet of this poor kingdom."

His Lordship concludes in this extraordinary style: " I was informed his Majesty had let fall some expressions to my disadvantage in the Parliament House; whereupon I again sent to him, begging him to believe that I had not a heart capable of a disloyal thought to him; and that *if I believed my brother had any, he should not be troubled with thinking how to punish him, for I had both a heart and a hand able to do it.*"

Here is an offer of assassinating his own brother, should that brother prove to be a traitor! What extremes of passion agitate politicians in their crooked course! Lanerick offers to return to court at the risk of his own life in the midst of his enemies, " confident that his Majesty knows not of the base design, though the King protects those who are accused." * This alludes to Montrose and his party.

The narrative by Lord Lanerick of the presumed immolation of the three Lords at the feet of his Majesty betrays such incoherence, that the whole pretended conspiracy was long considered as having no foundation in reality, and by many was treated as a subject of ridicule. The three noblemen were to be called into the King's drawing-room on parliamentary business — two Lords were then to enter at a garden-door, followed by two or three hundred men, when, proceeds the Earl, " they should either have killed us, or carried us aboard a ship of his Majesty's which then lay in the

* Lord Hardwicke's State-papers, ii. 299.

road." After all, the assassination might have subsided into a deportation. It is quite certain that in this novel political scene, Charles would never have endured to have been even a spectator; the assassination of the three Lords could never have taken place in his presence. Charles has never yet been accused, among the calumnies heaped on his head, of this sanguinary disposition. The stretch of his arbitrary command was an imprisonment.

Charles, indignant at the suspicions of the Hamiltons, insisted on a public trial of the presumed conspirators. We learn from that faithful recorder and actor in the passing scenes, Principal Baillie, that all parties considered it as most prudent to leave this dark and involved affair to a private committee; and in England it was consigned to the Privy Council. The Scotch Committee appear to have been strangely perplexed by the contrary depositions; the truth of some things could not be denied, and the falsity and absurdity of others seem to have been as evident. It was considered prudent that the original depositions should be suppressed; some notes of them however have been preserved.* In England it

* These notes or contents of the depositions are preserved by Balfour in his Journal of Parliament; and are in Malcolm Laing's Appendix to his Hist. of Scotland, iii. 515.

was resolved that all the documents relative to
" the Incident " should remain under the Secretary's care, to be inspected by any of the Peers,
but not to be published without the King's
command.* The chief point with Charles, was
the vindication of his own honour, so cruelly
implicated by the terrified Hamiltons. That
remarkable passage in Clarendon that the Hamiltons addressed the Scottish Parliament " not
without some reflections upon his Majesty," receives a fresh light from one of Secretary Nicholas's letters to the King, which has recently
appeared in the Evelyn papers. The Secretary
writes from London to the King at Edinburgh,
" The Marquis of Hamilton's second and third
letters to your Majesty, whereby he begs your
Majesty's pardon, which argues he is not so
faultless and innocent as we (the Privy Council) would here render him." This can only

---

* On inquiry, I do not learn that these papers are in the
State-paper office — they remained probably with Secretary
Nicholas, and if not lost, must be among his MSS. My
friend Mr. Amyott, to whom if his modesty would allow it,
I would apply the happy designation by Sir David Dalrymple of Lord Hardwicke, as " learned in British History," did
me the favour to examine the book of the Privy Council, but
not a single entry has been made of this singular transaction,
so careful were they, for the honour of the King, to bury it
in impenetrable obscurity.

allude to the Marquis having implicated the " King in the base design," as Lord Lanerick calls it. And therefore the Secretary congratulates the King on the result of the examination of the Privy Council, that " there was nothing which in any sort reflected on the King's honour." Nor has Charles been accused of any criminal act by the party. The Secretary designates " the Incident " as " that unhappy business "— and requests the royal command respecting the publication. The King simply notes on the letter, " There needs no more." *

What is more certain than " the Incident" is, that Lord Clarendon heard from Montrose himself that Murray, after having been the warmest encourager to the proposed impeachment of the Hamiltons, and offered himself to prove many notable things against the suspected noblemen, was the only man who discovered the whole " Counsel"—that is, the intended impeachment — to the Hamiltons ; and what is as mysterious as " the Incident " itself, Murray, the avowed enemy of the Marquis of Hamilton, suddenly deserted Montrose whom he had courted and whose intermediate agent

* Secretary Nicholas's correspondence in Evelyn. Pym's report of the Committee in the tenth volume of the Parliamentary History.

he had been with the King, and as suddenly
became the intimate friend of Hamilton.   The
alarm of the Hamiltons, occasioned by the dread
of assassination, I would ascribe to the same
manœuvres of Mr. William Murray of the bed-
chamber.   In betraying the projects of Montrose, he probably mixed up an exaggerated
account of that " frank" offer of assassination,
which the daring and vindictive Montrose
would not have hesitated to have had performed by his creatures, for he was himself then
confined in the Castle by the Covenanters.
The Marquis of Hamilton, practised on by
the artful insinuations of the faithless Murray,
evidently suspected that the King had consented to this inexpiable crime.   Hence his
regrets and requests of pardon, noticed in the
letters of Secretary Nicholas.   That Hamilton
had entertained this suspicion, though he certainly ought better to have understood the
character of Charles, is confirmed by an affecting circumstance.   Shortly after the mysterious
" Incident," and at the moment the Marquis
was created a Duke, Charles tenderly reproached him for having suffered so foul a suspicion
to enter his mind, reminding Hamilton that on
a former occasion, when a like charge had been
laid against Hamilton himself, he had instantly

rejected it with scorn, and as a proof of his unchangeable confidence had commanded Hamilton that very night to sleep in his chamber.

In a conspiracy of which we hardly know the conspirators, and in an " Incident" which never occurred, some reasonable conjectures may be allowed. Malcolm Laing, after an able review of this mysterious tale, concludes that " the Incident" was not altogether a fictitious plot, and that the proposed arrest of the Hamiltons, was probably assented to by Charles, under the influence of the extraordinary communications of Montrose : these, in fact, opened a scene of confederacy which extended to London as well as Edinburgh. At this moment Charles saw himself surrounded by conspiracies. One of his motives in hastening to Scotland had been to obtain possession of an engagement bearing the signatures of several English Peers, and, as he was told, of some Commoners with the Covenanters, and which we shall find he but " narrowly missed." If the arrest of the three Lords had the King's concurrence, what need was there of the three hundred men? That the King might have designed to arrest them is not improbable, but the rumour of the assassination, or the deportation, probably originated in the artful insinuations of Murray,

and in the confused accounts of the contradictory evidence of some officers, who seem to
have been let into a plot, which they did not
themselves understand. The plot, whatever it
was, may have been the contrivance of the
daring Montrose, who consigned the management to the Earl of Crawford ; but even this
point is difficult to conceive, for Montrose, who
was then soliciting the Royal favour, would
hardly have ventured to lose it, by an assassination which had been solemnly interdicted by
the King.

There was another circumstance which had
risen out of the mysterious " Incident" not the
least observable. When the news of the flight
of the three Lords from Edinburgh reached
London, it created the same consternation as
in the Scotch city : it was magnified by Pym
in Parliament* into one of those popular delusions which they began to practise ; it was
said to be a Papistical conspiracy against both
the Kingdoms ; and the Lord Mayor is directed to double guards and watches in the city
and suburbs ! A simple observer might suspect
the existence of some secret cause proportioned
to this strange effect. Why were the leading
members of Parliament thus panic-struck ?

---

* See Pym's Speech in Cobbett's Parl. Hist. ii. col. 915.

The revelations of Montrose evidently had affected them—that concealed intercourse which was shortly to be made apparent to the world, and which was yet imperfectly known to Charles, had cast the parties into confusion and dismay.

About the time of "the Incident" Scotland was a focus of political intrigues,—intrigues which have not entered into history, although they have left some obscure traces. The Scottish parties were so embroiled together, that Charles insisted, as each were ready to vent their mutual recriminations, on an act of oblivion on all sides. The King threatened that if the Covenanters accused the Earl of Traquaire and others, he would reserve three or four of their own party. The violence of their machinations we discover in the desperate style of the two great leaders of both the parties. When the Covenanters were insisting on having Traquaire tried by their Parliament, as "an Incendiary," which was the reigning party-name for any of the royal Ministers, more than once he swore that "before he perished he would mix heaven and earth and hell together!" In this chaos of his emotions, we may conjecture, that the wild elements combined the secret intrigues of some Englishmen

with the Scots, and of Argyle and other Covenanters with the Cabinet of the Louvre. The
desperate language of Traquaire was replied to
by the bold challenge of the Covenanter, Mr.
Archibald Johnston, who figures in Scottish
history as Lord Wariston. Wariston fiercely
offered the King, as he himself expressed it,
" to be yoked in one chain with the Earl of
Traquaire, and let him accuse me, and me accuse him, then let the judgment go free, and
the nocent suffer." Treasons hung on the lips
of every one; and Wariston tells that " these
recriminations deserve justice rather than
mercy." The Covenanter asks not for blood,
but surely he desires it. What scenes were
these for the unhappy Monarch! And what
a man was this Wariston, the head of the
Covenanters! This fierce Covenanter was one
who, as he describes himself, " did not weaken
his hands in the work of God." He was a
terrible being — the Talus with his flail of
iron, whom we have already noticed in the
history of the Puritans. He often discovers
the simplicity of his system of politics, — it
consisted of the strength of the Scottish army,
and his own unalterable intrepidity. He wrote,
with concise energy, from London to his brothers in Scotland, " Commend us to be stout —

prepare your armies.—The Lower House grow
in strength.—They have *Strafford's life* — are
thinking on *monies for us* — Lord! encourage
and direct them!" There is more dignity in
his patriotism when he declares that his only
end is that " the honour of the kingdom be
preferred to the King's point of honour." *
However, be it not forgotten, that this warm
patriot and inspired Covenanter closed his life
with the weakness which he said he himself
feared — he could not resist the seduction of
office. In Cromwell's time he begged not to
be sent up to London, dreading " the snares.'
Encumbered by a numerous family, and having
large sums not likely to be repaid for public
services, the Usurper, for so the Presbyterians
called the Protector, prevailed on Wariston
to have his accounts settled, and to serve him.
The offer was accepted, but deep was the
interior conflict of conscience and poverty.
We are told that it cast the fierce yet honest
Wariston into a state of melancholy ; with
a dejected spirit nothing went well with
him : and finally, it cost him his life at the
Restoration.

The close of " the Incident" was as curious,

* Dalrymple's Memoirs of Charles the First, 122 and
136.

though not as mysterious, as any part of it. The projected tragedy terminated in a perfect comedy. The Lords, who should have been assassinated were elevated into higher dignities. The Marquis of Hamilton was created a Duke; the Earl of Argyle had a Marquisate bestowed on him. Lesley, the Scotch General, was overcome by an Earldom ; a Scotch Laird was metamorphosed into a Viscount. Even the Covenanter, Mr. Archibald Johnston, was knighted, pensioned and commissioned as a Lord of the Sessions, and well known as Lord Wariston. Lanerick and Montrose alike, lost not a shade of the Royal favour. The very Presbyters, who were triumphing over the distribution of the Bishop's lands, which however were chiefly thrown to the devouring rapacity of the aristocracy,* and who so often had tried the gravity

---

* I refer the reader to a curious passage in the Diary-letters of honest Baillie (i. 334.) for an amusing specimen of the manner in which the vultures hovered over the great dead bodies of Episcopacy, till they were glutted by the carnage. It seems that when they came to the grand pillage the Presbyters were not allowed all the portion they had calculated on. " Glasgow was pitifully crossed by the Duke, who must needs have the temporality of that bishoprick ; the spirituality fell to the town-minister, which is but a small thing. But to content Glasgow, the bishoprick of

of Charles by their volume of a sermon—when like a true Scot the King even attended the Kirk—had their Henderson and Gillespie pensioned and preferred. Charles must have considered himself fortunate to have been permitted "to pardon" his own friends, with an understanding however that he was to neglect them; "the Incendiaries," as the Ministers of Charles were called, had been threatened with the recent fate of Strafford, and they were now rewarded for their zeal, by a Royal pardon! Some of the adherents to the King observed that should any of them be desirous of preferment, they had only to join the new rebellion which had just broken out in Ireland Charles indeed was now only exercising the weakness of sovereignty, for his real power was limited to granting concessions and conferring titles. Yet what availed this state-policy? In Scotland, Charles was only disappointing his

Galloway was given to the College. Aberdeen University got its bishoprick—Ross, Murray and Caithness are divided to North-land gentlemen of any small deserving; Argyle Isles, I suspect, to Argyle. The bishopricks were so quickly dilapidated, that we were near to have made a protestation in Parliament in the Church's name"—that is the Presbyters!

friends without conciliating his enemies, so
transient is the feeble gratitude for extorted
favours! It must be acknowledged that Monarchs incur misfortunes which are peculiarly
their own.

The King indeed had of late been so accustomed to grant concessions, without any
return of thanks, that the lip-service of the
vehement gratitude of some cunning Scots,
looked much like that loyalty from which he
had been so long estranged. Charles mistook
quiet for peace. Whatever was his design in
his present political journey, the policy proved
fatal; in going in person to Scotland, as
Clarendon forcibly expresses it, he had only
" made a more perfect deed of gift of that
kingdom," and what was not less fatal, the
management of the Scots indicated to their
English friends, who had watched their motions, and rejoiced with their rejoicings, that
the King must yield all to them; it would
indeed have reproached the incapacity and the
enterprise of the party, if Charles had not
shown himself as weak and as weakened a
Sovereign at London as he had done at Edinburgh. So contagious is the example of a
successful insurrection, that even the Irish
nation in their atrocious rebellion, now pre-

tended that they were only following the example of the Scots, and pleaded for their
liberties and their religion, as well as the
sons of Calvin — but these vulgar Papalists
proved to be more barbarous, even than the
Covenanters !

CHAPTER XI.

OF THE LETTER OF THE SCOTS TO THE FRENCH
KING — A DESIGN OF THEIR SEPARATION
FROM ENGLAND—BURNET'S ANECDOTE OF
LORD LOUDON EXAMINED.

THE Earl of Traquaire, who succeeded the
Marquis of Hamilton in the difficult and dangerous office of High Commissioner for Scotland, was a person of considerable abilities, who
from a private gentleman by name Stewart,
had been raised to distinction; an adventurous
intriguer unquestionably, and one whose fate
resembles that of many of this class, for according to the calamitous list of " Scot of Scot-
starvet's Staggering State of Scots' Statesmen,"
this versatile politician, after all his shiftings,
closed his career in indigence and obscurity.
Traquaire was now fixed in a dilemma, from
which by no artifice could he extricate himself
—he was secretly the great enemy to Epis-

copacy, and it was now his office to protect the very order which he sought to abolish.

The Earl of Traquaire was a favourite with Lord Clarendon, who in a suppressed passage declares that " He was one of the wisest men that he had known of that nation," and in his text, as formerly published, seems reluctantly to record the suspicions of others, that Traquaire was privy to the conspiracy against the Church. This his Lordship at first doubted. But in the suppressed passage the doubt seems to have disappeared, for we find a fuller detail of his ambiguous conduct.* Traquaire was openly accused by the Scottish Bishops before the King for his treacherous deportment in the Scotch business ; and Bishop Guthry with his strong feelings for Episcopacy, has ranked him among the rogues and traitors.

The duplicity or the versatility of this political character is strongly marked. Secretly hostile to Episcopacy, he had himself joined in ejecting the order of Bishops from the three

* Compare in the last edition of the first volume, page 192, with the Appendix, page 512. The contrast is very striking, and the confession of Clarendon, that the Earl designed by an alteration in the ecclesiastical, to make more reasonable a reformation in the temporal state, seems to settle the question.

estates of Parliament. But when he found the King still so tender on the point of Episcopacy, Traquaire, to help the King out of this difficulty, cunningly suggested that " Let the Parliament do what it would, there were still grounds for the restoration of Episcopacy, whenever the King could carry the point; for Bishops, by the laws of Scotland, forming one of the estates in Parliament, no act whatever that passed without them could have force in law, and much less the Act that had abolished them, since they never appeared there, and had protested against it." * This was what a modern French statesman has called an " *arrière pensée.*"

Traquaire's concealed feelings towards the Bishops, and his cabinet-opinion as Privy-counsellor, exhibits him in those very opposite positions into which the man of intrigue is sometimes so painfully thrust. The worldly wisdom of these Achitophels is to live on expedients—their only art is a trick of the moment; —but expedients will fail, and the deceiver is liable to be himself deceived.

The Scottish Commissioners, to quiet the people, published their own constructions of the

---

* Burnet's Memoirs of the Hamiltons, 119.

articles of the late hurried treaty of Berwick. As much had passed in loose conferences, where any harshness in the wording was softened by the Royal exposition, but not altered, that the honour of the King might suffer no degradation, and as these conferences were written down every night when the Commissioners returned to their camp, different persons would assign different results; what was set down as positive by one, to another would be dubious. The concessions which the Scots gave out were utterly disclaimed by the English, and " The Scots' false paper," as it was called,* was burnt by the hand of the common hangman, as a slanderous libel, " Every body disavowing the contents, but nobody taking upon him to publish a copy that they owned to be true." A curious instance of the absurdity of a treaty where the parties refer to what is not contained in it!

The Scots made an appearance of disbanding their army, by burning the tents which formed their camp, but they detained their officers, and Scotland presented the same unchanged scene. The Tables of democracy continued their sit-

* This paper is preserved in Frankland's Annals, 791. Malcolm Laing does not think " the Scots' Paper" to have been as false as the hangman proclaimed it.

tings. The new Assembly, to spare the King's
prejudices, avoided every allusion to the Assembly of Glasgow, which he had condemned
as illegal, but they were careful to reproduce
all its former resolutions.

Charles, though slowly, withdrew from that
last hold of his sovereignty — the contested
Episcopacy. The act of the Assembly declared that "Episcopacy was *unlawful* in the
Kirk;" that term on any explanation, Charles
firmly rejected. The King was willing to allow that Episcopacy might be declared to be
" contrary to the constitution of the Kirk," but
he never would acknowledge that " Episcopacy
was unlawful." " There may be," he observed,
" many several constitutions, but whatever is
absolutely unlawful in one Church, cannot be
lawful in another of the same profession of religion."

Such was the argument of Charles, which
has incurred the censure of two able historians.
Malcolm Laing considers it as " an immaterial
difference, unworthy to form an obstacle to a
national settlement;" and Dr. Lingard con-
demus it as " a mere quibble."

The historians of Charles the First rarely
place themselves in the perplexed situation of
this unfortunate Monarch. History requires
its abstractions as well as poetry ; the historian,

like the poet, should personate the character
he represents, placing himself in the condition
of the human being whose actions he records.
With the same fixed views before him, and
with the sympathy of the same feelings, he
should penetrate, like Tacitus or Clarendon, if
blessed with their art, into the secret recesses
of the mind. The instance before us is an illustration of this critical maxim.

When we discover the Royal Episcopalian
compelled to hang his wrath on this slight
thread, it serves at least to indicate the wounded sensibility which could not endure that
the obnoxious term *unlawful* and *Episcopacy*
should lie in such close connexion. But, in
the mind of Charles, there was a deeper dread
of this sweeping conclusion, for *cæteris pari-
bus*, had Charles acknowledged Episcopacy to
be unlawful in one Church, it would, or it
ought, to extend to the other. The King was
not raising a cavil, but opposing a principle,—
a principle which was striking at the Church
of England; and it proved to be an awful an-
ticipation,* nor was it unperceived by Charles

* The argument here used I had written before I discovered the same in Malcolm Laing himself, iii. 172. This
historian has even assigned another motive for Charles's
" Quibble,' as Dr. Lingard calls it. It is one not less forcible ; " If Episcopacy was condemned as unlawful in the con-

himself. He indeed was so fully aware of the perilous state into which his Anglican Church was thrown by the establishment of his Scottish Kirk; that he had drawn a solemn oath from the Chancellor of Scotland, (Lord Loudon,) the Earl of Argyle, and Lesley, that they would never interfere with the religious worship of England, and never on this subject aid the Puritans by their arms. This circumstance, which appears in the manuscript of the French Resident, was communicated by the King himself to that person, when, in 1644, Charles expressed his indignation at the conduct of the Scotch party at London.*

stitution of a Church, it could never be restored." Thus while this acute historian censures Charles for his hesitation at "an immaterial difference," when he comes to explain the King's views, he offers the most satisfactory apology for the King's conduct. It has been the peculiar fate of Charles, placed as he was frequently in the most trying positions, to be condemned in the same page which bears its refutation, whenever the historian has taken enlarged views. I have remarked this circumstance so often that I am provided with a copious chapter of instances, where several of our most eminent modern writers of the History of this period, while they condemn this hapless Monarch, have in the very same page contradicted themselves, correcting the popular notions they adopt, by a more intimate knowledge of their subject.

* I give the original passage. "Le Roi de la Grande Bretagne est tres malcontent des Ecossois. Il m'a juré que

The sons of Calvin expelled the Prelates, who constituted the third state in their Parliament, and excommunicated eight. They even procured three or four apostate Bishops to abjure Episcopacy as " an Order as hath had sensibly many fearful and evil consequences in many parts of Christendom."* And doubtless they inferred, that Presbytery is " an Order" guiltless of all crimes, and too wise to have troubled the world with any follies of its own.

For this time, however, the obnoxious term was softened — Charles had wholly succumbed —even his favoured Episcopacy was surrendered, to " the madness of the people." But the Scots had yet much to labour. Turning from their Presbytery, they looked towards a revolution in their Government. This was an advantage to Charles, for it convinced those of

lorsque par la necessité de ses affaires il fut contraint de consentir à cc que les Ecossois avoient fait contre la Religion, prévoyant que les Anglois se serviroient d'eux pour la revolte, il avoit tiré serment sur leur foi et sur leur honneur, du Chancelier d'Ecosse, du Comte d'Orgueil (Argyle) et Lesley, que jamais ils ne se mêleroient de la religion d'Angleterre, et ne l'assisteroient jamais de leurs armes en ce sujet." —*Sabran's manuscrit Négociations en Angleterre*, vol. ii. folio 148.

* The abjuration or renouncement of one of these apostate Bishops is preserved in Rushworth, ii. 957.

the English nation who were free from faction, that it was no longer " the Bishops' war," as it was termed, but a destruction of Regal authority at which some refractory spirits aimed.*

The Assembly decreed to ratify the Covenant. Traquaire had suffered every point to be carried, and, strange as it seemed to Charles, the Earl himself had subscribed the Revolutionary Bond. The name of Traquaire became popular, and resounded from the pulpits; Scotland blazed with bonfires! The half-timid.and half-daring Lord Commissioner hastened to Whitehall to plead his justification, averring that he could not prevail with the people, but by force, or by compliance. The Covenanting Earl was coldly received by the King, and again, as Baillie expresses it, " his credit was cracking."

Traquaire now in disgrace at Court, though popular in Scotland, either to redeem the Royal favour which he had lost, or not unwilling to check that political anarchy, with which the nation was threatened by the ambition of a few, contrived a new shift by which he strengthened the King's cause, and more clearly exposed the secret designs of the Covenanters. Traquaire had intercepted a letter addressed by

* Malcolm Laing, iii. 175.

some of the Scottish nobility " Au Roy," where
the subscribers offered themselves to be subjects of France ; to renew that ancient alliance,
that sympathy of common interests, which had
formerly reduced the Realm of Scotland to a
dependant province of France.

Charles now discovered sufficient cause for
alarm, and Lord Leicester, our ambassador at
Paris, in a private audience with Louis XIII.
sounded his Majesty's intentions. His Lordship attempted to take the King by surprise,
by artfully assuming that his Majesty had received a letter from the heads of the Covenanters. The King declared he knew of no such
letter. His Lordship then offered to read the
copy of an intercepted letter, of which the
King of England retained the original. Louis
observing that the letter was written in French,
read it himself, and then solemnly declared
that he had never had any thing to do with
them, and never would. " Le Roy, mon frère,
peut être assuré que je n'aime les rebelles et
seditieux"— Charles had desired the ambassador to say that the ground of their rebellion
was not conscience nor religion.—" Non ! Je le
croy, car c'est seulement une prétexte que tous
les rebelles cherchent pour couvrir leur mauvais
desseins."—" The true ground," continued the

Earl, "is their hatred to Royalty and Mo-
narchial Government, wherein your Majesty
and every King have a common interest."—
"Je le sçais bien, cela me peut arriver aussi
bien qu'à un autre, et comme vous dites les
Rois y ont grand interêt, et quant à moi je ne
favoriseray jamais les mutins et les rebelles."*

When I read, many years ago, the French
Monarch's replies, I was persuaded by the
naïveté of such blunt sincerity that it was clear
of all political artifice. I considered that the
witchery of the daring genius of the minister
had withered the faculties of Louis, and that
the French King knew nothing of the dispatch
of the Scotch Abbé Chambre to Edinburgh,
nor the continual intercourse with the Scottish
party; in a word, that Louis had yet no idea
that he was in reality the ally and confederate
of the insurgents of Scotland. Moreover the
existence of this French letter addressed " Au
Roy" by the Scottish Lords, has always been
denied by our historians from Hume to Brodie.
They have all asserted that no such letter was
sent, relying on the testimony of Lord Loudon,
one of the Lords who was implicated in the
treason, and sent to the Tower. He asserted that

* Sydney Papers, ii. Père d'Orleans Revolutions de l'Angleterre, iii. 19.

this intercepted letter was merely a rough copy, which, had it ever been intended, was never actually sent.

I became more intimately acquainted with the character and habits of Louis XIII. in the judicious history of Père Griffet. I discovered that never was there a monarch who carried the royal vice of dissimulation farther than this King; incompetent himself to govern, yet jealous even of his favourites on small matters, the sole political artifice he was capable of practising, was that of never betraying his own thoughts. The man whom he had condemned to imprisonment, or to death, in a last interview he would even dismiss with marks of particular regard. Louis XIII. was tutored by Richelieu, and never failed in the humble part of a pupil. That he deceived the Earl of Leicester by his apparent simplicity is probable, but modern researches often throw a new light over the dark passages of history, and communicate to posterity a knowledge of the times which no contemporary possessed. All the writers of English history have confided on the evidence of Lord Loudun; himself one of the conspirators. The letter in French by the Scottish Lords, addressed " Au Roy," we now know, was sent and was received. Monsieur

Mazure recently discovered it in the State-paper office of France.*

It is precisely the same as the letter which Charles had read to the Parliament. Calculating on the effect he imagined it would have produced by exposing the designs of the Scotch party, he was mortified to discover that the Parliament either passed it over as a state trick, or little cared whether the French assisted their " dear† brethren" of Scotland, to which they probably had no objection.

---

* Histoire de la Révolution de 1688, par Mazure, iii. 405.

† The letter Traquaire had intercepted was a duplicate. Modern research has also brought to light both a brouillon, and a corrected copy, different from the one dispatched to France. Dalrymple, Memorials of Charles I. 57—60. It is printed in Frankland, 810. The Scotch found the French idiom difficult. One of the Scottish Lords refused to sign, objecting to their use of " Raye de soleil," not because it was treason, but because it was nonsense ; for *Raye* is a Thornback, and it went to say, that " the glory of the French Monarch shone like that fish." However it went *une raye de soleil*, meaning *rayon*.

It may amuse the reader to see how party-histories have been written. Oldmixon, in his " History of the Stuarts" frequently referred to as authority by a party, describes in his peculiar style the scene which occurred when Charles from the throne acquainted Parliament of his having intercepted the letter to the French Monarch, which the Lord-Keeper read. " The Lord-Keeper, holding the letter folded, read

In these Scottish transactions, an important circumstance does not appear in our history. A party among the Scottish nobility seems to have designed a separation from England, and to have resumed their rank in Europe as an independent nation. This object was suitable to the policy of Richelieu. We may trace all the French Ambassadors who resided in England, even under the administration of that Cardinal's successor, holding secret intelligence with Scotchmen. In the manuscript papers of Sabran, I find many such confidential interviews. A political intriguer of this nation whose name does not ·appear, but whose eminence is indicated by his having received a gold chain from the King of France, and evidently some Scotchman intimately connected with the cabinet of

the superscription *Au Roy,* raising his voice very theatrically, showing that whoever writes so, acknowledges the King they address to be their Sovereign. Here's logic as well as rhetoric! This acting is not yet over. Then the Lord-Keeper read the letter, expatiating on it to prove the treason of the Lords who subscribed it. The artifice of the letter stared both Houses in the face. I can't write this incident no more than I could have seen it without laughing, to see the Lord-Keeper gravely folding up the letter, then turning *Au Roy* to the Lords and Commons; then the King speaking to it, then the Keeper speaking again to it; when all the while it was a farce in the opinion of that august assembly." 146.

the Louvre—the object of his interview with
Sabran was to point out the future danger to
France of an union of both the Parliaments of
England and Scotland in the design of establish-
ing one form of religion. He warned Sabran
that the Parliament had already their secret dé-
puties in Sweden, and among all the Protestant
Princes, as also with the States of Holland.
A league was ready to be formed against the
Catholic Princes. He complained that Scotchmen were not so well received at Court, under
the administration of Mazarine, as of Richelieu.
He designed, however, to revisit France before
he returned to his country. As Sabran entertained suspicions of this mysterious personage,
he encouraged him to open himself more freely ;
and it appeared that this Scotchman wanted to
establish the independence of Scotland by the
aid of France. He closed by a prediction.
" We shall have our Covenant and independence too at London, so that the Scots would
no longer be a province of England."

The information given by this mysterious
personage was shortly after confirmed. The
French Cabinet was thrown into a panic at
the Parliament's secret intercourse with Sweden by a concealed agent whose lodgings they
had not even been able to discover. This was

not wonderful; for he proved to be a Scotchman in the service of Sweden. Brienne, the
Secretary of State, who carried on the correspondence with Sabran, and whose views on
English affairs discover the most enlightened
sagacity, having been formerly acquainted with
all the parties in England, impresses on Sabran
to flatter and to gain over the Scotch, for more
than one purpose, either to be useful to the
King of England, or to oppose the Parliament
in the case of their erecting a Republic, which
might trouble France. Sabran was to lay
great stress on the ancient alliance which had
never been interrupted between France and
Scotland. If by money or by any other re-
compense he could gain over the Chancellor of
Scotland to the French, there was every disposition to gratify him. " Si vous venez à lui
tâter, mesurez vos parolles comme n'ayant nulle
charge de rien offrir, mais seulement de pres-
sentir quelle seroit sa disposition. Deux rai-
sons font qu'il ne s'en offencera pas; la pre-
mière qu'il est Ecossois, qui vaut autant à dire
qu'interessé; l'autre que c'est la France qui le
recherche, dont ils sont en possession de recevoir
des bienfaits." This Secretary of State was so
greatly alarmed at the projected league against
the Catholic powers, and at a combination with

all the Protestants, that as he writes to Sabran,
a long dispatch was sent to the Plenipotentiaries then assembled at Munster, to sound the
designs of the Chancellor of Sweden, (the famous Oxenstiern) who doubtless is the prime
mover of this proposition which threatens the
oppression and ruin of the Catholic Religion."

All these political terrors of the French cabinet produced a ludicrous incident.   Sabran
proved it as difficult as it was delicate to communicate with the Scottish Chancellor, as he
could only converse with him by means of an
interpreter; and such was the watchful jealousies of the parties, that he was hindered from
seeing him as often as he wished.   Sabran contrived an expedient.   He sent an invitation for
Twelfth Night to draw for King, to the Chancellor and his intimate associates, as a pretext
for their meeting.   " This was a difficult affair
to manage," continues Sabran, " for reasons
which he could not mention, but which you
may easily imagine." He probably alludes to
that feast-day, which was already condemned
as " a Popish superstition." The Chancellor
accepted the invitation; but the day after he
suddenly fell ill, as he said, so that the feast
really intended for the Scotch, Sabran found
necessary to keep, without obtaining its object,

by making up quite a different party, inviting the three Dutch Ambassadors and the Resident of Portugal to assist him in celebrating a feast which had never been intended for them, and which had balked the deep designs of the statesman who was regulating the affairs of France and Scotland.*

From the letter which was addressed " Au Roy," and from the particulars we gather from Sabran's Negotiations, we infer that there was a party among the Scottish nobles, who had contemplated, by an alliance with France, to separate themselves from England, and to establish their own national independence.

On this occasion a strange story has . been told, famous among those who would blacken Charles the First as the most arbitrary of tyrants. The Earl of Loudon, as we have noticed, was committed to the Tower, being the only Scottish Peer then at London who had subscribed the treasonable letter to the French King; and on this circumstance we have a surprising tale.

When Burnet was once accused of having suppressed several things in his Memoirs of Hamilton relating to Charles the First, from fear of offending the Court, he pleaded that

* Sabran's Manuscript Negotiations, ii. 17.

" some things could not bear telling." As an
instance, he mentioned that when the Earl of
Loudon lay prisoner in the Tower, Charles, in
his passionate resentment, sent a warrant to
Sir William Balfour, Lieutenant of the Tower,
to execute the prisoner for high treason the
next morning! The Lieutenant immediately
went to the Earl, and desired his opinion how
to avoid the execution. The Earl desired
Balfour to hasten to the Marquis of Hamilton,
whom, however, he could not meet with till
the King had retired to rest. The Marquis
and the Lieutenant are then represented as
waiting in the outer apartment in despair, till
one told Balfour that as Lieutenant of the
Tower he had a privilege to knock at the
King's chamber-door at any hour of the night.
The Groom of the Bed-chamber announced
to the King that the Lieutenant of the Tower
had come upon business. He was admitted,
when falling on his knees, he prayed to know,
whether the warrant for the execution of Loudon was legally obtained from his Majesty, and
whether he could legally proceed in the execution of it? The King replied, that the warrant was his, and must be obeyed. The Marquis of Hamilton, who had stood at the door,
then entering, on his knees begged the King

would not insist on such an extraordinary resolution. The King seemed peremptory. The
Marquis in despair taking leave, said that " He
would now ride post to Scotland, for I am
sure before night the whole city will be in an
uproar, and they will pull your Majesty out
of your palace. I will get as far as I can, and
declare to my countrymen, that I had no hand
in it." The King was struck at this, and bade
the Marquis recall the Lieutenant, when the
King, taking the warrant, tore it to pieces.

This story appeared in the shape of a memorandum made by Bishop Kennet in a blank
leaf of Burnet's Memoirs, as told to Kennet by
a Mr. Frazier, who had heard it from the vivacious gossip of Burnet; Frazier further added, that having once mentioned it to that
Duke of Hamilton who was killed in a duel,
his Grace said that he had often ran over the
papers in his collection, whence Burnet had
drawn his materials, and he recollected such a
relation. When Birch first printed the story,*
it produced a great sensation with the Whig
party of that day, as a complete evidence of the
arbitrary conduct of their English Nero.

* In an Appendix to the *second* edition of an Inquiry
into the Share which King Charles the First had in the
Transactions of the Earl of Glamorgan. 372.

The correctness of this narrative must, however, be questioned.   An extraordinary story
against Charles the First from Burnet, at that
day, was safe to tell and grateful to hear.   The
historical integrity of this warm and vivacious
memoir-writer, on the subject of Charles the
First, is impeachable, when we confront his
adulative style on the unfortunate Monarch in
the Memoirs of the Hamiltons, written early in
life, and the depreciated character which appears in the subsequent History of his Own
Times.   Had the tale run that Charles had
commanded the assassination of Loudon, it
would have borne more probability than one
of a private execution, which, at least, must
have taken place before witnesses.

Lord Loudon was at that moment one of the
Deputies of Scotland, confined to the Tower,
where he had been examined by the Attorney-
General and Secretary Windebank; and the
House of Lords thought fit to remand him till
further evidence was produced.*   It is against
all reason to conceive that Charles, while Loudon was thus placed in security, and pending
an examination before the Lords, could have
ventured to inform his Peers, whenever they

* Whitelocke's Memorials, 32.

chose to call for their prisoner, that he had been executed !

It is certain that the head of the Earl of Loudon was in imminent peril; for the act of treason, according to the laws of Scotland, could not be more evident ; and the King was certain that an open trial would have done that which he is represented to have sought by the most frantic impolicy ever recorded.

Dr. Birch, and other writers seem not to have known that the story itself had been already more largely told by Oldmixon, who refers for his authority to a " MS. MF," as " an authority too noble to be called in question, and known to all the people of the first quality in North Britain." But Oldmixon, as I have frequently detected, is such an infamous interpolater, that his history is faithless as any of the French Varillas, who referred to manusrcipts which were at length found to be the chimeras of his own brain. He is much fuller in his story, than the one said to have descended from Burnet. Among his *dramatis personæ*, he has introduced the Queen in bed, complaining of Hamilton's intrusion at two or three in the morning; " but the Marquis taking her up short, let her know she was a subject as well as himself."* Secret history wonderfully improves under the pens of certain writers.

Dr. Birch, a warm Whig, is very tender on the political tergiversation of his favourite historian, Burnet. To Bishop Burnet we are unquestionably indebted for a mass of very curious secret history, sometimes tinged by his prejudices, but much of which is veracious. Birch says, " It was not to be expected that the historian writing (the Memoirs of Hamilton) in such times and circumstances, (under Charles II.) should venture to relate at length the remarkable story to which he evidently alludes in a passage of those Memoirs." The passage

---

* History of the Stewarts, 140. It is amusing to observe this vile writer delivering his opinion on Historical composition. " One great advantage the Ancients had over the Moderns in writing history, was the liberty of their genius ; and they had another which was the credit they were in with their readers ; we do not find the margents of Thucydides and Livy crowded with authorities. The Historian's own word was taken." Yet so blind is party, that Micaiah Towgood in his " Essay towards attaining a true idea of the character and reign of King Charles the First," accepts the impudent and vulgar writer's history " as a good collection of *fucts;* though his zeal, perhaps, breaks forth into too frequent and warm sallies." When I shall give the history of this writer, my readers will learn on what principle he acted and he wrote.

of Burnet is, " There were some ill instruments about the King who advised him *to proceed capitally against Loudon, which is believed went very far.* But the Marquis of Hamilton opposed this vigorously, assuring the King that if it were done, Scotland was for ever lost." If Burnet, in his loose and inaccurate style, alluded to the story which he told twenty years afterwards, he has certainly not afforded any indication that he had such a statement lying before him. What he says is true, as we find confirmed by Whitelocke; that " the King was *advised* to proceed capitally against Loudon."

Another circumstance, in my mind, seems fatal to the authenticity of the story. When Lord Hardwicke carefully examined this very Hamilton collection, and published the important papers which Burnet had only alluded to, or had passed over unnoticed, I find none of this strange history. Would Lord Hardwicke, the zealous patron of Dr. Birch, have neglected such a curious piece of secret history, which also would have authenticated the fugitive and suspicious tale of this execution before a trial?

Would the present noble owner of this collection once more open his archives, and in-

spect those family documents which have entered into the history of the nation, it is probable that he may have it yet in his power to inform us about Oldmixon's manuscript MF, and
Bishop Burnet's tale which " could not bear the
telling." *

The true close of this history of the Earl of
Loudon we have already given in the chapter
on the Marquis of Hamilton.

---

* Since this chapter has been written, I observe with pleasure that Dr. Lingard, whose unbiassed judgment is always
to be highly valued, " gives no credit to Burnet's hearsay
story." He does not seem to be aware that Oldmixon had
told it so long before. I have sometimes thought that Oldmixon's mysterious manuscript MF. of which he does not
assign the place where it may be found, was some collection
by the Mr. Frazier who told Burnet's tale. Oldmixon also
notices in his preface a Dr. Fraser who had lent him pamphlets and papers.

CHAPTER XII.

THE SECRET MOTIVE OF CHARLES THE FIRST'S
SECOND JOURNEY TO SCOTLAND. — THE
FORGED LETTER OF LORD SAVILLE.

THE motive of the second journey of Charles
to his " ancient and native kingdom " so late as
in August 1641, after the many extraordinary
events of that and the preceding year, has been
variously conjectured by historians. Among
the most important of those events, the King
had witnessed the imprisonment of Laud, the
execution of Strafford, and the abolition of
Episcopacy in that very kingdom to which it
seemed as if the King were flying as to a last
refuge. Since the death of Strafford, the regal
power of Charles was reduced to a shadow of
sovereignty ; his personal distresses and the
confusion in his councils were such at this moment that the King could not endure to be
near Westminster, where one of the Bed-cham-

ber said that nothing made the King more anxious to remove from his Court and his Council, than that variety of intelligence which at every minute was brought to him, and on which every one gave the most contrary opinions and the most alarming comments.* Charles was evidently too sensible of the decline of his power, for he did not conceal it from himself. In his frank confession to honest Secretary Nicholas, who at this time alarmed for their common safety, was earnestly requesting the King " to protect his faithful servants," there is a melancholy and pathetic feeling. " I shall not fail to protect you according to my power, and (according to the old English compliment,) I would it were better for your sake."†

A secret motive instigated Charles to hasten to Scotland; and his determination would suffer no impediment from friend or foe. The rapidity with which the King performed his journey, and the small retinue with which he entered Edinburgh, betrayed his impatience. This was no longer a Royal progress. Charles rode from London to York in less than four days.

* Hackett's Life of Williams, ii. 163.
† Correspondence of Secretary Nicholas in Evelyn, ii. 60.

It is a curious fact that this Royal journey to Scotland was equally dreaded both by the friends and the enemies of Charles; the one imploring him not to leave England where his presence was deemed most necessary, and the other alarmed at this closer intercourse with Scotland. When the Scotch Commissioners at London were consulted by both parties on the propriety or the necessity of the King's journey to Edinburgh, they delivered an oracular response. " It was desirable," they said, " but the time might be made convenient :"—too subtle to press that which their English friends did not wish, and too prudent to refrain from the chance of partaking of those Royal favours which they were sensible were ready. to be showered on them.

At length when the King was at Edinburgh both parties were equally anxious to urge his return home. That such similar results should have proceeded from such opposite principles and such contending interests, has perplexed our historians.

It was thought by those who were in the King's interest, that he could not reasonably expect any great reverence to his person from the triumphant democracy of Scotland, and that the affairs of that Kingdom could be more advantageously transacted at a distance.* The Patriotic or County Members, and the presbyterian and puritanic party in the House, at first protested against the King's journey to Scotland, and for this purpose even sate on a Sunday, excusing this profanation of the Sabbath by issuing a declaration of the urgency of the occasion. And when they found that no arts which they tried could change the Royal decision, they appointed a Committee of their own party to attend on the King, on the plea of these gentlemen being present at the act of pacification, to cherish the kindly intercourse between the two nations. It is quite evident that a Committee of Three, consisting of Lord Howard of Escrick, a malcontent Lord who " had delivered himself soul and body" to the party, and Sir Philip Stapelton, a young political adventurer, both under the guidance of the wary Hampden, were only spies on the King, who in truth was thus placed *en surveillance;* and as Clarendon sarcastically observes on this Committee, and on their new office, that " It was their first employment, and the first that ever Parliament had of that

* Clarendon, i. 490.

kind."* The English Parliamentarians were morbidly jealous of their "dear brethren," and they entertained some reasonable suspicions that the Leaders of the Scottish faction had betrayed, or might betray, their new friends in their copartnership of Revolution. A stricter intimacy of the King with the Scots might reverse the state of affairs, and the more dangerous and doubtful issues seemed to them to threaten to be the result of this political journey.

Unquestionably, among other expectations, the King looked forwards for a balancing power against his English Parliament among the Scots; while the Parliament itself had calculated on their support as the only means to carry on their own measures. Scotia was now the northern Mistress courted, alike tremblingly, by the King and the Parliament. She who was the abject creature of their favours, held their destinies in her hand.

When the last hope had vanished that Charles could manage his inexorable Parliament by yielding to them, humbled and degraded as the Monarch felt by the fall of Strafford, there is no doubt that Charles would have

* Clarendon, ii.

leaned on the affections of his native kingdom, and by conciliating a whole people, have
resumed that monarchical independence which
he had lost. The King had already succeeded
in gaining over some of the heads of the Covenanters—the Earls of Rothes, of Montrose, and
others ; and Charles was now hastening to his
Scottish throne, thence to touch with his sceptre every act of concession to the Scottish people, and from the fountain of honour to shower
his Royal graces on their chiefs. At this moment we discover that even the Queen " began
to speak honourably and affectionately of the
Scottish nation," and Henrietta, desolate in her
own palace, and trembling amidst the menaces
of the Parliamentarians, appears to have had a
serious intention of accompanying the King.
The motive assigned for this change of feeling
is, that " this hearty agreeance would be a sovereign help of the continual harsh rencounters
of the English Parliament.*

But, besides the present, there was also a
more secret motive concealed in the breast of
the King. From the communications of Hamilton, and the disclosures of Montrose, Charles
had gathered many intimations, many surmises,

* Baillie, i. 327. who informs us of the Queen's resolution.

and no dubious conviction of a treasonable correspondence carrying on by the popular leaders of the Parliament with those of the Scottish party. To invite, as well as to aid foreign forces to invade England, is treason by law; and a great object in this political journey was to detect this secret confederacy, and to procure irrefragable evidence of this treasonable correspondence, of which Charles had formerly received intimations from his late unfortunate minister.

Charles, in the preceding year, had already learned of a written engagement to the Scots, subscribed by several English Peers, and as he was told, by several leading members of the House of Commons. On the first proposal of the treaty of Rippon, in September 1640, Sir Henry Vane, the Secretary, notices the curious fact that on the morning of the 24th of that month, when the King at York took his chair, the Lords desired justice upon Sir William Bartley for having said that the rebels had thirty-seven of the heads of the nobility who had invited them to come into England. Lord Hardwicke observes, that this was the first getting out of the story of the letter and subscription said to be forged by the Lord Saville.

Charles had eagerly sought to possess himself of so undisguised a document of treason. The King appears to have tracked it to its secret covert—it was deposited with Archibald Johnstone, afterwards the well-known Wariston; as we learn from Burnet, who was the nephew of Wariston, that the King earnestly pressed his uncle to have it delivered up into his own hands. Charles did not succeed in obtaining it, but in a remarkable passage in the Icon Basilike the King evidently alludes to this circumstance, and which could only have been known to himself. " I had discovered, as I thought, the unlawful correspondence they had used ; (alluding to the incident of the seizing the six members) and the *engagements* they had entered into, &c. of all which *I missed but little to have produced writings under some men's own hands* who were the chief contrivers, &c." *   During the treaty of Rippon, Charles in vain renewed his efforts to obtain these " written engagements." The stern Covenanter Wariston does not appear to have denied that such a writing existed, but he pleaded the sacredness of his oath as an apology for his refusal to betray the trust.

" The forged letter of Lord Saville," as it is

* Laing's Hist. of Scotland, iii. 520.

called in our history—a document of treachery
and treason, for it was compounded of both—
no historian, save one of no authority, pretends
to have seen, and the particulars concerning it
vary, as usual in relations of obscure incidents.
We have to pursue this fictitious and invisible
fugitive through an obscure labyrinth of circumstances ; but by what is known among
much which remains unknown, we may show
its reality, and even detect its purpose. We
cannot ascertain the moment when the King
discovered the existence of the "written engagement," but we have evidence that he did
discover it ; we cannot appeal to the document
itself, for we may suspect the authenticity of
that which has been given as the original.
We cannot harmonize some discordant accounts from authentic writers, as Clarendon
and Burnet, yet we shall show that it would
be absurd to question its existence, or even to
doubt the forger. We are surprised when Dr.
Lingard tells us, that "he does not mention
the letter said to have been forged by Lord
Saville and sent to the Scots ; the assertion
rests on very questionable authority :" an historian in his researches must conquer difficulties, if he loves the labour of truth.

The Scots after their first invasion were

doubtful of their reception in England on a second; well might they have faltered, for it was a fearful step. Uncertain how the English people would countenance their own English friends, the Covenanters had some dread of provoking the national jealousy, which once roused might have sided with the King; and the invaders, who themselves were but ill-prepared, might have been involved in the endless conflicts of a civil war. They required something more palpable than advice and encouragement from their English allies. During this indecision, while hovering on the borders, they received an engagement subscribed by several Lords, whose names and principles were well known to them. These Lords dispatched an invitation to the Scottish army to enter England; they offered unlimited promises of support, and they expressed their confidence that the Scots were their best friends to remove their own grievances. It is said that this written engagement decided the doubts and quickened the march of the Scots. A rumour spread through the Scottish camp that " they were sure of a very great and unexpected assistance, which, though it was to be kept secret, would appear in due time."

These English Lords, however, did not come

forward to aid their new confederates; the Scots who had been lured to pass the borders, found that they had only to depend on their own arms, and to make their own way, by fair words and meek pretences.

When the English and Scotch Commissioners met together to open the Treaty of Rippoń, Lord Loudon and Sir Archibald Johnston, afterwards the famous Wariston, requested a private interview with Lord Mandeville, better known as Lord Kimbolton, and finally as the Earl of Manchester. The Scots opened with severe expostulations, charging Lord Mandeville and other Lords with a shameless breach of their promise and the violation of their solemu engagement, declaring that never would they have invaded England, had they not entirely confided in the faith of those English Lords, according to the articles which they had signed.

Lord Mandeville seemed lost in astonishment; he solemnly declared his perfect ignorance of any such articles. Lord Loudon again urged it as an act of great ingratitude towards them who had hazarded all that was dear to them, on the faith of this solemu engagement. Loudon observed that when he was a prisoner in the Tower, Lord Saville had treated with

him in the names of several of the nobility and
gentry, and on his return to Scotland, Saville
had sent him this very agreement subscribed
by these Lords, by the hands of Mr. Henry
Darley.* And this the Lord Saville, they
doubted not, would avouch to be true. A
meeting with this Lord was agreed on. Without any knowledge of what had just occurred,
Saville was taken by surprise, and in his confusion acknowledged that he had never acquainted those Lords with the business, whose
signatures appeared to this deceptious engage-

---

* In a narrative of obscure and secret transactions, differences appear, even in telling the same circumstance. We
may instance this in Burnet's account. Lord Saville is there
made to show Lord Loudon and another Scotch Lord, about
the period mentioned, an engagement under the hands of
these Lords, to join with them on their entrance into England, provided they refused any treaty but what should be
confirmed by an English Parliament. The Scotch Lords
desired leave to send this paper into Scotland, to which,
after much difficulty, Saville consented. It was inclosed
in a hollow cane, and one Frost, afterwards Secretary to the
Committee of both Kingdoms, was sent down with it in the
disguise of a poor traveller. It was to be communicated
only to three persons, the Earls of Rothes, of Argyle, and
Wariston. Burnet's Own Times, i. 47. This is a detail,
which we cannot discover in the authentic narrative of Lord
Mandeville—yet the secret mode of the conveyance of the
Engagement is evidently alluded to.

ment ; he openly confessed that he had counterfeited their hands ! The apology the guilty
Saville offered was, that observing a backward-
ness in the Covenanters to hazard an invasion,
he considered those names would have most
weight with them ; that since this expedient,
he added, had answered its design, and that a
Scotch army in England would serve their best
purposes, he desired their silence, that all discoveries might be prevented, exhorting them
to improve the occasion which this fictitious
instrument had the merit of having presented
to them.

The honour of the noblemen implicated in
this extraordinary transaction was thus cleared,
all but that of the faithless Lord to whom it
cost no blush to own the infamous forgery.
Yet at this conjuncture it was not deemed prudent on either side, to express their indignation
by rejecting Saville from their party. Lord
Mandeville, however, requested that he might
be allowed to acquaint those Lords whose
names had thus been used without their privity,
and that the Declaration, or Engagement,
under their counterfeited names might be delivered up to them. A few days after, the
deceptive instrument was sent for from New-
castle, where lay the Scottish camp ; and in the

presence of Lord Mandeville and the other Lords, who declared that their signatures had been so skilfully imitated that they could not distinguish them from their own writing,* the names were separately cut out and burnt, but the Engagement itself the Scottish Lords insisted should be preserved. Afterwards when the Scots laboured under difficulties and danger by the failure of supplies for their army, and seemed to lose confidence in their new confederates, they were once on the point of retreating and petitioning for the King's grace, and proposed to allege for their excuse that invitation from the Lords which they still retained.†

Such is the narrative of the singular political forgery by Lord Saville, drawn from the authentic Memoirs of the Earl of Manchester, the only one of the party who has left any memorials of their more secret transactions.

* It is said by Oldmixon, whose authority has no other weight than the probability of the fact, that Lord Saville wrote letters to all the supposed subscribers on purpose to get answers to them, and by their names to those answers he so well counterfeited them that when they saw their pretended hand-writing, every one of them declared that they could not swear they did not write their names, though they could swear they had signed no such letter.

† Nalson, ii. 427.

It establishes the existence of the forged document, and even authenticates the forger.
But the very precaution which was taken to
bury it in secrecy, and to secure the supposititious subscribers from the danger they incurred, cast into great uncertainty the very existence of the document itself; and it even
enabled the subdolous Saville, afterwards, as
it appears, when he had ingratiated himself
into the favour of Charles, to insinuate that
the signatures which the King had heard of,
were the real ones of those Lords whose names
he had counterfeited.

It is said not only that Charles had nearly
obtained possession of this paper, as the King
expresses himself, " of which I missed but
little," but that it was the foundation of the
impeachment which Strafford was preparing to
bring against the popular leaders in Parliament when he was himself impeached.* This
is one of the obscure points in this history of
deception. If none but certain Peers were the
subscribers, Strafford could not hope by this
instrument to discover those Commoners who
were so deeply engaged in the Scottish intrigues; nor could he have brought forward
as evidence a document so cautiously concealed,

* Laing iii. 520, who refers to Acherly and Oldmixon.

seen by none but those whom it concerned
to hide it, and which, in fact, by the preven-
tive care of Wariston had ceased to exist, as
soon as it was seen. The rumour which Sir
William Bartley spread at the opening of the
treaty of Rippon in 1640, and the pressing desire of Charles at that time to have the unknown document delivered up to him, are
evident proofs that this secret instrument of
treason was not unknown, but in a manner too
indistinct and uncertain to be acted on. Strafford was not unprepared to impeach Lord Say
and some of the patriots on more certain information and correspondence, such as the
King afterwards himself obtained when in
Scotland, probably through Montrose.

It is, however, curious to observe that had
we not had the fullest account of this fictitious
document from Lord Mandeville, its existence
might still have been questioned, as well as the
person who forged it. A later historian, indeed, furnishes not only much information respecting the forgery, but drags into open light
the invisible document itself, which had hitherto resisted all the researches of preceding historians. Oldmixon has given it entire—but
he is an author so utterly disingenuous and
depraved, so guilty himself of historical forge-

ries and interpolations, that we know not how
to trust the man, whose honour has suffered
the brand of infamy.

The extraordinary style in which he gives
this historical document raises our suspicion
of its genuineness. " This," he exclaims, " is
the important letter which most authors make
mention of, but none ever saw, and all are
mistaken in ;" nor less extraordinary is his
mode of authenticating it; instead of simply
assigning the place where it was deposited, he
has thrown out a cartel of defiance. " These
original papers relating to the affairs of Scotland carry with them sufficient evidence of
their truth. But if that should ever be called
in question, they will be so well vouched as
will leave no room for suspicion, and be much
to the confusion of those who suspected it."
Never, in the sobriety of history, was ever a
grave authority thus thrust on us, by the blus-
ter of a literary bravo. We may, however,
question the quality of his vaunted document.
He tells us, " Welwood says twelve noblemen
signed it, Mr. Acherley puts the Earl of Mul-
grave, the Earl of Clare, and Earl of Boling-
broke's hands to it, as also the hands of several
leading Commoners ; whereas, in fact, there
were no hands but those of the seven Lords,"

whose names he has subscribed to the letter. Oldmixon is now fixed in this dilemma. If he transcribed the original, which Wariston appears to have detained, after having cut out the names of the pretended subscribers, on what authority does Oldmixon affix the names of the seven Lords? If he transcribed from a presumed copy of the original, he well knew that such a paper was no certain authority. The truth seems, that this treacherous historian was desirous of disguising the real nature of his communications, which probably would not bear too close an inspection, as happens to some other anecdotes of his Scottish papers.*

The intention of Lord Saville in encouraging the Scots to march into England, and in sending besides the present forged engagement,

---

* In the recent edition of Burnet's History of His Own Times, is a remarkable, though it be only a private reference by the Speaker Onslow to " a note in his copy of Oldmixon's History of the Stuarts, p. 145." Burnet i. 48. We regret that this note remains unpublished; it may hereafter be consulted, should the volume be in the library of his noble descendant. I suspect that the Speaker entertained doubts of the authenticity of Oldmixon's communication. This egregious writer of history has collected and exaggerated many loose rumours and many scandalous tales, which there is great reason to conclude are entirely apocryphal.

letters of his own invention full of illusory statements, was at first to get his great rival Strafford prosecuted by that party as an Incendiary. The implacable hatred and rankling jealousies long felt by the Savilles against Strafford in their rival dominion in the North, were the inherited and unextinguishable animosities of two great family feuds; when Saville was made a Lord, Wentworth placed himself in the opposition, and when Wentworth was created a Viscount, Saville changed sides, and left the Court to act against it.

The pre-eminent fortune of Strafford for a time had prevailed over his baffled and indignant enemy, who had now no other arts to practise than that of the most desperate malice. Saville was therefore at first in earnest in his advice and projects with the Scots, but when these had all the success he desired, and the Scots entered England, and Strafford fell, Saville found himself slighted and despised among the party whom he had flattered himself he should have led. It was then he determined that the Scots and their friends in their turn were to be immolated to his ambition. The reckless double-dealer looked round for the advantages which he might derive from betraying secrets of state of his own contrivance, and

implicating those Lords in an act of treason
which he had himself forged. The utter
worthlessness of this ignoble Peer would render even this nefarious scheme not improbable
— it is however quite certain. After the fall
of Strafford, Saville made ample discoveries to
Charles. He hesitated not to avow the faithless part which he had acted, but he presumed
that his returning loyalty and contrition had
survived the early days of his conspiracy.
This is explicitly told us by Lord Clarendon—
" when all the mischief was brought to pass
that he desired, he very frankly discovered the
whole to the King, and who were guilty of the
same treason, when there was no way to call
them in question for it." * Saville then appears to have insinuated to Charles, as we may
judge by the King's allusion to " the written
engagement" which he said " he missed but
little to have procured," that the signatures
which he had himself forged were real ones.
Charles who appears to have rarely exercised
any critical judgment on the characters of those
about him, not only invested this servile traitor
with the white staff, but at length created him
the Earl of Sussex. But the faithless never
cease their treacheries. The day at last arrived

* Clarendon, ii. 600.

when this despised Lord, with whom most men refused to associate, was refused by the King himself ever to be admitted into his presence.

Such is the history of the forged letter of Lord Saville. Can we now doubt the real existence of the forged instrument, or the person who contrived it? Neither Clarendon nor Burnet had seen it, but their accounts in the main are confirmed by the Earl of Manchester, an undeniable witness of the transaction. Dr Lingard must allow us to conlcude that no incident in history, so purposely obscured and so secretly conducted, could rest on more substantial evidence.

CHAPTER XIII.

THE IRISH REBELLION.

PUBLIC men have been often placed in a position quite at variance with their real circumstances; thus he, who has been looked on as the favourite of fortune, at that moment was its victim. Charles the First, apparently, had even become popular in Scotland. The King had yielded to the Presbyterial nation, and had showered his regal favours on their great ones; he was, as the Scots described Charles the First, "the contented King of a contented people." Yet amidst this festival of state, the King would rather have entered into the house of mourning. His thoughts were occupied by two events equally painful — the Irish Rebellion, and the menaced Remonstrance of the Commons. Charles beheld himself the Monarch of three kingdoms alike engaged in revolution, or in rebellion, from very opposite

motives, and not always from his own mis-
government.

Before the King left Scotland, he had received the first intelligence of the memorable
Irish revolt; at the very moment he had con-
ciliated the jarring interests of that divided
land, on the same principle of his present proceedings with Scotland — by conceding to the
full, the requests of the Irish deputation.
These persons were hastening home in peace-
ful triumph only to be mortified by the artifice,
or the incapacity, of their governors ; and to
witness the greatest of national calamities, in a
land of blood.

The King had granted two bills, one for the
security of lands to their possessors, and the
other for renouncing all claims on the part of
the Crown. This happy settlement, which
would have " attached the whole population of
Ireland to the Royal interest," was prevented
by the extraordinary conduct of the two Presbyterian Lords Justices of Ireland ; the Lord-
Lieutenant, the Earl of Leicester, not having
yet left London. These Lords Justices are accused of being wholly devoted to the party in
the English House of Commons ; and it is
alleged that being aware that the passing of
these bills would have secured the King's po-

pularity, desperately disappointed the successful deputies and the whole body of Catholics
by proroguing the Parliament, a few days
before their return from the King at Edinburgh.*

Terror and amazement ran through the
nation. The history of the Irish massacre, as
this rebellion is emphatically called, has been

---

* Lingard, x. 161. Mr. Hallam inclines to think the
conduct of these Lords Justices is rather to be ascribed to the
weakness of their character. They may have been weak, and
yet criminal. They had been warned by Charles as early as in
March 1640-1, that there was a design of raising commotions
in Ireland, many Irish officers in foreign service, and others,
were passing over to Ireland, by intelligence which he had received from Spain : this appears by a letter many years after
discovered among the papers of Sir William Parsons, one of
these Lords Justices; yet the intimation led to no active
measures on their part.—Nalson, ii. 566. It is said 'that
this Irish Rebellion was at first but a spark which might
have been put out. They appear to have zealously persecuted the Romanists; Parsons, it is said, had declared, that
" within a twelvemonth no Catholic should be seen in Ireland."—Nalson, ii. 567. Strange is the history of religious
parties! Scotland had risen, and the English Parliament
adopted their cause against Charles's attempt to force Episcopacy on a Presbyterian land; and yet this very Parliament were intent on changing a land of Romanists to a land
of Protestants. The King, who was called a tyrant, yielded ;
the Parliament, who were advocating the cause of freedom,
would not even allow a toleration !

officially drawn up by Sir John Temple, a
Privy Counsellor; its pathetic picture may be
viewed in Hume; its frightful details in Macaulay. So shocking is the representation to a
delicate mind, that the female historian warns
her readers that should they dwell on it, their
imagination would be impressed by images of
the most horrid kind. At present more than
one terrific cause was at work; their faith had
combined with their vengeance. A religion
which has shown itself too often sanguinary,
opened Heaven for them, in covering themselves with the blood of their companions; and
the eternal hatred which the conquered had
vowed to their conquerors, took no note of
the unnumbered slaughters of the helpless and
the innocent. The very animals in the field
were deemed heretical, and lay in heaps, un-
touched even by robbers! Some fugitives,
famished and crazed, having witnessed so many
inventive cruelties, declared on their oaths that
the ghosts of the murdered had flitted before
their eyes! They deposed to scenes and
listened to cries, which could only have been
the apparitions of their own terrified reveries.
An involuntary shudder even now disturbs us
in the repulsive minuteness of such detestable
scenes. What seems most incredible in the

history of these Sicilian vespers, repeated in
Ireland, is its authenticity. The Eastern tale
of the slaughter of the Innocents is less strange;
the dragonades of the French Huguenots were
more humane ; and the massacre of St. Bar-
tholomew seems but a single scene of this
direful tragedy.

To us who only read the history of this
massacre with the indignant emotions of out-
raged humanity, it is curious to observe, how
coolly the politicians of both parties contemplated this national calamity. The Royalist,
Sir Philip Warwick, tells us that " the Parliament, it was observed, were not displeased ;"
and the Commonwealth-man, General Ludlow,
assures us, that " the news of the Rebellion, as
I have heard from persons of undoubted credit,
was not displeasing to the King." They both
use identical words, though they could not
have had any knowledge of each other.
Hardened politicians ! who thus could coldly
calculate the political consequences of such
revolting barbarities, and cast aside the sympathy they owed to a whole people of suf-
ferers, for the malignant delight of a party-
reproach !

A successful rebellion is contagious. The
revolt in Scotland had been servilely copied by

their English allies. Now Popery claimed her freedom as well as Presbyterianism. But if the sons of Knox had offered the Romanist the bewitching form of triumphant revolution, the rude democracy of the Kirk seemed contemptible to the passive obedience of the Mass-Priest. Unhappily for Charles, the Irish in arming against a Puritanical Parliament, offered him their loyalty in the shape of rebellion. They pretended to hold a commission from the King, and proclaimed themselves to be the Queen's army. The situation of Charles was as critical as it was perplexing. He could neither countenance the loyalty, nor punish the rebellion of the Irish. Should he temporise with those who had risen in his name, it would be a confirmation of the malicious insinuation of the Commons, that the King himself had encouraged the Revolters; and when he offered himself, and his life, as he did, to suppress this unnatural rebellion, he excited the perturbed jealousies of the prevalent party in the Commons; for of all events which they most dreaded, was that of seeing the King at the head of an army.

Deprived of the power of Government, amidst this conflict of feelings and of interests, Charles wrote to the Parliament that to them

" He committed the care of Ireland." Charles little suspected that in such few words, he was delivering a deed of gift of his last remaining realm.

The deeper heads of the party in the Commons grasped at their prey with avidity—but the prey was not Ireland—it was the King himself! Affecting to interpret a casual expression in an unlimited sense, they at once assumed the entire management of the war, independently of the King. "In this manner," writes Mrs. Macaulay with an air of triumph, "they at once disarmed the Crown of that part of the executive power, which on this occasion had been universally apprehended." The cunning and the quibble, are at least equal to the wisdom and the candour. It is mortifying to detect Legislators and Patriots, congratulating themselves on a flaw in the indictment, and catching at subterfuges which might delight a senate of petty lawyers. Even the panegyrical historian of their deeds, was not insensible to this artful interpretation, and this act of violated justice; for she apologizes for their conduct, assuring us, that they were only enabled to adopt this false interpretation by " the affections and opinion of the public." * But

* Macaulay, iii. 93.

" the Public" is a peculiar phrase in our political history, where we shall usually find that there are at least two Publics.

The conduct of the Commons is very remarkable. They took on themselves the management of a war, but studiously neglected it.

It seemed unaccountable how they, who to the world seemed shaken by so many panics at Popish plots, now that a whole land had proclaimed their Papistry, and a people of Protestants were cast into their last extremity, should remain unmoved, and delay any efficient measures, while they were protracting the daily miseries of devoted Ireland. The King reproached the Parliament for their dilatory conduct, and offered to hasten in person to quell this sanguinary rebellion. " It was a business," observed the King, " which one man might conclude better than four hundred." But they would not trust the King even with an army of Covenanters, for at Edinburgh, their Committee, who served as the Parliamentary spies over the King, had advised, that is, we presume, the only head among the party, Hampden had advised, that " if the Parliament agreed to this, the King would insist on the command." Ten thousand Scots would have marched at a day's notice, but the Commons in London refrained

from voting to send a Scottish army till Charles
was secured at Whitehall.

Meanwhile every day brought more dismal
intelligence, and miserable men who authenticated the worst.   In vain the Lords and gentlemen of Ireland, despoiled of their lands, petitioned—in vain the ruined merchants supplicated—in vain the last of an extirpated race
invoked their vengeance.   In vain they urged
that a three hours' sail would relieve the nation, for no longer was required for a Scottish
army to land in Ireland.

The patriotism of the stoical Commons lay
not towards a land of misery; all their sympathies were absorbed in their deep councils, to
confirm their past and to secure their future
labours.   Secretary Nicholas, writing to the
King, observed that " the preparations for Ireland go on but slowly, and may come too late
to prevent great mischief, notwithstanding the
care of our Parliament."*   The Secretary was
judging by the exterior appearance of the language of the members and the votes of the
House; he discovered no deficient indignation
in the one, nor resolutions in the other, nor any
languor in their preparations, but he probably

* Evelyn, ii. Correspondence

wondered at the result — for Ireland was not relieved !

Hume acutely observes of the Commons on this occasion, that " their votes breathed nothing but death and destruction to the Irish rebels; but no forces were sent, and little money was remitted."

The truth is, that the Commons did not consider that the Irish rebellion was quite inopportune, at a moment when the King seemed to have become popular; his concessions in Scotland had satisfied that nation, and all those he had made in England, had satisfied the moderate among the English, and the Commons now discovered that their friends were falling off. At this critical moment this new rebellion served as a pretext to aggrandise their own influence by throwing into their hands an universal patronage; forces were raised which furnished them with an army of their own; the royal depots were emptied of their arms, which at once strengthened their hands, and weakened the King's. Monies were levied, which were disposed of, for their own particular purposes. In all this bustle, there was no haste to relieve Ireland !

Some among the Commons felt a secret pleasure in viewing the King entangled in new and more intricate difficulties. Had this insurrection not broken out, Charles would have returned in peace from Scotland. Some painful jealousies, too, the party in the English Commons, had experienced in the prodigal caresses which had mutually passed between Charles and his Scottish subjects. Their Committee of espionage must have been startled at the overflowings of the old soldier Lesley, now the Earl of Leven, on his knees consecrating. his oath—with so many others of the Covenant, who in their holiday of honours had sang such courtly hosannas. They were somewhat fearful that even their " dear brethren" were no longer to be rebels.

The Irish rebellion by the appearance it assumed, and by the imposture of a. Royal commission, which the rebels asserted that they held,* was not unfavourable to re-excite the populace, or "the Public," against the unfortunate Monarch. The Commons appealing to the declaration of the Irish, boldly ascribed the rebellion to the evil councils of the King, and even to a less pardonable cause, for they insinuated that Charles himself was the concealed

---

* Sir Phelim O'Neale, the head of these Insurgents, it was afterwards discovered, had torn off the great seal from some deed, and affixed it to a pretended Commission.

instigator of this unnatural rebellion. They
insolently menaced that if he chose not Ministers in whom they could confide—and where
those Ministers were to be found was obvious
—the Parliament would hold themselves absolved from granting any aid to avert the destruction of Ireland.*

Charles was returning from Scotland with
melancholy forebodings; perhaps these were
somewhat diverted by the assurance of a loyal
reception by several bodies of gentlemen in the
country who were earnest to meet the King
on his way. It is certain that many independent men sympathised with the difficulties by
which the King was surrounded, after he had
concurred in so many popular measures. At

---

* This undisguised avowal, at the time it was made was
checked by the more prudent, or the more moderate Members. It does not appear in the Parliamentary history, but
it was conveyed to the King by his faithful Secretary. Evelyn, ii. 62. Correspondence. It was evidently thrown out at
a moment when even politicians, in their hearts, expose
nakedly some of their arrière pensées, by one who was familiar with the design of the party, which was to make the
King wholly dependent on themselves. And this is amply
confirmed by their subsequent conduct in this affair of Ireland. It was about this time that a Member talked of de-
posing Princes, but that was premature, by some years, so
this prophetic seer was sent to the Tower. Nalson, ii. 714.

no period since his reign, was public opinion among honourable men so strongly disposed to protect the Royal honour. Among these now were also the citizens of London; a circumstance to which Charles had been little accustomed.

It would seem that the loyalty of the City depends on that of the Lord Mayor. Gournay, the present Chief Magistrate, in his zeal had resolved on a public reception of the King on his return, and to entertain the Sovereign at Guildhall. The Lord Mayor consulted Secretary Nicholas to learn the day of his Majesty's arrival. The Secretary pressed on the King its policy, and as Charles too much avoided these popular representations, and was not over-gracious in his manners, the honest Secretary found it advisable to insinuate some pretty forcible hints. " I humbly conceive it would not be amiss to your Majesty, in these times, to accept graciously the affections of your subjects in that kind, and to speak a few good words to them, which will gain their affections, especially of the vulgar, more than any thing that hath been done for them this Parliament." The King was docile to the sage council. But the zeal of the Lord Mayor exasperated the party in the Commons. Was their elaborate

Remonstrance which would render the King quite odious to the people, and which had been so long hatching, and was now quite ready, to be preceded by the most popular testimony of the loyalty of their City of London? They would have intimidated the Chief Magistrate, but Gournay was equally indignant and intrepid; a character which his subsequent conduct to the last maintained. He was indeed never forgiven. They afterwards discharged him from his Mayoralty and lodged him in the Tower, putting the gold chain round the neck of their faithful creature Isaac Pennington.

In this reign of stormy politics so trivial an incident as the banquet of a Lord Mayor has become a subject which requires even a critical investigation.

I will not detain the reader among the pomps and solemnities of the morning procession. On the King's entrance at Moorgate he stopped his carriage by the side of a splendid tent, where he was received by the Lord Mayor and addressed by the Recorder, to which having graciously replied, the King left his coach, and mounted his horse. As he passed, everywhere the streets resounded with the cries of " Long live King Charles!" He viewed every house adorned with tapestries. He was accompanied

by a cavalcade of five hundred citizens, vying
in the richness of their dresses. Not a voice
murmured, not a hand was lifted in scorn.
Monarchs may well be excused if they deceive
themselves, when a whole people create the
illusion. The King was feasted with unusual
civic magnificence.* Charles had graciously
delivered " a few good words," and it was remarked that he took his hat off more frequently than he was accustomed to do. It was
late in November, and " the days being short,"
the Royal carriages drew up at four o'clock,
and the whole *cortège* returned from the city
dinner ; the King, however, mounted his horse.
All the attendants carried torches, and " the
night seemed to be turned into day." " The
noise of trumpets which at their different stations in the morning had announced the approach of the King, was now changed for
softer sackbuts, and dispersed bands of musi-
cians were playing their voluntaries. On passing St. Paul's, the choir, standing in their sur-
plices in the porch, chaunted an anthem, which

---

* Nalson has devoted six folio pages to a minute description of this great city feast and grand ceremonial. Some of
the details might amuse those who are more experienced
than myself in Lord Mayor's dinners on such Royal visits.
Nalson, ii. 677.

extremely delighted the musical Charles, who stopped till its close. In taking leave of the Lord Mayor, whom with his son-in-law Charles had knighted, and who had reconducted the King to his palace, warm was the Royal gratitude, when breaking from the accustomed reserve of his manners, Charles embraced the Lord Mayor, charging him in his name, to return the Royal thanks to the whole city. The populace, excepting some, perhaps, whose steps had been detained at the great conduits of Cornhill, Cheapside, and Fleet Street, which were " running with claret wine," had gone on in their attendance on the King to Whitehall ; that scene of their recent tumults, and now of their hailing acclamations !

The King, in addressing Parliament, laid great stress on this public testimony of loyalty ; and though some may lowly rate a king's speech in Parliament, yet it is probable that its sincerity was the consequence of those grateful emotions which had been so long estranged from his breast. " I cannot but remember, to my great comfort," said Charles, " the joyful reception I had now at my entry into London. I bring as perfect and true affection to my people as ever Prince did, or as good subjects can possibly desire—I will yet grant what else can be justly desired, for satisfaction in point of liberty."

" And yet within a month, a little month,"

shall the King, in personal danger, become a fugitive from his palace to escape from those hailing citizens, in a state of insurrection. There are events incalculable by any moral arithmetic; and it is not strange that the most sagacious have not always foreseen approximating events, which at the distance we view them, appear more closely connected together than they were to a contemporary observer.

The public reception of the King was but an evanescent scene of popularity, and the adversaries of Charles have represented it as a mere state-trick. The sudden contrast which soon followed makes the suggestion plausible, but yet it was not so! The great subsequent change in the conduct of the citizens was the consequence of that hazarded act of Charles, when he went down to arrest the five Members in their House.

On the present occasion there required no Court influence, since the loyalty of a courageous Lord Mayor, with his friends, and the state of public feeling at that moment, were

abundantly sufficient to account for this public reception. But as this notorious testimony
of civic loyalty has always mortified a certain
party, and seems to call in question their general representation of affairs, Mrs. Macaulay observes that " The Queen had taken a great deal
of pains that the King should be received with
a more than ordinary magnificence on purpose
to mortify the Parliament."* " The great deal
of pains taken," however, seems to have been
entirely with those who would have put aside
the reception altogether. It is curious to observe on this ticklish affair, of the public loyal
reception of Charles the First, how it sharpens
the anger of our Republican lady. She who
on certain occasions appeals to " the disposition
of the public," and has said, alluding to the
tumults, that " the popular leaders had recourse to the spirit without doors to get the
better of the opposition they found within,"†
now irreverently scolds at " the majesty of the

---

* It is fair to observe that Madame de Motteville says,
" The Queen endeavoured to make the King all the friends
she could. She brought over the Mayor of the city of London." i. 212. I have only the English translation of her
Memoirs, and we cannot lay much stress on this vague
style. We have other and better evidence on this head.

† Macaulay, iii. 118.

people." She concludes, and not untruly, that
" the sottish multitude are influenced by a
variety of state-tricks." As Gournay, in the
language of Mrs. Macaulay, was " a bigoted
Royalist," and as his loyalty, at least was courageous, there required no Court influence nor
the intrigues of Henrietta, with this Lord
Mayor, to account for his conduct. In fact,
this piece of diplomacy ascribed to the Queen,
she was in no condition at that moment to have
ventured on. Abandoned in her palace, watched by a hundred eyes, and often terrified by
the artful menaces of Parliament, the Queen
could hardly have had either influence or intercourse with the Lord Mayor. And indeed
in respect to the Queen's interference with that
functionary, the recent publication of Secretary
Nicholas's Correspondence with the King will
set that tale at rest. Here we discover Gournay's application, backed by the recommenda-
tions of the honest Secretary.*

---

* I give the passage to show how facts, however unau-
thorised, pass current in party histories ; where one liar
makes many. " If your Majesty please to give leave to my
Lord Mayor and the citizens here, to wait on you into this
town, I beseech your Majesty to command that timely notice may be given of the day, that they may provide for it,
for the best of the citizens express a great desire to show

The King had been well informed of the activity of the party in the Commons during his absence; of their private juntos, as well as their more open courses. His concessions, and his promptness to redress all grievances, had served them but for triumphs, which they counted up only to multiply. Their diligent proceedings when the Houses were but thinly attended on some of the most important resolutions concerning both Church and State, were not the only causes of his uneasiness—there was something more latent, and because it was not yet brought into shape and light, but had long been mysteriously hatching in all the darkness of secrecy and intrigue, hung like a night-mare in the Royal slumbers.

During Charles's stay in Scotland, his faithful Secretary was furnishing the most alarming intelligence of " a Declaration," which afterwards appeared as the famous " Remonstrance." He was troubled to think what would be the issue of it, for he saw at once through the whole mischievous design, sagaciously observing, that " if there had been in this nothing but an intention to have justified the proceedings of Parliament, they would not have begun so

their affection, which I humbly conceive will not be convenient to decline." Evelyn, ii. 60. Correspondence.

high as the third year of your Majesty's reign
to the present." The Secretary then did not
know that they began much earlier, from the
day Charles ascended the throne. These communications, however alarming, were not however so novel to the King as the Secretary
imagined. Ere Charles's departure from England he had received an intimation from a
quarter whose intelligence in secret affairs was
well known to him.

Before Charles went into Scotland he had
been warned by his old and active intriguer,
Bishop Williams, of the pending grievance;
for it must be confessed, that the King had his
grievances, as well as the people. Williams
had been diving into the secrets of these masters of revolution. He had turned short on
them; and they who had been the occasion of
liberating him from the Tower, naturally counting on the vindictive spirit of an aggrieved
man, to join with them, now repented evoking
a spirit of darkness who startled them, and
whom they knew not how to lay. " I wish
we were well rid of him!" exclaimed one of
the party. The future Archbishop, on his side,
was himself in terror, and had anticipated the
pending stroke of late repeatedly aimed at
Episcopacy itself. The policy of Williams

had ever been the most emollient; and he had concluded, whether judging from himself, or from some in the ranks of public spirits, that every patriot had his price; and that a place, provided it did not disappoint the expectant, was a bed of roses for the most restless. He had all along been desirous of postponing the King's journey to Scotland, for another season. I give his conversation with Charles as characteristic of this political character.

"The Scots," said Williams, "are sear boughs, not to be bent. Keep near to the Parliament, all the work is within these walls; win them man by man, inch by inch. Sir! I wish it were not true what I shall tell you. Some of the Commons are preparing a Declaration to make the actions of your Government odious. If you gallop to Scotland, they will post as fast, to draw up this biting Remonstrance. Stir not till you have instigated the grand contrivers with some preferments."

"But is this credible?" said the King.

"Judge you of that, Sir," replied Williams, "when a servant of Pym's, in whose master's house all this is moulded, came to me, to know in what terms I was contented to have mine own case in Star Chamber exhibited among other irregularities. And I had much ado to

keep my name, and what concerns me, out of
these articles; but I obtained that of the fellow,
and a promise to do me more service, to know
all they have in contrivance, with a few sweet-
breads that I gave him out of my purse."*

Such was the clear warning which Williams
had given Charles. In this curious conversation, we detect not only the place where this
memorable Edict of the party was hatched, but
we are also let into the grand mystery of its
incubation.

But we must now take a view of the proceedings of the Commons, before we arrive at
the history of the famous Remonstrance; it is
the symphony before the opera.

* We learn from a manuscript note of Sir Ralph Varney's,
to which Mr. Hallam refers, that " the Remonstrance" was
projected in August before the King's journey, but was then
considered as unnecessary, for the King was rapidly conceding their demands. However, it remained à favourite
object with the Remonstrants, who were only waiting for an
opportunity to revive it.

CHAPTER XIV.

THE COMMONS PERSIST IN NOT RELIEVING IRELAND.

AT this critical moment when Ireland was threatened by universal desolation, the Commons opened an interminable discussion with the Lords; interminable were it to have depended on arguments. The Upper House had of late become refractory; it became necessary to hold up a sharper rod, and the Commons now assumed a dictatorial tone, which must have shaken the falling aristocracy.

In bringing in a bill for pressing, they prefixed a preamble which declared this Royal prerogative to be illegal. This was at least a debateable point. The King asserted " his ancient and undoubted privilege," as practised by his Royal predecessors. It was, indeed, a grievance to the subject, and liable to great abuse. When the Crown was desirous of

relieving itself of any obnoxious member in
the House, or any other person in any rank of
life, the King had the power of pressing—that
is, of appointing them to do some public service at their charge; and in some cases, as in
a time of war, they might be sent out of the
kingdom to the army.* The Commons were
secure of the popularity of their protest, and
the King was as tenacious of his ancient rights.
.It was one of the great misfortunes of Charles
the First, that while the Commons were pursuing the most popular objects, they appeared
to Charles only intent, by their encroachments,
on reducing the Monarchy. to the state of a
Venetian Doge. . To the Lords it seemed, that
under the cloak of the urgent necessities of the
state, the Commons: were carrying a great
party-measure. . The Lords already had been
thrown into some alarm for their own privileges. The style of the Commons was autho-
ritative, and soon became menacing. It was
to be a struggle between the two Houses. .

The Lords objected to the preamble, which,
to say the least, was ill-timed; and the bill
could not pass with it, without a deliberation
and a discussion, which would impede the
momentous interests at stake. They offered

* I have shown some cases in Curiosities of Literature.

to pass the bill, laying aside for the present the preamble. The Commons adhered to the preamble. Neither House would yield — and Ireland was not relieved!

Pym, at the head of a Committee, told the Lords, that the Commons, being the representative body of the whole kingdom, and their Lordships being but as particular persons, and coming to Parliament in a particular capacity, that if they shall not be pleased to consent to the passing of those acts and others, that this House together with such of the Lords that are more sensible of the safety of the kingdom may join together.*

When we combine this menace, with what we shall find Hampden afterwards declared on passing the Remonstrance, we discover, that at this period the project of annihilating the House of Lords was now matured. The Hierarchy was to be rooted up; but the Peers were in the branches. All this was proceeding, day after day, and Ireland was not relieved!

Charles, as he had formerly done in the business of Strafford, imagined that he should reconcile the parties by his fatal interposition; and thus dispatch the more urgent business of

* Nalson, ii. 712.

Ireland. The King came down to the House and offered to pass the bill with a *salvo jure*, for King and people,* leaving the discussion to a fitter time.

This interference of the King on a bill which was still in debate with the two Houses, and particularly an unhappy allusion, that the King was " little beholding to him whoever at this time began this dispute," was declared to have broken into the fundamental privileges of Parliament. Both Houses alike caught fire. Those Peers, who were the friends of the Commons, did not fail to aggravate this violation of the Constitution. The Commons desired that a humble petition should be delivered to the King, that " he should take notice that the privilege of Parliament was broken, and to desire him (the King) that it may not be done so any more hereafter." The Lords agreed to this stern " humbleness."—And the King made an ample apology, simply assuring both Houses that " he had not the least thoughts of break-

* Mr. Brodie seems to limit the *salvo jure* Charles proposed, as if merely for the preservation of his own right— but this necessarily included that of the people's claim for exemption. He says " this usurped power had already been pronounced illegal." By whom? As yet only by the Commons themselves. It was a subject for future discussion.— Brodie, iii. 243.

ing the privilege of Parliament, which he would protect and support."

What must the Commons have now conceived of their own prevalent power, when, at the same time, they witnessed the King — the Bishops—and the Peers, all apologizing and all equally submissive!

While both Houses were occupied in the common cause of their privileges, they had proceeded with unanimity; but when the Commons pressed for their preamble, the struggle was renewed, till the Lords refused to join in some petitions of the Commons. All this while Ireland remained unrelieved!

The mobs again were called out. " No Bishops!" was the watchword, and they were nearly anticipating another cry, " No King!" for in passing Whitehall, they said " They would have no porter's lodge, but would speak to the King themselves without control, and at their discretion." The Commons would have three fast-days appointed, and one monthly—for Ireland. No other relief was yet held out, to use the expression in one of their own " Petitions," for " a land weltering in blood."

The Lords still eluding the preamble, proposed that ten thousand English should join the same number of Scots. And the King

offered to raise the men if the House undertook
to pay them.   The Commons now resented
the proposal of the Lords as an improper interference of the Upper House.   One of the answers of the Commons to the Lords is remarkable for its terse insolence.

"They were not used to be capitulated
withal.   Their actions are free as well without
conditions as capitulations ; and the House of
Commons desire it may be so no more.   Further they desire that their. Lordships would
pass the Bill for pressing, in regard they conceive that the ten thousand English cannot go,
unless that is done."*

In vain the King, again and again, urged
them to put an end to the miseries of Ireland,
while the rebels were encouraged in their barbarities by the slowness of the succours which
they had voted, but never sent.   The Commons, on their side, again and again, pressed
the Lords to pass the Bill, with the preamble—
without which Ireland would not be saved.
They noticed the King's offer to furnish the
ten thousand men, in the most extraordinary
way imaginable—for a rumour spread that the
King was coming down with his Papists to cut

---

* The " Smart answer of the Commons" to two propositions
of the Lords, is given in Nalson's Collections, ii. 771.

the throats of the good citizens of London, and fire the City!

Thus the Commons persevered in imputing the loss of Ireland to the obstinacy of the Lords. At length they sullenly ordered their Committee on Irish affairs to meet no more!

Such was the conduct of the Commons on this occasion, which requires to be explained. Even by the confession of their ardent eulogist Mrs. Macaulay, this endless discussion occasioned a fatal pause in the military preparations.* With all the artifice of a partisan, that lady lays the whole weight of her censure on the heads of the Lords : them only she accuses of the guilt of this unpardonable remissness in the suppression of this unnatural rebellion. But in truth, all its criminality originated with the Commons.

For an Englishman nothing is more instructive in his national history than a calm scrutiny into the shiftings of partisans when they are fixed in the torture of an inextricable dilemma. Mr. Brodie affords me a remarkable instance. The Scottish Advocate will not allow his clients, the Commons, should yield a point. He declares, "Had the Commons halted now, they must have been held to recognize it"— the privilege of

* Macaulay, iii, 111.

pressing —" They had therefore no alternative now." This representation is incorrect, since the *salvo jure* left the discussion open at any future day. Mr. Brodie says the King insisted not to pass the Bill without " a salvo jure, or preservation of *his right.*" This seems to me unfairly given; it seems to restrict the benefit of the *salvo jure* merely to the King; but in the King's speech it is positively declared thus, " To avoid farther debate at this time, I offer that the Bill may pass with a *salvo jure both for King and People.*"* Probably aware of the futility of this argument, Mr. Brodie suddenly mystifies the simple reader by a disclosure of certain secret motives in these transactions, on both sides, " Considering what had occurred on former occasions," continues Mr. Brodie, " it is scarcely to be imagined that this Prince had profited so little by experience, as not to anticipate the result of this illegal interference with a Bill depending before both Houses." Mr. Brodie has justly expressed his surprise that Charles gained little from experience — but his wide inference is quite his own. " And *therefore we may conclude* that he was actuated by deeper motives than a mere desire to have his assumed right preserved." He reveals " the deeper motives,"

* Rushworth, iv. 457.

—" When the King proposed, as a compromise, to raise ten thousand volunteers, provided the House would support them, and as that would have evaded what the Commons," as Mr. Brodie assures us, " had *resolved* upon,"— namely the appointment of the officers —" *it is likely* to have been one view which influenced him and his secret advisers from the beginning." Thus it appears by Mr. Brodie that the real contest was " the appointment of the officers," and farther that the Commons had resolved on this, without communicating with the King or the Lords !

The object is changed : it was not for " the preamble," but " the officers," which the Commons were disputing : they were clamouring for one thing but intended another. Had the King and the Lords been as much in the secret as Mr. Brodie, it would have fully warranted their firm resistance. But it is clear that had the Commons first succeeded in passing their " Preamble " against Pressing—it could have had no connexion with " the appointment of the officers," and " therefore," to adopt Mr. Brodie's hypothetical style, " it is likely," that they had no such intention in the origin of their discussion.*

* Brodie, iii. 244.

The country was thrown into jeopardy by this party-question raised by the leaders in the Commons. One of the most vituperative calumniators of the King, in a rare moment of his dispassionate politics, has acknowledged that on this occasion " The Parliament *connived* at the Irish rebellion, in order to charge King Charles with fomenting it."*

Can we now refuse to agree in one opinion, that true patriotism, undegraded by criminal intrigue, would have instantly relieved Ireland, and left " the Preamble " as a grievance to be resumed, as the King had said, " at a fitter time ?" The ruling-party in the Commons on so many occasions, were alert at similar contrivances; and by practising more artifices than accord with the dignity of patriotism, have stamped their character, too often, with the subtilty and cunning of Faction.

* Lord Orford, Memoires, i. 150. 4°.

CHAPTER XV.

THE GRAND REMONSTRANCE.

THERE is great obscurity among our historians respecting the origin of this memorable
and elaborate party-production. It is evident,
that it could not have been drawn up in haste,
for a temporary purpose; for in fact it is an
historical memoir of all the infelicities of the
King's reign, with a very cautious omission
that all the capital grievances there commemo-
rated had no longer any existence.

The secret history of this anti-monarchial
attack, for such it is, and such were now a
rising party in the House; the persons who
framed it; the Councils which must have been
held on it; the mode of their inquiries after
some of " the grievances;" and the time occupied in its composition, for we find that it was
long in preparation, and even laid aside in suspense, would all be matter of deep interest in

the history of the artifices of a subtile party.
We are at present * deprived of any memoirs
of these persons; they appear not to have cbro-
nicled their acts of patriotism. We can only
get glimpses of them as in a dark chamber,
without light enough to see their faces, but,
not without evidence which yields us more
than suspicions of the persons themselves. The
reader has already heard some important intelligence from that great revealer of political
events, Bishop Williams, and from the watchfulness of the vigilant Secretary Nicholas.

The Remonstrance at length was brought
into the House. The party was sanguine.
They had numbered their votes, and moreover
had practised a trick on those Members who
disliked the violence, and deemed this act to
be uncalled for at a moment when the Sovereign had shown by so many acts of his own,
and by a recent change of councils, that wearied by opposition, he now was only seeking
for public tranquillity. The trick practised
was this. They assured these moderate men
that the intention of this Remonstrance was
purely prudential; it was to mortify the Court,
and nothing more! The Remonstrance, after
having been read, would remain in the hands

* I say at present, for Lord Nugent has long announced a
Life of the Patriot Hampden.

of the clerk and never afterwards be called for.
When it was brought forward, to give it the
appearance of a matter of little moment, the
morning was suffered to elapse on ordinary
business, and the Remonstrance was produced
late. They overshot their mark; the very
lateness of the hour was alleged as a reason to
postpone entering on the debate, for to the
surprise of one who afterwards rose to be the
most eminent person in the nation, and also of
some of the authors, it now appeared that the
Remonstrance was to be submitted to a very
strong opposition.

At nine the next morning the debate opened, and several hours past midnight it fiercely
raged, with every dread of personal violence
among the Members.* It was a full House,
and was only carried by the feeble majority of

---

* As a curious instance how difficult it is sometimes to
ascertain the plainest matter of fact, from even those who
were present, Rushworth says, the Debate lasted from three
in the afternoon till three in the morning : Sir Philip Warwick says it was three in the morning when the Remonstrance passed. Whitelocke differs from both, prolonging
it from three in the afternoon till ten the next morning. It
is certain that the House was debating hard at midnight, but
began earlier than Rushworth mentions; for Secretary Nicholas writing to the King, says, " The Commons have been
in debate about their Declaration since twelve at noon, and
are at it still, it being now near twelve at midnight."

eleven; Clarendon says only by nine. We
find some notice of the calmness and adroitness
of Hampden, during this disorderly debate.
When the Remonstrance had been carried, he
moved for the printing, that it might be dispersed among the people. According to constitutional usage it should first have been communicated to the Lords, and afterwards presented to the King. But this appeal to the
people against the Sovereign, as it avowedly
was, he observed run in the sole name of the
Commons — an all-sufficient authority! Already this great man was meditating that separation from the Lords, which in due time occurred. This had been indicated by several
signal unparliamentary courses, for the House
of Lords had of late been refractory.* Even
Hampden failed in the division for printing, on
the first night; but it was a favourite measure,
and his cool and determined diligence renewed
the motion three weeks after, when the printing was carried by a considerable majority. So
out-wearied, or so supine were the Royalists,
though the King was excessively anxious that
this cruel record of his disturbed reign, reflect-
ing such an aggravated picture of tyranny and
himself the tyrant, should not be sent forth

* Macaulay, iii. 99.

among the people, unaccompanied by his defence, or his apology. Thus it happened that
when the King desired that they would not
print the Remonstrance till they had his answer, Charles discovered that it had already
been dispersed.

This edict of Revolution had been nearly
rejected, and unquestionably it would have
been thrown out, had it not been for an accident to which it would seem our Parliaments
are liable. The length of the Debate, as much
as its vehemence, exhausted the physical condition of the elder Members; many through
utter faintness had been compelled to retire,
and honest Sir Benjamin Rudyard not unaptly
compared the passing of the Remonstrance to
the verdict of a starved Jury. Clarendon complains on the present occasion, that while the
party themselves had secured the presence of
all their friends, the hour of the night had
driven home the aged and the infirm, who
could no longer await the division. Mr. Hallam has shrewdly remarked on Clarendon's
complaint of the friends of established authority, that " sluggish, lukewarm and thought-
less tempers, must always exist, and that such
will always belong to their side." A simple,
but important truth! and since the wisdom,

or the virtue, of a free people, must often depend on the subtraction or the multiplication
of voices, it is a curious fact in the history
of an English Parliament, that some of the
most eventful changes in our Constitution, have
been carried by the feeble majorities of two or
three votes; and that the majority and mino-
rity on the same question, at different periods,
have changed sides.* Thus it happens that
the age and the health of the Members become
a material circumstance in the highest concerns
of the nation, and nothing seems more desirable than that even an absent Member should
not be deprived of his vote, provided he

* The great points of the National Religion, under Elizabeth, were carried by six, and some say by a single vote; the
Hanover Succession was voted in by a single vote! Calamy,
ii. 2. It is certainly difficult to get at "the sense of the
Nation." On a question whether the Protestant religion
was in danger under Queen Anne's government, 256 saw no
danger, and only 208 remained in a state of alarm. Calamy's
Life, ii. 279. But it often happens that Parliaments correct their own errors; for we find questions which had been
frequently lost by the weakest minorities, afterwards carried
with little or no opposition. The *Nemine contradicente* is
always rare. How can we hope to reconcile so many opposed interests, to convince such different sizes of understandings, and conciliate tempers which no art of man can
ever accord! In this imperfect state of human existence,
we can only trust to the *Ayes* and the *Noes!*

had been present at the debate. An artful party in that case, could not steal a majority from a thin House; and the robust, the diligent, or the juvenile, would possess no fractional advantage over the infirm or the supine, in that great sum of human wisdom which is to appear in the numerical force of a division of the House.

After the numerous concessions of the King, and the humiliated state to which the party had reduced the Sovereign, certain as they were that they could scarcely demand any thing short of the throne itself, which Charles would now have denied, what motive induced this ungenerous Remonstrance of grievances redressed; of painful reminiscences; of errors chastened, and of passions subdued? Mrs. Macaulay tells us that " this Remonstrance was looked on by the opposers of the Court as absolutely necessary to their farther curtailing the power of the Crown, which was essential to the preservation of those privileges the public had already obtained." Such is the diplomacy of revolutionary democracy, and with the present party it was an irrefragable argument: we will not add with Hampden and Pym, though there is sufficient reason to suspect their designs; but the result proved that this party had decided on overturning the English Constitution by setting aside the Crown altogether.

But, in truth, this was not the first motive of the present personal persecution of the Monarch. " The Remonstrance" was an act of despair. Those who have written since the day of the female historian, with less passion and closer research, though not with more ability, nor even with any undue sympathy for this unfortunate Prince, have agreed that a far different motive than the one alleged in favour of the Commons, was the real inducement of this ungenerous attack.

That motive was a conviction that their own supporters had visibly diminished; some of the most eminent names in our history. had abandoned them; and their violent courses, contrasted with the sacrifices both of personal feelings and Royal authority, of which Charles, of late, had given so many striking evidences, had affected the moderate, and alarmed the honest. Nor was it unknown to themselves, that their clandestine practices in their inter-course with the Scots, of which Strafford had made some discoveries, and Montrose had re-vealed more, were rankling in the mind of Charles. The King had lately accepted for his advisers some from themselves — and under more prudent councils than Charles had been accustomed to, the heads of the party felt themselves in personal danger ; for the throne might appeal to the people, and patriots might be impeached, as well as ministers attainted. They dreaded nothing more than a popular King. An able judge of these times has observed, that " Their Remonstrance was put forward to stem the returning tide of loyalty which threatened to obstruct the farther progress of their endeavours."*

The Remonstrance was made such a point to be carried with the Commonwealth-men, who though not yet in their strength, were so sanguine, that Cromwell, as yet a new name in our history, expected that it would pass with little or no opposition ; and after it was carried with the greatest difficulty, and by means in which the parties were not fairly balanced, Cromwell swore, for at that time he was not half "·the Precisian" he turned out to be, that had it not passed, " some other honest men would the next day have sold their estates, and abandoned Old, for

* The same true statement occurs in Dr. Lingard, x. 157, and Mr. Hallam, i. 584. Let me add my feeble testimony.

New England." It is quite clear that the anti-monarchists considered this desperate act of theirs to be the test and ratification of their triumph; and some of those " other honest men," might probably have been found among the contrivers of this piece of political machinery.

CHAPTER XVI.

THE HISTORY OF LORD DIGBY.

THE King's new private advisers were eminent for their patriotism and their ability; the virtuous Lord Falkland, the active Sir John Colepepper, and the sagacious Mr. Hyde. Their names were even popular; they had gradually retreated from the Opposition, and now stood by the side of the King, without extinguishing their honourable principles. Another person, whose councils, on more than one remarkable occasion, Charles adopted, and who appears not to have closely connected himself with the other ministers, was the fascinating Lord Digby. The restless imagination and the reckless audacity of this extraordinary man, made him the most dangerous adviser of a Monarch, who himself was liable to do precipitate acts, repented often as soon as done, and whose temperament was the most sanguine that a Prince so unfortunate has ever shown.

George Digby, the second Earl of Bristol, should rather be the hero of a romance, than of history. He was himself so much a creature of imagination, that an imaginative writer would seem more happily to record the versatility of his fine genius, and the mutability of his condition, that we might contemplate through a wider scene so many glorious enterprises. Should a writer in some Biographical Romance—for the wantonness of our taste may find novelty even in such a Fiction—make this hero independent of circumstances, by adding only a termination to the adventures of Lord Digby, which he himself never could, this Romancer, in the simple narrative of his life, could place before us an extraordinary being—a perfection of human nature, the very idealism of Romance; and the truths he would have to tell, would at least equal the fictions he might invent.

Among other peculiarities in the fate of this nobleman was the place of his nativity. Born during his father's prolonged embassy at Madrid, he did not leave that Court before his thirteenth year; he spoke the Spanish language with native elegance, and stole some of

the fancies of its literature. This circumstance,
scarcely noticeable in another person, in this
Lord's romantic history becomes an incident,
as we shall see, in which the fortunes of Spain
might have revolved. He acquired the French
idiom with the same vernacular felicity to the
admiration of the Parisians, and this too might
have changed the face of the administration of
Mazarine! But in the language of the land of
his fathers, he was neither Spaniard nor Frenchman, but a Briton. Thus Lord Digby was
master of the languages of all the countries, in
every one of which he was to become so variable and so conspicuous an actor. His eloquence, elevated and forcible, has the elegance
which we imagine to be the acquisition of our
own days; his indignant spirit, bold in expression as in thought, sharpens his sarcasm, or
stings with scorn, often sliding into graceful
pleasantry. It is not Canning we are listening
to, it is Demosthenes! His patriotism seems
vital; for no man in Parliament, at that troubled and critical period, marked his way so
distinctly between the conflicting interests;
just to the Sovereign, he asserted the rights of
the nation. He maintained the necessity of
frequent Parliaments without calumniating the
Monarch, or flattering the people; he could

condemn Strafford without becoming an acces-
sory in that judicial murder; and we shall see
that he spoke in favour of the Test Act, though
he was himself a Roman Catholic.

Several years of studious residence at his
father's retreat, when the Earl, on his return
home, was banished to his seat, was a fortunate
circumstance in the life of the son.   Surrounded by the learned and the ingenious, who resorted to Sherborne Castle, Lord Digby became
equally learned and skilful in the prevalent
theology and philosophy of that day, and accomplished in elegant literature.   One of the
fruits of these early studies was his letters to
his relation, Sir Kenelm Digby, against the
Roman Catholic religion.   When he himself
chose to be converted, it is said, that he never
would take upon himself to answer himself,
except by a subtile apology, or rather a fanciful
distinction, which he made between the Church
of Rome and the Court of Rome.

Lord Digby's first step into life was strongly
indicative of its subsequent events.   His impetuous passions brought him into notice.   On
a casual visit to the Metropolis, from the quiet
shades of Sherborne, he engaged in an amour,
and a duel; both of which were none of his
inferior delights through life.   He chastised an

insolent rival, who was a favourite at Court,
and it was done in the purlieus of Whitehall.
His Lordship was committed to prison.   The
severity of this treatment, with the remembrance of his father's, now qualified him by his
discontent, to become an able coadjutor in the
patriotic band of Opposition.

A lovely countenance, and an innate gra-
ciousness of person, which instantaneously fas-
ciuated the beholder; a voice, whose tones
thrilled some obdurate beauty when on his
knees he would creep, with prodigal sensibility
bewailing his own want of merit; or which,
could throw an irresistible charm over his elo-
cution, insinuating his own confidence to the
listener; these were the favours of Nature;
and hers, too, that temperament which courts
danger, and the fearlessness which scorns death.
There was something chivalric in his courage,
quick to assert his honour by that sword which
had often signalized his glory in the field.   But
the utmost refinement of art had accomplished
a perfection beyond the reach of nature.   With
the emotions and the imagination of a poet, he
often penned views of things as if they had a
present existence, when, in truth, they were
only events which had not yet occurred; events
in which he was himself so often disappointed,

and had so often disappointed the unreasonable
hopes of others. Lord Digby was never wise
by experience and misfortune; for his working
genius was only invigorated by the failure of
one event to hasten on another; nothing seemed lost, when so much remained to be acquired;
and in his eager restlessness, the chace after the
new soon left the old out of sight. By the peculiarity of his situation, Europe was opened
for his career, and when he had wrestled with
his fate at home, he met her as a new man, in
France or in Spain.

But those who had prematurely blessed their
good fortune, for having met with a wonder of
human kind, and clung to him as their pride
and their hope, were left desperate at a single
mischance; these persons had set all their venture on his single card; they could not repair
their ruined fortunes by new resources; and
thus it happened, that those who had been his
greatest admirers were apt to become his
greatest enemies. None so easily won admiration and esteem, none more rapidly lost their
friends. It was remarkable, as Clarendon observes, that Lord Digby's keenest enemies had
been connected with him by the closest friendships. Digby accepted their esteem as a tribute to his own virtues and transcendent

genius, and as he deemed it, as an evidence of his own skill in the management of men; but their enmity he ascribed to their own inconstancy and their jealousy of his superiority. Lord Digby on all occasions was easily reconciled to himself.

Deliberation and resolution with him were hardly separable; and the boldness of his conceptions was only equalled by the promptness of their execution. Digby had that hardiness of mind which is called decision, and that hardihood of heart which is courage; qualities not always found in the same individual. It was his constitutional disposition to embrace the most hazardous exploits, not only from an impatience of repose, but from a notion that the audacity of the peril would cast a greater lustre on his genius and his actions. Cardinal de Retz has finely observed on this feeling, that "the greatest dangers have their charms if we perceive glory though in the prospect of ill-fortune; but middling dangers have only horrors when the loss of reputation is attached to the want of success." Digby's designs were sometimes so hazardous that he would reserve some important point to himself, and not confide it to those whom he appeared to be consulting; and this, as Clarendon observes, not

so much out of distrust that they would protest against it, for he was very indulgent to
himself in believing that what appeared reasonable to him would appear so to every one
else, but from a persuasion that by this concealment, he was keeping up his own reputation, by doing that which had been unthought
of by others. It was this unlucky temper in
his nature which produced so many inconveniences to the King and to himself — for
Charles the First was himself too prone to
sudden enterprizes, and a counsellor so daring
and so fanciful as Lord Digby was the un-
fittest minister for a Monarch who though
easily induced to adopt such rash attempts, as
quickly was startled at their difficulties.*

No man dared more than Lord Digby, and
few had greater abilities to support that daring
nature; but no man's life, who had entered
into such a variety of fortunes, was more un-
prosperous, nor were ever such great designs
left unaccomplished by the genius which had
conceived them. If Lord Digby possessed
some extraordinary qualities, he had also others
which were not so, and which worked themselves into his character only to weaken it;
like those roots and branches which grow out

* Clarendon, ii. 102.

of the fractures of battlements and turrets, and come at last to loosen, or undermine, even such solid strength.   It was his fatal infirmity, says Clarendon, that he too often thought difficult things very easy, and considered not possible consequences, when the proposition administered somewhat that was delightful to his fancy, by pursuing whereof he imagined he should reap more considerable glory to himself, of which he was immoderately ambitious. *

How did it happen that this extraordinary man so frequently acted in contradiction with himself? The character of Lord Digby has furnished some sparkling antitheses to the po-lished cynicism of the heartless Horace Wal-pole.   Insensible to the great passions of a mind of restless energies, but petulantly alive to the ridiculous, Lord Orford could easily de-tect the wanderings of too fanciful a genius, but he wanted the sympathy, or the philosophy, to penetrate to their causes.   This man, who in so many respects may be deemed great, had some fatal infirmities.   He would carry his dis-simulation perhaps beyond the point of honour. On the trial of Strafford he appears to have left his party from his indignation at their mea-sures; his eloquence on that occasion has reach-

* Clarendon, ii. 101.

ed posterity. But when with deep impreca-
tions he protested that he knew not of the abstraction of an important document, which was
long after discovered copied in his hand-writing
among the King's papers, whatever might be
the policy of his solemn oaths, and however desperate the predicament in which he stood, it
has involved his honour. In the proposed arrest of the six members, when his Lordship discovered how ill that measure was resented by
the House, he immediately rose and vehemently
spoke against it, declaring that it was absolutely
necessary that the King should disclose the
name of the proposer of that pernicious counsel; and whispering to Lord Kimbolton, who
was intended to have been one of those State
victims, that " He now clearly saw that the
King was hastening to his own ruin." Yet we
are told by Clarendon that it was he only who
had advised the measure, without any communication with the Ministers. Even on this
occasion his own character rose paramount.
For a moment he had been " the creeping
thing" which has left in the dust the trail of his
political cunning, but his dauntless spirit soared
as high as it had sunk, for Digby could not dissi-
mulate when his courage and intrepidity were

in question. He who had reprobated the dangerous and unsuccessful design, on the next day offered the King to hasten with a few gentlemen and seize on those very Members who had flown to the City, and bring them, dead or alive. Charles was startled at this greater peril than the memorable one of which he had already repented. In so chivalric a genius, one could hardly have suspected a selfish being, as we shall see his repeated deeds have stamped him to be; his feelings were concentrated within himself. Clarendon tells us that he was never known to have done a single generous action even to those who had claims for their disappointments in their unwary dependence on him. He sacrificed his protestant daughter to a Flemish Baron for his own convenience. He was habitually addicted to gaming and to his amours, and lived even at a time when in the receipt of a considerable revenue, a mean life, unworthy of his rank and name, and to his last days, after the Restoration, he seems to have been so maddened by personal distresses, that his violent behaviour to Charles the Second had nearly incurred an act of treason, and it banished him from the Court.

Such is the anatomy of the mind and genius

of this accomplished Statesman and warrior; his actions only exhibit him in the motion of life.

The Commons excepted Lord Digby from pardon, in a negotiation for a treaty of peace. They pursued Digby with the same violence they had hunted down Strafford, designing that another Minister should bleed on the scaffold. Digby flew to Holland. But he was not a man to repose in security at a moment of great agitation. We soon find him at York, where in a midnight interview with the King he arranged his return to Holland to procure arms. Taken, and brought into Hull, an adventure occurred which perfectly displays his versatile and dauntless character.

When Lord Digby found himself in the hands of the Parliamentarians, he appeared as a sea-sick Frenchman, and retiring into the hold of the vessel, he there concealed his papers; their detection would have been fatal. The Governor of Hull was Sir John Hotham, a man of a rough unfeeling nature, sordid, and influenced entirely by his meanest interests; moreover he was an enemy. Digby, in his usual way, deliberated, and resolved. The seasick Frenchman opened his part, by addressing

one of the sentinels in broken English, till by
his vivacious gesticulations, the man, at last,
was suffered to comprehend that the foreigner
had secrets of the King and Queen, which he
would communicate to the Governor.   Introduced to Sir John, the disguised Digby took
him aside, asking in good English, " Whether
he knew him ?"   Surprised, Hotham sternly
answered " No !"   " Then," resumed Lord
Digby, " I shall try whether I know Sir John
Hotham, and whether he be in truth, the same
man of honour I have always taken him to
be."   Digby revealed himself, and in his per-
suasive manner left to Sir John the alternative,
of an ignoble deliverance of him to his implacable enemies.   Hotham was mastered by
the greatness of mind of Lord Digby, and so
touched by the high compliment to his own
honour, that the stern and covetous man, who
had now in his hand whatever his interest, or
ambition, could desire for their ends, spontane-
ously declared that such a noble confidence
should not be deceived.   The only difficulty
between the two enemies, now was to concert
the means of the escape of the other; it was
considered to be the safest that the Frenchman should be openly sent to York, with a

promise that he should return to Hull. Such hair-breadth escapes were the delight and the infirmity of this romantic hero.

In the civil wars, from the first battle of Edge Hill, we trace Lord Digby's gallant at- chievements, and on one signal occasion his desperate bravery. He seemed as careless of death, as if he had been invulnerable to bullets, which, however, he was not, for he received many wounds very little short of life. As active in the cabinet as in the field, he was concerting very ingenious schemes to obtain a city by an intrigue, or to project a visionary treaty, but he did not command success. Whatever might be the skill of the sculptor, his marble was of too rough a grain to take his polish. His good fortune was always of short duration. He suffered a great defeat—quarrelled with his officers—and was sent by Charles to Ireland. There his busied brain planned to fix the Prince on an Irish throne; but the Queen in- sisting that her son should hasten to Paris, Digby followed; a circumstance which first brought him in contact with the French mi- nister.

On the death of Charles the First, Lord Digby at St. Germain addressed Charles the Second, offering his devoted services in a style which could only have been dictated by a nobleman, the intimate companion of monarchs, and by a genius even more distinguished than his rank.*

Lord Digby now was the servant of fortune. France opened a scene favourable to the genius of the man. The commotions of the Fronde had broken out. The insurrectionary state of England seemed to have been reduced to a French *petite pièce,* as if the comedians of the *Théatre Italien* were performing one of their own ludicrous parodies. The French in Revolutions were then but childish mimics.

Lord Digby, not without difficulty, having procured a horse, entered as a volunteer in the Royalist army. One of those extraordinary occasions which can only happen to extraordinary men, for others are incompetent to seize on them, made his fortune in one day.

The two armies were drawn up against each other, at no great distance. One of the insurgents advanced out of the ranks, and in' a bravado offered to exchange a shot with any single man who would encounter him. Lord Digby,

---

* It would be irrelevant to our subject to insert this admirable letter, which is the most striking evidence that the style of the present day has degenerated in its changes. It exists in the Clarendon Papers.

without speaking to any one, leisurely moved
his horse towards this vaunting champion, who
stood still, apparently awaiting his antagonist.
It was a dishonourable feint; for the bravo
dexterously receding towards his own party as
Digby approached, the whole front of the
squadron fired. His Lordship was shot in the
thigh, and though he still kept his seat, it was
not without difficulty he got back to his own
side. Such intrepid gallantry, performed in
the presence of the French Monarch, Cardinal
Mazarine, and others of the Court, raised an
universal inquiry. At that moment few knew
more of the remarkable gentleman than that he
was an Englishman. All pressed forward to
admire the chivalrous Lord, and on his recovery
the King and the Cardinal instantly gave him
a regiment of horse, with the most liberal ap-
pointments.

Every thing about Lord Digby was in unison with his imaginative character. The impress on his standard was noticed for the ingenuity and acuteness of its device. An Os-
trich, his own crest, was represented with
a piece of iron in its mouth, and the motto,
Ferro vivendum est tibi, quid præstantia plumæ?
" Thou who must live on iron, what avails the
lustre of thy feathers?" But the motto in-

cludes a play upon words; the iron alluded to his sword, the feathers to his pen, to whose excellence he himself was by no means insensible.

Lord Digby's troop of cavalry was chiefly composed of English emigrants, who flocked to the standard of their idolized commander. He charmed them by the seduction of his imagination, the shadows of his fancy; they flattered themselves in flattering him. But neither the Commander nor his followers had patience and industry. Victories and promotions were equally rare in the puny warfare; and the adventurers gradually fell off in murmurs, abandoning the hero who, they were induced to conclude, if he had the power, would never have performed his prodigal promises.

But Lord Digby, at the French Court, was in the element in which he was born, and had been trained; and there he was more idolized than by his military dependents. The beauty of his person, the delightfulness of his conversation, the softness of his manners, his elegant literature and his political sagacity, and above all his alacrity and bravery in action, put him in full possession of all hearts and eyes. His Lordship was even admitted into the councils of the King and the Cardinal. He was in-

vested with a high command in the French
army, which gave him the full privileges of
tolls and passes and licences over the river to
Paris, so that his profits were considerable as
his honours. Such a prosperous state might
have terminated the career of other men.
Digby was more gratified at having attracted
the eyes of both sexes on him, than on the
honours which had no novelty for him, and
the fortune, which however abundant, could
never supply his invisible necessities. His
revenues were so large that it was imagined
that his Lordship designed to accumulate a
vast fortune, for he maintained no establishment, was without an equipage, lived meanly,
was never bountiful nor even charitable, yet
ever moneyless. Deeply involved in amorous
intrigues and romantic exploits, more adapted
for some folio romance than for the page of
grave history, he was however not less intent
on political ones, of the boldest nature his
inexhaustible invention had ever conceived.
When Cardinal Mazarine was compelled to quit
France and retire to Cologne, while the popular clamour was at its height, that sage statesman recommended Lord Digby to the Queen,
as an able and confidential adviser. In one of
the flights of his erratic genius his Lordship

projected supplanting Mazarine, and himself
becoming the Premier of France. He counte-
nanced the popular cry against Mazarine, and
suggested to the Queen, Anne of Austria, that
her personal safety was concerned in keeping
the Cardinal in exile. But though this fascinating nobleman had deceived an old Statesman, he could not make a woman his dupe;
for the Queen accepting his zealous councils
with complacency, was equally cautious in in-
forming Mazarine of his accomplished friend's
conduct. When the Cardinal returned in triumph, it was contrived to send his Lordship
on a very hazardous expedition to Italy, where
success seemed next to an impossibility. Digby surmounted the difficult task, and returning
to Paris was highly complimented by the Cardinal, and rewarded — at the same time that
he was cashiered and ordered to depart from
the territories of France.

Here was a kingdom lost! Digby now re-
paired to the obscure Court which Charles the
Second held at Bruges, and where some of the
courtiers wanted half-a-crown for a dinner.
Digby announced that he brought money
which would last him a twelvemonth, but at
the end of six weeks he had drained his trea-
sury. As neither the Monarch nor the Peer

could be of any use to the other, it was not
found inconvenient to part. Digby had now
to create a new scene of action, and he designed to enter into the Spanish service. He asked for no recommendation from Charles, but depended on his own resources — half Spaniard
as he was; for the gaiety of his disposition prevented him from being wholly Spanish. But
here he found obstacles ; his person was far
from being agreeable in the Spanish army in
Flanders, where about two years before, in a
predatory incursion, rapine and conflagration
had marked the progress of his troops through
many villages and towns, and he listened to his
odious name in lampoons and ballads. The
poverty of the Spanish Court in Flanders offered no promise to a military adventurer.

But Digby knew the character and taste of
Don Juan, the Governor of the Low Countries,
who unlike other grandees of Spain, was addicted to universal literature, and had a passion
for judicial astrology ; and Digby was an arbi-
ter in literature, and an adept in the mystical
and the occult.

The Spanish ministers and officers gave but
a cold and reserved reception, but they soon
marvelled at the delectable Spanish idiom
from the lips of an Englishman ! He, who had

been, as it were, a native in all the Courts of
Europe, was many men in one man : one who
interested all in their various stations, according
to their tempers and their pursuits. The confidential Minister of the Governor, Don Alonzo
di Cardinas, had personally known our mercu-
rial genius at London, and was the most obdurate, from " his own parched stupidity," till
Digby, as Clarendon says, " commending his
great abilities in State affairs, in which he was
invincibly ignorant, the Don suspected that he
had not known Lord Digby well enough before." Whoever listened was lost, and none
more than Don Juan himself. No one indeed
was so capable of appreciating the luxuri-
ant genius of this accomplished man. At
every leisure hour Don Juan sought the company of Lord Digby ; frequently at his meals,
and in the evenings, the Prince indulged in
literary conversations, and, more retiredly, in
whispering the secrets of the skies.

Nothing was now wanting to convince Don
Juan that he had by his side the greatest genius in Europe, but some signal service, which
might fix with the Spanish army the worth of
their new compatriot. The Spaniards had long
been annoyed by a fort, five miles from Brussels, which Marshal Schomburgh had rendered

impregnable.   The Spanish Prince had suffered
repeated repulses in his attempts to reduce this
fort.   Many Irish regiments, who had followed
the fortunes of their Sovereign, were in the
service of France, and the garrison of this fort
was chiefly composed of this soldiery.   Charles
the Second had lately been abandoned by Mazarine, in his terror of Cromwell, and the King
was now a fugitive in the Spanish Netherlands.
Digby one day surprised Don Juan by an assurance that the Spaniards should possess the
fort.   He had been privately negotiating with
the Irish officers, and having convinced them
that as their Sovereign was no longer protected
by France, it could not but be agreeable to him
that they should unite with Spain who had
afforded him an asylum, to the Irish it was
perfectly indifferent in whose service they engaged, and they found no difficulty in resolving
to pass over to the other side.   The great Marshal Schomburgh, who was convinced that he
was secure from all attacks, suddenly discovered that his orders were disobeyed, and himself
in the midst of unaccountable mutinies.   The
Marshal was constrained to march out of his
impregnable fort, and had the mortification to
witness most of his garrison wheel about to the
Spanish camp.   The dexterity and secrecy which

Lord Digby had displayed in this transaction to the Spanish Prince, looked as if he had ma-gically changed the scene; and Don Juan declared that there was no reward equal to that service. From this moment Lord Digby, who no longer viewed any prospect of the Restoration, devoted himself to the Spanish Court.

Digby now anticipated some active part in the state; and to be an entire Spaniard he deemed it necessary to become, what they call at Madrid, "a Christian." There was never wanting a favourable opportunity to execute what he had resolved on. Falling ill at a monastery where he visited his daughter, Father Courtnay, the Provincial of the English Jesuits, converted the able assailant of the Romish faith. This rapid conversion was not considered miraculous, even by the Spaniards, — and yet it seems so, for Father Courtnay was a person of no talents, and the learned Digby must have known the arguments of the Jesuit before he listened to them.

This step irretrievably lost him with the English. Charles laughed at the ascendancy of Father Courtnay over the understanding of the great philosopher, but, with his country-men, Digby was not to be quit for their ridi-cule, and the King found it necessary to conceal his own sentiments, in pursuance of the advice of Clarendon, in commanding Digby's absence 'at all future councils; and moreover, ordered him to resign the signet as Secretary of State, which though now but a titular office, was important, for it conferred on him a political character at the Court of Madrid. Even Don Juan, who had not read this portentous conversion when they had conned the stars together, cast a cold glance on the wonderful young proselyte. The Prince. indeed had incurred a reprimand from the Spanish Cabinet for suffering himself to be so powerfully influenced by Lord Digby; the jealousy of the Ministers was at work. No place, no pension came from Madrid; no compliment from Rome, but an exhortation, which relished of irony, that " since his Lordship had been converted, it behoved him now to convert his brothers."

When Charles the Second was invited to be present at the treaty between France and Spain at Fontarabia, Don Louis de Haro, the Spanish Minister, pointedly excepted against the King being accompanied by Lord Digby. Yet such was the spell of Digby's genius that Charles, though his crown might have been at stake, could not part with his delightful companion, who leaving the negotiators with the fate of Europe in their hands, as matters not very pressing, proposed to the King to take a circuitous route in their way, from city to city. His Lordship had been a curious traveller, who knew when to post, and where to loiter; thus delighting and delaying, a rumour reached them that the treaty had been concluded, and the Plenipotentiaries had taken their departure. The lounging Monarch then discovered how far he had been carried away by the fancies of his erratic conductor, to the detriment of very urgent affairs. The report however proved premature; but the adventure was auspicious to Lord Digby, for no sooner had he come in contact with Don Louis de Haro and the Spanish grandees, than that Statesman was as deeply captivated by this admirable man, as had been Don Juan. On Charles's return to Brussels, Lord Digby was invited to Madrid, where he was well received by the King; his wants were amply provided for, and he remained at that Court till the Restoration.

The Earl of Bristol, such Digby had now become, returned home Spanish in heart, but he had lost an old friend in the Chancellor ever since his adventure with Father Courtnay. He retained however the personal affection of the King, who on the Restoration had been more munificent to the Earl of Bristol than the Royal forgetfulness had allowed with so many others. As Digby could not be of the Privy Council, nor hold any ostensible post in the administration, but had free access at all hours to the King, he ambitioned to be the head of the English Roman Catholics, but he found that the Jesuits would not divulge their secrets. That he could not be the Prime Minister of England, possessing as he did the King's ear, I suspect rankled in his spirit.

A curious incident now occurred, which shows that the genius of the Earl of Bristol, unmitigated by age, still retained the restless invention of his most fanciful days. The treaty of the Portuguese match, already advanced, was confidentially revealed by the King to the Earl, who, provoked that he had not a greater share in foreign affairs, than his old friend the Chancellor admitted him to, determined to exert his rare faculty of puzzling, and obstructing any project which was not of his own contrivance. He startled the King by an assurance that this proposed political marriage must be followed by a war with Spain; he described the critical situation of Portugal, and of that miserable family who would shortly be compelled to ship themselves off to their Brazils, as Spain in one year would overrun the whole country. He caricatured the Infanta, as repulsive in person, and known to be incapable of having any progeny, an objection which was fully verified by the event. There were, however, two accomplished ladies of the House of Medici, whom he luxuriously painted forth to the voluptuous Monarch, and whom Spain would consider as a Spanish match. He suggested that the King should send him incognito to Italy to make his election for a Queen of the most favoured of these two ideal ladies. He prevailed over the weakness of the Monarch; kissed hands, and took his departure; and though a letter was dispatched after him to stay any farther proceedings, he pretended that he had received the communication too late, and would have closed his secret negotiation with one of the ladies, but, as Clarendon sarcastically observes, " he had not the good fortune to be believed."

The same improvidence in his domestic affairs which had marked the wanderings of his emigrant life, ruined his happiness. Jealous of Clarendon's influence, he thought that the Chancellor had lessened his favour with the King. One day, in a closet interview, in a state of great agitation, he upbraided the King in unmeasured terms for " passing his life only in pleasure and debauchery, while he left the government to the Chancellor—but he would do that which should awaken him!" The King was equally surprised and confused; otherwise, as he declared, having been personally menaced in his private closet, he had called the guard, and sent his old companion to lodge in the Tower.

This extravagant conduct was the prelude of the Earl of Bristol exhibiting charges of high treason against his estranged friend the Chancellor. When these were brought into the House of Lords it was resolved, that by the statutes of the realm no Peer can exhibit a charge of high treason against another Peer in their own House; and further, that in the matters alleged there was no treason. What is extraordinary, the Earl himself fully concurred in these resolutions, but what is still more so, he preferred the same charges a second time. " Follies of the wise!" The King was so greatly offended, that warrants were issued for his arrest; and during two years, this baffled and eccentric statesman was forced to live *au secret*. But this singular man was familiar with the mutability of fortune, for on

the Chancellor's final disgrace, we find that the
Earl of Bristol came to Court and Parliament
in triumph!

In the enmity of an ancient friendship, like
the unnatural feuds of civil war, the hatred is
proportioned to the former affection. In the
persecution of Clarendon the Earl of Bristol
was his own victim. His vindictive passion,
perhaps, on this single occasion, blinded his
luminous intellect and subdued the natural
generosity of his temper, for that was such,
that though he loved and hated violently, the
softness of his disposition would easily reconcile him even to those who had injured him.
Digby had more imagination than sensibility;
his love, or his hatred, appeared by the most
vivacious expressions; but it was his temper,
more than his heart, which was engaged. His
friend, or his enemy, in his own mind, was but
a man, with whom he considered that a single
conference would be sufficient to win over to
his own will.

His glory was now setting, when Digby
was yet to show himself to all the world, as
the most elevated of human beings.

Lord Orford, among the contradictions in
his character of Lord Digby, has sneered at his

conduct on a remarkable occasion. " He spoke
for the Test Act, though a Roman Catholic."
Thus an antithesis, or an epigram, can cloud
over the most glorious action of a whole life.
This statesman, in the policy of that day, and
at that critical hour, above all other considerations, held, that the vital independence of this
country was in the firm and jealous maintenance of the Protestant interest. On this occasion he delivered his sentiments with his accustomed eloquence, but above the eloquence
was the patriotism.

The present work will not admit of a developement of the fine and original genius of
this remarkable statesman. From his speech
on the Test Act and his " Apology" addressed
to the Commons* might be selected passages,
as important for their deep sense, as for their
splendid novelty. The noble speaker avoided to decide, whether the boon of greater freedom to be granted to the Romanists would
be dangerous; or whether the unreasonable
ambition of any Roman Catholics had afforded
any just grounds for the alarm which had so
violently seized on, and distempered the major
part of his Majesty's Protestant subjects? It
is these fancies which he would now allay, and
he thus illustrates the nature of popular fancies.

* It is preserved in Nalson's Collections, vol. ii.

" My Lords, in popular fears and apprehensions, those usually prove most dangerous that are raised upon grounds not well understood; and may rightly be resembled to the fatal effects of panic fears in armies, where I have seldom seen great disorders arise from intelligence brought in by parties and scouts, or by advertisements to Generals, but from alarms on groundless and capricious fears of danger taken up we know not either how or why. This no man of moderate experience in military affairs but hath found the dangerous effects of, one time or other; in giving a stop to which mischiefs the skill of great commanders is best seen." He closes the speech with these words - " My Lords, however the sentiments of a Catholic of the Church of Rome, (I still say not of the Court of Rome,) may oblige me, upon scruple of conscience, in some particulars of this Bill, to give my negative to it, when it comes to passing, yet as a member of the Protestant Parliament, my advice prudentially cannot but go along with the main scope of it, the present circumstances of time and affairs considered, and the necessity of composing the disturbed minds of the people."

However we may be disposed to censure the eccentricity of this singular personage, his public character was always decided, and at the most critical moments of his political life his path was clearly traced before him. Lord Digby, from his first eloquent speech on the trial of Strafford to his last on the Test Act, poured forth the feelings of a patriot with the calm sagacity of the statesman. Had he lived in our times, it is probable that Lord Digby would have spoken against this very Test Act, and afforded Horace Walpole one more ungenerous sneer.

Little did Lord Digby imagine that he would only be known to posterity by the pen of his immortal adversary, the Chancellor, who in his solitude, though feeling himself personally aggrieved, had suffered no vindictive passion to cross the seas—a sad exile from his country and his glory ; yet in his leisure hours at Montpellier, his great mind found a delightful task, in commemorating the splendid accomplishments and the daring virtues of his great enemy, which he felicitously distinguishes as " the beautiful part of his life." " It is pity," continues the noble writer, " that his whole life should not be exactly and carefully written, and it would be as much pity that any body else should do it but himself, who could only do it to the life, and make the truest description of all his faculties, and passions, and appetites, and the full operation of

them; and he would do it with as much ingenuity and integrity as any man could do."
And his Lordship finely concludes—" If a sa-
tiety in wrestling and struggling in the world,
or a despair of prospering by those strugglings
shall prevail with him to abandon those contests, and retire at a good distance from the
Court, to his books and a contemplative life,
he may live to a great and long age, and will
be able to leave such information of all kinds
to posterity that he will be looked upon as a
great mirror by which well-disposed men may
learn to dress themselves in the best ornaments,
and to spend their lives to the best advantage
of their country."

This had been a fortunate suggestion, had it
ever reached Lord Digby ; but this Earl of
Bristol lived eight years after this noble effu-
sion, and though no man was more partial to
his own genius, he has left his adventurous life
unwritten. We have lost a tale of the passions, warm with all the genius which prompt-
ed his actions. The confessions of Lord Digby
might have afforded a triumph over his vanities ; Statesmen would have been lessoned, and
men of the world, through his versatile conditions, and in his reckless life, would have
contemplated a noble and enlarged image of
themselves.

CHAPTER XVII.

THE FLIGHT FROM THE CAPITAL.

THE menaced Remonstrance had been the secret terror of Charles the First: even in Scotland, at its first intimation, the King had earnestly impressed on his faithful Secretary that his friends should put a stop to it by any means. Heart-stricken at its presentation, the King desired that this Remonstrance should not be published, unaccompanied by his answer; he learnt that it was already dispersed!

The style of the Monarch, in alluding to this Remonstrance and to the seditious libels of the pulpits, betray his dread. " We are many times amazed to consider by what eyes these things are seen, and by what ears they are heard." With this envenomed satire on himself and his government, the very populace were now to sit in judgment over their rulers, and to comment with all their passions and their incompetence, on evils often aggravated, and evils which though they had ceased to exist, by their cruel recollections seemed to increase the number.

Rushworth has printed this memorable States paper in the extraordinary manner of a chapter in the Bible, consisting of 206 verses; every verse a grievance which had been redressed, or a grievance which Charles was now willing should no longer exist.* He appealed to them in his replies "whether he had not granted more than ever King had granted?—whether of late he had refused to pass any Bill presented by Parliament, for redress of those grievances mentioned in the Remonstrance?" This Remonstrance was an elaborate volume, which might serve as the text-book of every Revolutionist in the three realms; and it laid open his infirm government to the eyes of Europe; or, as it was described in one of the King's Declarations, "rendered us odious to our subjects and contemptible to all foreign Princes."

This anomalous Remonstrance was the first formidable engine of that great Paper-war which preceded the civil, sad and wrathful image of the fast-approaching conflicts! This Remonstrance may also be distinguished as the first of those decisive acts by which the

* Rushworth, iv. 438.

Commons usurped the whole Sovereignty of Government. It was an appeal to the people against the Sovereign, by the Commons themselves, and an actual announcement of the separation of the Lower from the Higher House, since it had not been deemed necessary any longer to require the concurrence of the Lords. " Our presumption may be very strong and vehement, that though they have no mind to be slaves, they are not unwilling to be tyrants; for what is tyranny but to admit no rule to govern by, but their own wills? And we know the misery of Athens was at the highest when it suffered under the thirty tyrants."*

The Remonstrance received an able answer, the secret production of Hyde, which Mr. Brodie candidly acknowledges " was calculated to make a great impression," but which Mrs. Macaulay could only perceive " was vague, and totally deficient in justifying the King's actions." As if the King's actions were to be justified, any more than the proceedings of the Commons! It is however remarkable for the positive statement of that important circumstance in the reign of the calumniated Monarch, which, had it been fictitious, could hardly have

* His Majesty's Answer, Husband's Collect. 284, should be 283.

been ventured on, in such an unreserved appeal to the whole nation—namely, the present prosperity of the people, and the national happiness during a period of sixteen years; " not only comparatively in respect of their neighbours, but even of those times which were justly accounted fortunate."

The style of Charles had become more popular; the moderate councils of Falkland, Colepepper, and Hyde would have tended to tranquillize the disturbed state of the public mind; and Charles himself had evinced his own disposition for conciliatory measures, by all which he had himself done in Scotland.

The violence of the Commons now strikingly contrasts with the subdued conduct of the King. They seemed to have acquired a renovated vigour; their agitation was more intense; their hostility more open. The sovereignty of England now depended on the single vote of the Commons. The more the King was driven to yield, seemed only to inflame their consciousness of power. Secret motives were instigating this fiercer activity.

One motive was their dread of a change in public opinion; the stream which had hitherto carried them on, was ebbing, or turning from its course. Charles, left to discreeter councils, might win the affections of the honest and the honourable, who were not enlisted into a party. When Hampden reproached Lord Falkland for having changed his opinion, his Lordship replied to the patriot, that he had been persuaded at that time to believe many things which he had since found to be untrue; and therefore he had changed his opinion in many particulars, as well as to things as persons. This, at least, was an unbiassed opinion, for the virtuous Falkland had accepted office on the repeated entreaties of his Sovereign, but with the greatest repugnance. The Commons were now despotic. They ridiculed even Parliamentary customs when these thwarted. their immediate purposes; when on one occasion Pym declared that the established orders were not to be considered like the laws of the Medes and Persians. When the shadow of the House of Lords was yet suffered to show itself, an extraordinary motion was made by Pym, that " the *major* part of the House of Commons, and the *minor* of the Lords, should be an authentic concurrence of both Houses.*

---

* Sir Philip Warwick, 187. Abstract propositions little influenced the conduct of the demagogue who publicly pro_ mulgated them. He who thus violated the laws has himself delivered for posterity one of the noblest descriptions of law

Mr. Godolphin, objecting to this novel Parliamentary reform, observed, that if the *greater* part of the Lords went to the King with the *lesser* part of the Commons, it would be exactly the same thing. Pym was too resolute to be embarrassed by a dilemma. Godolphin was instantly commanded to withdraw, and an order entered in the Journals, that " the House should take into consideration the words spoken by Mr. Godolphin." It ended, as usual, wih the threat, and Godolphin escaped without the treason ! It would be difficult to determine whether the King had made, or the patriots were making, the greatest encroachments on the Constitution.

Another secret motive was at work which instigated the violence of the Commons. It

which the whole compass of our language can produce, in a passage which rivals the splendour of one of the common places of Cicero, and the logical force of Lord Bacon's profound meditations. " The law is that which puts a difference betwixt good and evil, betwixt just and unjust. If you take away the law, all things will fall into a confusion ; every man will become a law unto himself, which in the depraved condition of human nature must needs produce many great enormities ; lust will become a law, and envy will become a law ; covetousness and ambition will become laws ; and what dictates, what decisions, such laws would produce, may easily be discerned."

was known to some in the House, that the
King possessed from Strafford, Saville, and
Montrose many discoveries concerning themselves. The patriotic leaders had betrayed their
sensitive state on various occasions. They had
clamoured against the King's journey to Scotland, and sent their Commissioners at his back;
they had felt even a jealousy in the King's
personal communication with his Scottish subjects; when the mysterious " Incident" occurred at Edinburgh, the parties at London
were struck by the sympathetic terror. Charles
possessed evidence for their impeachment, they
imagined for their destruction. To maintain
the power they had usurped, it was necessary
to push on to every extremity; it was also
a desperate effort for their own self-preservation. They decided to annihilate the House
of Lords, beginning by the Bishops, and to
degrade, to calumniate, and to terrify the Sovereign; dreading nothing so much as that
reconciliation which seemed fast approaching
between the King and the nation.

It is important to observe, that the inevitable
results of these persevering persecutions of the
Commons led to the fatal imprudent acts of
the various parties who on their side alike

urged by their despair, fell the victims of the Commons.

The Lords now perceived their own danger in resisting the Commons; the mobocracy again triumphed! Many Peers absented themselves from disgust, or from terror; and thin houses supplied a majority for the Commons. The cry of " No Bishops" had been for some time bellowed by the mobs, who more explicitly threatened " to pull the Bishops in pieces." One evening, at torch-light, the Marquis of Hertford hurried to the Bishops' bench, and greatly agitated, prayed them to remain all that night in the House. The terrified Bishops earnestly desired their Lordships that some care might be taken of their persons; messages to the Commons were totally disregarded; some Lords only bestowed a smile. The Earl of Manchester at length undertook to protect Williams the Archbishop of York, and some Bishops his friends. Some escaped by secret passages, others by staying great part of the night in the House.

The final ruin of the Bishops was hastened by the rashness of one, who on so many critical occasions had never been deficient in self-possession, nor in dexterous manœuvres. The

Archbishop of York, the wily Williams, in this extremity, maddened by despair, committed an act of greater imprudence than were even some of the King's precipitate measures.

Archbishop Williams hastily drew up a protest, and by his artful representations, assuring them of the legality of the act, obtained the signatures of twelve Bishops, wherein they declared that " All laws, orders, and votes were void, and of none effect in their absence." This Protest was not to be used till it had received the Royal consent. The Lord Keeper Littleton, however, to ingratiate himself with the Commons, as more than one testimony confirms, read it openly in the House, aggravating its offence. When this protest reached the Commons, it was instantly voted " high treason." " We poor souls, who little thought that we had done any thing that might deserve a chiding, are now called to our knees at the bar—astonished at the suddenness of this crimination compared with the perfect innocency of our own intentions." Such is the language of Bishop Hall in his " Hard Measure." At night, and in a hard frost in January, the Bishops are dragged to the Tower. The news of their committal is announced by the ringing of bells and the blaze of bonfires, so preva-

lent was now the novel passion for **Presbytery**!
The infamy of the Bishops was blazoned in
scurrilous pamphlets both at home and abroad,
and their " treasonable practices" were reiterated, till some discussed what sort of death
could expiate such unheard-of crimes? After
a tedious prosecution of these victims of state,
huddling them together, " standing the whole
afternoon in no small torture, struggling with
a merciless multitude," and in that dark night
sending them all in a barge to shoot London
Bridge, where the chance of escape was doubtful—the Commons did not make out their pretended treason. One of the party, to prevent
involving them in any greater crime, desired
that they should only be voted " stark mad,
and sent to Bedlam." Another of their oracles
being asked for his opinion, declared that they
might with as good reason accuse these Bishops
of adultery, as of treason. They remanded
them for another day, which day never came.
The truth is, many in the nation did not conceal their abhorrence of their barbarous conduct in hurrying to their dungeons these dignified and learned personages. It is observable that in more than one instance the party
evinced the sagacity of retreating when they
discovered that they were in danger of losing

ground in popular opinion. But though the
bold design of the Commons was frustrated in
condemning the Bishops as traitors, they persisted in renewing the Bill for taking away
their votes at the same time with the bill for
pressing, both which, as Clarendon states, had
lain so long desperate while the Lords came
and sat with freedom in the House. Both
afterwards easily passed in a very thin House.*

Thus had the Commons signalized their
triumph over the Lords; nor had they ceased
to harass the hapless Monarch; and the injuries and indignities offered to his person were
"scorns put upon the kingly office," degrading
it in the eyes of the very populace. The King
was reduced to a state nearly of destitution,
" Beggar as I am!" he exclaimed; once he
pathetically reminded them of his personal de-
privations; " we have and do patiently suffer
those extreme personal wants, as our predecessors have been seldom put to, rather than we
would press on the great burdens our people
have undergone, which we hope in time will
be considered on your parts." There was a
bitter mockery in their pretended elevation of
the character of majesty; they sometimes promised " to make him a great and glorious

---

* Bishop Hall's " Hard Measure."

King," but they also told the Sovereign, that they had done him no wrong, for he was not capable of receiving any ; and that they had taken nothing from him, because he had never any thing of his own to lose. About this time the Commonwealth-men raised their voices ; Harry Martin, in a novel strain had asserted, unreproved, that " the office of Sovereignty was forfeitable," and that " the happiness of the kingdom did not depend on the King nor any of that stock." Sir Henry Ludlow, the father of the celebrated General who has left us his Memoirs, had openly declared that " Charles was unworthy to be King of England." The King had long witnessed the petitioning mobs; he daily heard how their pulpits sermonized sedition ; and gay ballads were chorusing the fall of the Bishops, and menacing his own, under the palace windows. All seemed a merciless triumph over the feebler Sovereign.

Charles seemed abandoned amidst his new council ; his old ministers had been forced to flight, or had been compelled to resign their offices to his new and suspected friends. The Sovereign afterwards had been placed amidst a council whom he could not consult on his most immediate concerns, and whose advice, it has

been conjectured, on more than one occasion,
had proved treacherous. His new Solicitor-
general, the dark-browed St. John, was meditating his ruin; Lord Say and Sele had led
him into perilous measures. With his new
ministers, Falkland, Colepepper and Hyde,
however honourable, his personal intercourse
had been but recent, and there was yet wanting on both sides that confidential intercourse
which time only matures. Meanwhile Charles
was betrayed in his most retired hours; the
apartments of the palace were surrounded by
watchful spies, by corner, listeners — and by
mean creatures, who on the denial of any
favour would fly to the Parliament, where they
were certain of being enlisted among the re-
cruits of patriotism. Pym unreservedly told
the Earl of Dover, that "if he looked for any
preferments he must comply with them in their
ways, and not hope to have it by serving the
King." Hence it happened that the most
secret councils, and the future designs of
Charles were anticipated by his great enemies.
These confederacies explain many extraordinary
occurrences which could not have happened in
the ordinary course of affairs, and which must
have often surprised Charles himself as much
as they have done the readers of his history.

The artifices practised on the infirm faculties of the Queen, who lived in continual panics during the King's absence, was not surely with Charles one of their least offences; he felt them as personal injuries. Threatened with impeachment, she was reminded that several Queens of England had perished on the scaffold. The tremendous secret had been revealed to Henrietta, by those who were acting by connivance with some of the party in the Commons. When the party petitioned to be informed who were the "Malignants" who had done that malicious office, they well knew who it was; and could they have been compelled to confess to whom they stood indebted for their information concerning the Queen, the juggle would have been manifest. The same person who had so confidentially acquainted the Queen with the design must have conveyed to them the alarm, and the language, which broke forth from this terrified Princess.* But they well knew that the Queen could not betray those whom she held as her friends, and she was in consequence compelled to assure the very persons who she believed would willingly have required

* Clarendon, ii. 232. The recent edition furnishes a material verbal correction from the manuscript. The passage as given by the former editors to me is unintelligible.

her life, that "although she had heard such a discourse, she had never considered it credible."

The King was often driven to similar compulsions. At length when the Commons desired the execution of seven priests, in which the Lords were made to join, the King would only consent to their banishment. Among such numerous claims, which the Commons were daily urging, this sanguinary measure was the only one to which the King would not yield. Amidst the humiliating state of contumely which Charles was enduring, it was not among the least hopes of some who entertained deeper designs than the rest, that this Monarch, of a temper hasty and indignant, would be provoked into some fatal indiscretion, and so it happened!

It was on the 3rd of January, 1642-3, without any conference with his ministers, that Charles commanded the Attorney-General to impeach the five members, and the Lord Kimbolton. A Serjeant-at-arms demanded that the House should deliver them into his custody, and returned with a message, but not an answer. That very night a printed order from the Commons was issued that no member can be arrested without the consent of the House, and every person might lawfully aid any member in his

resistance, "according to the Protestation taken
to defend the privileges of Parliament." This
was an open defiance of the Royal authority!
In strictness, however, there was an irregularity
in the form of Charles's arresting the members;
they alleged that their consent must be had
before any proceedings were instituted against
a member of their House — a subject, however, which admitted of many opposite arguments when the privileges of Parliament were
afterwards discussed, and which might lead to
some ridiculous results. " The Protestation"
on which the irregularity is grounded, had been
a recent act of the Commons. The King afterwards complained, that when he resolved on
the arrest of the members, having no design to
invade their privileges, " he had expected an
answer as might inform us if we were out of
the way; but we received none at all. This
was the first time that we heard 'the Protestation' might be wrested to such a sense. We
confess we were somewhat amazed having never seen nor heard of the like, though we had
known members of either House committed
without so much formality as we had used, and
upon crimes of a far inferior nature to those
we had suggested. Having no course proposed
to us for our proceeding, we were upon the

matter only told that against those persons we were not to proceed at all; that they were above our reach, or the reach of the law, so that it was not easy for us to resolve what to do."* Amidst this unhappy conflict of prerogative and privilege, new and hurried ordinances were often recurring; and most of the dissensions between the King and the Commons seem to have sprung from the latitude, and even opposite sense, in which both parties received them. As formerly in the " Petition of Right," Charles discovered in the exercise of his authority, that he had been deprived of it, by some unexpected explanation of a recent Act of the Commons.

On the following day, the 4th of January, Charles, to the astonishment of all men, went down in person to the House of Commons, to repeat his injunctions, if not to arrest the members, in their open House. He came, too, attended by a formidable company. This memorable incident in the history of Charles the First cast his affairs into irretrievable ruin, at a moment when Pym is said to have acknowledged that " If that extraordinary accident had not happened to give them new credit, they were sinking under the weight of the ex-

* Husband's Collections, 245.

pectation of those whom they had deluded, and
the envy of those whom they oppressed."*

Clarendon positively assures us that the
King's adviser on this occasion was Lord Digby. Mr. Brodie observes that the proceedings
against the six members had been resolved on
before the King left Scotland, and the utmost
that can with propriety be imputed to that
nobleman is, that he recommended what he
saw had been determined upon.† Had this

---

* Clarendon, ii. 183. The noble writer in delivering the
Patriot's confession has evidently interpolated it with his
own feelings.

† Brodie, ii. 151 and 280. Mr. Brodie refers generally
to the correspondence between the King and Nicholas in
Append. to Evelyn's Mem. This would be an authority
recently published, which could confirm that of preceding
writers, who were not contemporary with the events. But I
cannot discover any passage which specifically shows any
such decision. Oldmixon, however, asserts, that the articles
of High Treason were prepared by the King when in Scotland, and that the impeachment of the members was the
consequence. *Hist. of the Stewarts*, 176, col. 2. We know
that the King had been very assiduous in obtaining information in Scotland, and probably collected enough to satisfy
himself of what he deemed treasonable practices ; but on his
return home, and the Act of Oblivion having passed, it seems
not probable that he would have ventured to impeach these
powerful leaders, had they granted him that tranquillity
which he flattered himself to have restored in Scotland.

impeachment been solely the consequence of a long settled determination, it is remarkable that on so important a State-measure, the King should never once have discussed it with those three ministers who possessed his entire confidence.* Whatever we may deem the policy of this bold act of impeachment, we must not condemn it as any exercise of arbitrary power, since the King professed to put the members on their legal and fair trial. What the treasonable practices precisely were we can only conjecture; for the patriots were never brought to the bar. The articles exhibited by the Attorney-General seem to have been common between the impeached members and the Parliament. Did Charles imagine that he could compel the Parliament to condemn themselves or accomplices with their own leaders? Hume has profoundly observed that " the punishment of leaders is ever the last triumph over a broken and routed party; but surely was never before

* Mr. Hallam solves this historical poblem, not perhaps untruly. " The King was guided by bad private advice, and cared not to let any of his Privy Council know his intentions lest he should encounter opposition," i. 588. I suspect, however, that Mr. Hallam imagined at the moment of writing this, that Charles had " listened to the Queen." 583.

attempted in opposition to a faction during the full tide of its power and success." Had the King in reserve some of their later intrigues, some yet unrevealed occurrences which had passed in their Divan, for Whitelocke informs us, that they had of late held frequent private meetings? The King was fully convinced that he possessed particular proofs of " a solemn combination for altering the government of the Church and State; of their designing offices to themselves and other men, &c."* Charles even considered that " the people would thank him for disclosing some of his discoveries."

It was the subsequent act of going down to the House in person, and with a considerable force, which was, as the King afterwards called it, " a casual mistake." The King went reluctantly and not without hesitation, till quickened by a woman's taunt:—of what nature was that famous taunt, I must refer the reader to a preceding passage.† This reluctance seems to indicate that the project was not his own; it has even been surmised that the rash council came from that irresistible quarter; and Hume, taking his ideas from Whitelocke, ascribes it to " the Queen and the Ladies of the Court," who

* Husband's Collections, 534.
† See vol. iii. 130.

had long witnessed the personal indignities the King was enduring. It was quite in character that the vivacious Queen of Charles should have been transported at this " brisk act," as Clarendon might have called it, and rejoiced to see her Consort become " master in his own dominions," at least over those who were threatening her with an impeachment. Such a *coup d'état* would charm her toilette politics, which were always the echo of some one who had her ear at the moment; she had no political head of her own. That person was now Lord Digby, who had equally fascinated Henrietta and Charles. The King was not likely to be swayed on such a strong and decisive measure, by the sudden freaks and fancies of womanish councils, which on many occasions he had treated with raillery or dismissed with argument. The irritated Monarch was in more danger at this moment of having his natural impetuosity worked upon by " the sanguine complexion" of Lord Digby; an expressive designation which some years after, experience had taught the Monarch to apply to his romantic adviser.

All that perilous boldness which characterises the singular genius of Lord Digby is stamped on this memorable impeachment, as well as on the more extraordinary occurrence of the succeeding day. His wonderful dissimulation in the House of Lords, the instant he discovered the fatal effects of his own councils, on the impeachment, reprobating the measure even to Lord Kimbolton, the very victim on whom he expected to have laid his hands, was not unusual with this versatile man. That he instigated the King to hasten in person to the House, if any one did, appears from this remarkable circumstance. After Charles had been baffled in the attempt, and found to his surprise, that " all the birds had flown," the reckless Digby offered the King to take a dozen picked military men, Col. Lunsford and other soldiers of fortune, and hasten to the City, and in the House where the fugitive members lodged, by a *coup de main*, to seize on them alive, or leave them dead. Charles, who had grown more sage than his counsellor, by some hours, forbade this double rashness. The man who would willingly have cast himself on such a forlorn hope, was the sort of genius who only could have suggested, if any one did, the wild romantic scheme of the King coming down, with men armed, to the House of Commons.

On a hasty knock, the door of the Commons was thrown open, announcing the arrival of their extraordinary visitor: already warned, from more than one quarter, of his approach, the House had a little recovered from their consternation; still the presence of the Sovereign in the House of Commons, for all parties, was a moment of awful novelty,* and our actors had now to perform a new part for the first time. The Speaker was commanded to keep his seat with the mace lying before him. Charles entered, solely accompanied by his nephew the Palsgrave. Immediately uncovering himself, the Members stood up uncovered. The King took the Speaker's chair " by his leave." He stood some time, glancing around, but seemed perplexed by the multitude of faces ; he more particularly directed his looks towards Pym's usual seat by the bar, whose person he well

---

* An explanatory apology for this unusual proceeding was afterwards given by Charles. " We put on a sudden resolution to try whether our own presence, and a clear discovery of our intentions, which haply might not have been so well understood, could remove their doubts, and prevent those inconveniences which seemed to have been threatened; and thereupon we resolved to go in our own person to our House of Commons, which we discovered not till the very minute we were going — the bare doing of which we did not then conceive could have been thought a breach of privilege, more than if we had gone to the House of Peers, and sent for them to have come to us, which is the usual custom."— Husband's Collect. 246.

knew. Charles in addressing the House assured them, that no King that ever was in England should be more careful of their privileges ; but in cases of treason he held that no person hath a privilege. On the word of a King he declared that he intended no force, but would proceed against those whom he sought in a legal and fair way ; he subsequently said, " according to the laws and statutes of the realm, to which all innocent men would cheerfully submit." He took this occasion again to confirm that whatever he had done in favour, and for the good of his subjects, he would maintain. He now called on the impeached members by their names. None answered. Turning to the Speaker, who stood below the chair, he inquired whether they were in the House? The Speaker, Lenthall, a person who never afterwards betrayed any sign of a vigorous intellect, and who, had he acted with less promptitude and dignity, might have fairly pleaded the novelty and difficulty of his unprecedented situation, seemed inspired by the greatness of the occasion. Kneeling to the King, he desired the Sovereign to excuse his answer, for " in this place I have neither eyes to see, nor tongue to speak, but as the House is pleased to direct me, whose servant I am here." The King told him that " He thought him right, and that his own eyes were as good as his. I see the birds are flown!" He concluded by strenuously insisting that the accused Members must be sent to him, or he must take his own course.

On this occasion none but the Speaker spoke. All were mute in sullenness or in awe. No generous, no dignified, emotions broke forth from that vast body of Senators. The incident itself was so sudden, and so evidently unpremeditated that Charles had not discovered his intention to a single friend. All were astonished or indignant. It was, however, a fitting and a fortunate occasion for some glorious patriot to have risen as the eloquent organ of the public opinion, and have loyally touched a nerve in the heart of a monarch, who would not have been insensible, amidst his sorrows and his cares; he might have been enlightened by solemn truths, and consoled by that loyalty of feeling from which he had been so long estranged. Charles having spoken, and no friendly voice responding, left the House as he had entered, with the same mark of respect. But the House was in disturbance, and reiterated cries of " Privilege! Privilege!" screamed in the ears of the retiring Monarch.

We are told by Clarendon that the King deeply regretted the wild adventure, and that " He felt within himself the trouble and agony which usually attends generous and magnanimous minds upon their having committed errors which expose them to censure, and to damage." Should it be imagined that this colouring exceeds the reality, we may at least trace the King's whole conduct after his late error day after day, to retrieve " the casual mistake," and to adopt measures, the reverse of those which would argue a design of arbitrary rule.

All parties agreed to censure this bold and hazardous measure; for on unsuccessful enterprises men are judged of by the results. Fatal as was this false step, yet Charles was always conceiving himself justified in the impeachment; the King was desirous that the nation should be rightly informed of his own notions. On his return in the evening he sent for Rushworth, whom he had observed at the Clerk's table, taking down his speech. The King commanded him to supply a copy. Rushworth, at all times in due dread of his Lords the Commons, who in their tyranny were already preparing the sad fate of the Attorney-General for having obeyed his Master's commands, and who honestly avows that he wished to be excused, reminded the King that the House was so jealous of its privileges, that Mr. Nevil, a Yorkshire member, had been committed to the Tower only for telling his Majesty what words were spoken by Mr. Bellassis son to Lord Faulconbridge. Charles with remarkable quickness observed, " I do not ask you to tell me what was said by any Member of the House, but what I said myself." This fortunate distinction allayed the fears of the wary Clerk of the Commons, and is one among the other abundant evidence of the logical head of Charles. Rushworth transcribed the Speech from his short-hand, the King staying all the while in the room. The King instantly sent it to the printer, and it was published on the morning.

These transactions passed on the third and fourth of January, 1641-2. The impeached Members had flown to the city. The Commons on their adjournment formed a select committee at Grocers'-hall, at once to express their terror, and not to be removed from the council of the five. On the fifth, Charles having utterly rejected the wild bravery of Digby's resolution to seize on the Members, went to the Guildhall accompanied by three or four Lords and his ordinary retinue. He

addressed the people in the hall, regretting
their causeless apprehensions, and still relying
on their affections; the accused Members who
had shrouded themselves in the city, he hoped
no good man would keep from a legal trial.
He aimed to be gracious and condescending;
and to be popular, he offered to dine with one
of the Sheriffs, who was a known Parliament-
man, and by no means solicitous of the royal
honour. But Charles was mortified when the
cry of the Commons echoed from the mouths
of the populace. A daring revolutionist flung
into the King's coach a pamphlet bearing the
ominous cry of insurrection, " To your tents,
O Israel!" for this Puritanic Israelite, de-
signated as an Ironmonger and a Pamphleteer,
only saw in Charles a sovereign who was to
be abandoned, like the weak and tyrannical
Rehoboam. Rushworth says on the King's
return there were no tumults, however the loyal
Lord Mayor was pulled from his horse, and
with some of the Aldermen, after manifold
insults, was fortunate to escape on foot.*

Events, fraught with the most important
results, pressed on each other at every hour.
Both Houses of Parliament, as if in terror,
adjourned from time to time and from place to

. * Nalson, ii. 822.

place. The city was agitated, and the panic spread into the country. All the plots and conspiracies which they had formerly heard, and had almost ridiculed, they now imagined to be very credible. Such rumours were the talk of the day and were cried at night. A conflict of the disordered multitude raged through Westminster. Their language was as violent as their motions. " It was a dismal thing," says Whitelock, " to all sober men, especially Members of Parliament, to see and hear them." It had become necessary to fortify Whitehall.

On the sixth, the King ventured to issue a Proclamation for the apprehension of the five Members who were to be lodged in the Tower. They were however more secure at a house in Coleman-street, in hourly communication with the Committee, till they were carried in state to Merchant-Taylors'-hall, to sit in the Committee itself.

On the seventh, the Royal Proclamation was declared to be false, scandalous, and illegal, and the Attorney-General was committed for having preferred the articles against the five Members.

An inflammatory narrative by the Committee of the King's unhappy entrance into the House of Commons, was prepared with considerable

art. They assiduously collected every loose
expression, and every ridiculous gesture of
some inconsiderate young persons who appear
to have joined the King's party on their way.
From such slight premises the Committee had
drawn the widest inferences, till in the climax
of this denouncement of their " Rehoboam,"
they alleged, as evidence, the opinion of these
blustering blades themselves, that had " the
word" been given, "questionless they would
have cut the throats of all the Commons." It
is certain that Charles had enjoined his company not to enter the House " on their lives."
A news writer of the day acknowledges that
" they demeaned themselves civilly ;" and Lilly,
by no means prejudiced in favour of " the
gentlemen with halberts and swords," says—
" Truly I did not hear there was any incivility
offered by those gentlemen then attending to
any Member of the House, his Majesty having
given them strict commands to the contrary." *
But the party had calculated on the effect of
deepening the odium which the King had
incurred ; and though this aggravation of the
idle words of some idle men, little comported
with the dignity of the Commons, it was an
artifice which served their purpose, of ex-

* Lilly's Life and Death of Charles the First.__108.

citing the public feeling against the indiscreet Monarch.

A people already in tumult, were flax to the fire; the populace seemed now only waiting to be led on to any desperate enterprise. Most of the shops were closed, and the wandering rabble, here and there, were listening to any spokesman. At such a crisis, orators and leaders shot up, certain to delight themselves with an indulgent audience, or to head compliant associates. A person of some consideration exclaimed, "the King was unworthy to live!" another that "the Prince would govern better." The rage of the infuriated Leviathan was at its height. The tub was thrown to the whale. It was proposed to conduct the accused members in a grand triumph to their House. A thousand mariners and watermen fly to the Committee to guard them on the river; a mob of apprentices proffer their services by land.

During the preparations for the triumphal procession of the five, Charles deemed it necessary to remove from Whitehall.

Such a resolution was not made without difficulty, and the unhappy result is alleged to prove that a contrary conduct was the preferable one. The flight of Charles from the

capital has been condemned. Some dreaded
a civil war, should the King abandon the
capital. The Lord Mayor, with many of the
King's friends from the city, offered to raise
a guard of ten thousand men, but that itself would have been the very evil for
which it offered a preventative — a civil war.
" If your Majesty leaves us," observed a
sage citizen, " we are undone, and the Members will carry all before them as they
please." Presciently he added, " Sir, I shall
never see you again !" Moreover, it was urged
that the King had yet a strong party in the
nation—a majority among the Peers, and no
inconsiderable number of the Commons, who
though they were separated by their fears,
were not yet lost, and even his late error might
be redeemed. But the King had lived of late
without honour ; the Queen not without peril ;
every hour was multiplying personal injuries
which he dared not resent. His late false step
had ruined his hopes, and his confidence in
his Lords had long been shaken since they
could no longer protect their own privileges.
At a distance from this rule of terror, these
scenes of insurrection, perhaps his fortune
might change ; he might show himself to his
whole kingdom, the Sovereign he desired to

be; his presence in the Capital had only surrounded him by conspiracies in his palace, and
dethronement from his Parliament.

On the tenth of January the King with his
family, and a few of his household, took his
melancholy departure from Whitehall, which
he never again saw but to die before his palace-
window.

On the eleventh, at noon, the Committee,
with the five Members, came by water to
Westminster. The river was covered with
long boats and barges—their appearance was
warlike—" dressed up with waist-clothes "* as
prepared for action; their guns pealed and their
streamers waved; at land the drums and the
trumpets responded. Clamouring against Bishops and Popish Lords, as they passed by
Whitehall they jeeringly asked " What had become of the King and his Cavaliers?" The multitude rolled on from the city and the suburbs,
with loud acclamations, following the citizens

* As Clarendon calls them. The term is not in Todd,
and perhaps the use is obsolete. They are explained in
Kersey's dictionary, as " all such clothes as are hung about
the cage-work, or uppermost hull, to shadow the men from
the enemy in an engagement; whence they are also termed
Fights." The *Wark* or waist of a ship, is described as that
part of her which lies between the two masts, the main and
the fore-masts.

and the trained-bands, who carried "the Protestation" tied to the tops of their pikes, and
several troops of volunteers, who, instead of
feathers, decked their hats with "the Protestation." This "tumultuary army" was led by
a Captain of the Artillery-ground, for whom
an extraordinary commission for that purpose
bore the novel title of Major-General of the
Militia. Major Skippon, who had risen from
the ranks, became an able officer in the Revolutionary war. The double triumph was complete by land and water. Its military character was the most striking novelty; and without
a war, the Parliament could show an army.
All these scenes remind one of Revolutionary
Paris.

The King had flown to Hampton Court; this
was the first flight in his life, that was afterwards to be so fugitive. Here, however, the
distance was not found inconvenient for the
march of that army of Petitioners, for such
they appeared to be, by their number and their
hostility. It was now the apprentices, the
porters, the beggars, and the " good wives" of
the city,* grew eloquent on paper. The most

* Hume, vi. 477. The philosopher is perfectly Lucianic
in his descriptions, particularly in his profane scoffings of
these female zealots.

remarkable petitioners who went to the King, were the deputation of a formidable body from Hampden's County of Buckinghamshire. Four thousand, as they were computed, says Rush-worth, some have said six, riding every man with the cockade of a printed copy of " the Protestation" in their hats, had presented them-selves at the doors of the Commons, calling themselves " countrymen and neighbours of Hampden." As they were probably expected, this Buckinghamshire cavalcade excited no asto-nishment, and they were sure of a flattering re-ception. It must be confessed this muster did great honour to the Patriot, but the fact could not be concealed, that here was a formidable squadron of cavalry of Hampdenites; of which the Colonel had not yet been appointed. It was a regiment which might have given Charles more reasonable alarm than the Commons affect-ed to feel when Lord Digby drove one morning in a coach and six, attended by a single servant, to deliver a message to about fifty disbanded officers at Kingston, for which he was com-pelled to fly the country, and attainted of trea-son for " levying war."

On the twelfth, Charles flew to Windsor, having first dispatched a message to the Com-mons. He told them that some finding it

disputable whether his proceedings against the
Members were agreeable to their privileges, he
waived them—but would adopt others in an
unquestionable way.

Between this day and the twentieth, a committee, for now the government seemed entirely at the mercy of a select committee, proposed a new Remonstrance on the state of the
kingdom. To disperse this storm, the King
sent down a remarkable message to both
Houses. He offered that if they would digest all their grievances into one entire body,
for settling the affairs of the nation on a secure
basis, he would convince them that he had
never designed to violate their privileges, and
was ready to exceed the greatest example of
the most indulgent Princes.

This healing message rejoiced the Lords,
who implored the Commons to join with them
in accepting this unreserved confidence of the
King. But the Commons had to walk in their
own path, not in that of the King's or the
Lords'. On the next day they pressed the
King to proceed against the members. The
King inquired whether he is to proceed by impeachment in Parliament, or by common law;
or have his choice of either?

After these repeated attempts on the King's

side to maintain the justice of his impeachment, it came to an almost incredible conclusion—the King grants a general pardon to all
the parties! The style is singular: "As he
once conceived that he had ground enough to
accuse them, so now his Majesty finds as good
cause wholly to desert any prosecution of
them." Charles would not falsify his late proceedings by declaring the innocence of the accused Members, but assigns a reason which
only leaves to posterity a testimony of his inextricable difficulties.

It might be imagined that the whole Incident of the five Members, had now closed all
farther negotiations. But while Charles existed as the Sovereign, there remained for the
Commons, particularly for the Commonwealth-
men, much to be done. They had not yet
obtained possession of the sword, though they
had wrested the sceptre from Royalty. They
advanced a step farther than the ingenuity of
malice could easily have contrived. They petitioned the King to disclose the names of his
informers against the five Members, and to
consign them to the Parliament! This "humble petition" never could be answered by the
King, and this they well knew.* Such was

* Rushworth notes, "What answer his Majesty returned to
this petition, or whether any, I do not find, or remember."—

their Machiavelian policy; to close their discussions they usually forced the King into a
predicament in which he must either have
been the most contemptible of Princes in sacri-
ficing his friends, or in exposing the secrets of
State, which involved his honour; or appear
odious to the people by a concealment of what
he dared not avow, or for having alleged what
he could not maintain.

At this moment the King was left abandoned amidst the most urgent wants. He
could no longer draw the weekly supplies for
his household, for the officers of the customs
were under the controul of the Commons.
The Queen had pawned her plate for a temporary aid. His friends in terror were in flight;
and the Sovereign sate amidst a council whom
he could no longer consult. He was betrayed
by the most confidential of his intimates. He
was deserted by those who like Lord Holland
had depended on his bounty, or whom like the
Earl of Essex he had unaccountably neglected.

Rushworth, iv. 492. I observe by Mr. Brodie that a bill in
vindication of the accused Members, was immediately prepared, but Charles justly alleging that it reflected on him,
which it certainly did, refused to pass it. Parl. Hist. x.
388. Cobbet, ii. 1134-46. This fact completes the proofs
of the rancorous personal persecution of the helpless
Monarch.

" In this sad condition," says Lord Clarendon,
" was the King at Windsor, fallen in ten days
from a height and greatness that his enemies
feared, to such a lowness that his own servants
durst hardly avow the waiting on him."

Amidst the perplexities of State, and these
personal distresses, the anxieties of Charles
were increased by the fate of his Queen, and
the pressure of his own immediate plans of
operation. Henrietta's fears were restless since
the menace of impeachment. The pretext of
the Queen to accompany her daughter, be-
trothed to the Prince of Orange, to Holland,
covered more than one design. There, in security, not unprovided with the means, carrying with her the crown jewels, she might execute some confidential offices, while the King
resolved to fly to the North, as yet untainted
by the mobocracy of the Metropolis.

There was yet an agony to pass through for
the husband, in the separation from his adored
companion—that hapless foreigner, now chased
to a still more foreign land, to live alone among
a people who never cast a sorrowing look on
suffering Royalty. Charles accompanied Henrietta and the Princess to Dover; many an im-
portunate message was received from the Commons on his way, and the last hours of the

parting of the family were disturbed by many
a gloomy presage. When the Queen had
embarked, Charles stood immoveable, watching
the departing ship with the most poignant emotions. There was an awful uncertainty whether they should ever meet again. He stood
on the shore to give them the last signal, the
last farewell!—gazing with moistened eyes till
the shadowy sails vanished in the atmosphere.
When the vessel was no longer visible, Charles
lingered for some time, pacing along the shore,
wrapped in deep and sad thoughts. The King
had of late been accustomed to the deprivation
of his power—to the destitution of personal
wants, and it was doubtful whether he had a
kingdom which acknowledged its Monarch, or
a soldier who would obey his commands, for at
this very moment, and on his road, he had been
assailed by reiterated messages to deliver up
the militia to the Commons. But he had never yet lost his wife—he had never felt that
pang of love—the loneliness of the soul.

Yet he was still a father, and Charles contemplated on a melancholy pleasure on his
return to Greenwich, to embrace the Prince.
On this last tendril were now clinging his domestic affections; yet of this object of his
tenderness the Commons hastened to deprive

him. While at Dover, a worthless courtier
had been refused to be admitted of the Prince's
bed-chamber. With men of this stamp a
favour denied implies a wrong received; and
thus injured, this man declared that " since
he could not be considerable by doing the
King service, considerable he would be, by
doing him disservice." Posting to the Parliament, he gave some pretended information
of a design to remove the Prince into France,
but more intelligibly offered himself as " their
bravo" at taverns, and meetings, not deficient
in insolence and audacity. This worthless rejected creature of the Court, though without
talents, and having long lost his character,
was publicly embraced and eulogised, even by
Hampden. In the spirit of party no man is
too mean to court, no arts too gross to practise. Charles had desired the Marquis of Hertford, the governor of the Prince, to bring him
to Greenwich; on this an express order from
the House forbade his removal. But the command of the father was preferred. Several
Members hastened to Greenwich to convey the
Prince to London, but the King had arrived;
and they were silent in the presence of the
father. Charles had been greatly agitated on
his road by a message from the Commons

respecting the Prince. Embracing his son, the melancholy Monarch, shedding some joyful tears, exclaimed, " I can now forget all, since I have got Charles !"

The King had granted so much, that he had nothing left to bestow, save one great object of the ambition of the triumphant party —the army itself.

They had first proposed to nominate the Lords Lieutenant of every county, chiefly their adherents, who were to obey the orders of the two Houses; the two Houses were now the House of Commons. The King had not refused even this point, reserving to himself a revocable power. But their policy was now, observes Hume, to astonish the King by the boldness of their enterprises. They declared that their fears and jealousies had so multiplied on them, that it was necessary for them to dispose of the whole military force of the kingdom, both for the safety of his Majesty and the people; this they had resolved to do, by the authority of both Houses—that is by their own authority. And they mercifully invited his Majesty to fix his residence among them.

It is remarkable of Charles the First, that whenever he acted unembarrassed by the distracting councils of others, there was a promptness in reply, and a decision in conduct; which convey the most favourable impressions not only of his intellect, but of his intellectual courage. When the Committee of both Houses went down to Newmarket to deliver this astonishing message, instead of finding the King subdued into pusillanimity, an object of the contempt they had so studiously shown him, they were answered by such an unexpected denial, in a style so vigorous and indignant, that it startled the Committee, who had relied on what of late had so often passed. They had come to vanquish a deserted Monarch, and were themselves repulsed. Lord Holland would not venture to report the King's words, without a written memorandum. By this circumstance posterity receives an authentic specimen of Charles's colloquial discourse; we trace his warm undisguised emotions expressive of his anger, or pathetic from deep and injured feelings.

From the King's interviews with the Committee I transcribe those passages which will interest the readers of his history.

" I am confident that you expect not that I should give you a speedy answer to this strange and unexpected declaration.

" What would you have ? Have I violated

your laws? Have I denied to pass any one
Bill for the ease and security of my subjects?
I do not ask you what you have done for me?

"Have any of my people been transported with fears and apprehensions? I have
offered as free and general a pardon, as yourselves can devise. All this considered, there is
a judgment from Heaven upon this nation if
these distractions continue. God so deal with
me and mine that all my thoughts and intentions are upright for the maintenance of the
true Protestant profession and for the observation and preservation of the laws of the land."

On the following day the Earl of Holland
endeavoured to persuade his Majesty to come
near the Parliament. Charles replied, "I would
you had given me cause, but I am sure this
Declaration is not the way to it. And in all
Aristotle's rhetoric there is no such argument
of persuasion."

The Earl of Pembroke pressed to learn of his
Majesty what he would have them say to the
Parliament? Charles smartly replied, that "He
would whip a boy in Westminster School that
could not tell that by his answer."

Again pressed by the Earl of Pembroke,
after all that had passed, to compromise the demand of the Commons, by granting the militia

for a time : Charles suddenly swore, " By God ! not for an hour ! You have asked that of me in this, was never asked of a King, and with which I will not trust my wife and children."

Well might Charles the First exclaim, as once he did, in addressing the Commons, " Surely, we too have our grievances !"

SUPPLEMENTARY CHAPTER UPON

SIR JOHN ELIOT,

WITH HIS CORRESPONDENCE DURING HIS

IMPRISONMENT IN THE TOWER.

As no personal history of Sir JOHN ELIOT was known before I wrote, I considered myself fortunate in having been enabled to discover many positive facts, hitherto unknown, of this memorable patriot ; their results assisted in the developement of his character.

When I had discovered that Sir John Eliot had formerly been the intimate acquaintance and fellow-traveller of the Duke of Buckingham ; that so late as 1623, Sir John had written in a strain of court flattery and humble intercession ; that he had then suffered an imprisonment, and declared that " having served his Grace with all affection, he had preserved the rights and liberties of the Duke, though with the loss of his own,"—could I pass over so many important circumstances, which hitherto no one had noticed ? Could I avoid combining them together, and then drawing the evident conclusion, that he who was so intrepid a patriot in 1626,

had in 1623, been very differently affected towards this
State-victim ?

What I had said attracted the attention of the very
amiable descendant of that great Patriot.   Lord Eliot
favoured me with a correspondence on that occasion, in
which the ability of the noble writer is only equalled
by his urbanity.

I had said that Sir John Eliot was " of a new family,"
an expression retained from a contemporary writer, who
at the time seems to have considered that a family in
Cornwall, not of ancient Cornish descent, was there " a
new family."   I read with delight his Lordship's accurate researches relative to the Family of the Eliots.   I
rejoice whenever I observe the junior branches of our
Aristocracy sensible, that they have had Ancestors, and
that there is a Posterity.   Some appear to consider that
they stand unconnected with either.

His Lordship writes, " Without attaching any undue importance to Antiquity of Family, one may be
permitted to entertain some little feeling on this subject ;
and I trust that you will not think that in mentioning
the following circumstances I have dwelt on them at an
unreasonable length."   I am confident, since I have
known his Lordship, that he entertains not a little, but
a great deal of feeling on this subject.   The descendant
of an illustrious man has always to consider that a great
Ancestor is a perpetual Rival.

Lord Eliot's researches in the antiquity of his family
will interest some of my readers, as a Record preserving
several curious particulars ; although his Lordship observes that " These statements may not be of any interest to the world in general, but they are still of some
importance to the descendants of Sir John Eliot."

His Lordship then proceeds,

" The assertion that Sir John Eliot was of a new family is incorrect. The great Uncle of Sir John, who was the first possessor of Port Eliot, was, it is true, not of antient *Cornish* descent, but his family had been seated in Devonshire for many generations; the name of one of his Ancestors being found in the Sheriff's Returns of the Gentry of that County made in 1433, 12 Henry VI." as may be seen in Fuller's Worthies. Prince likewise, in his Worthies of Devon, mentions the family of Eliots as being ancient. The Priory of St. Germans and its Lands were obtained from the family of Champernowne, (to whom they had been granted by Henry VIII.) in exchange for property possessed by Sir John Eliot's great Uncle at Cutlands, near Ashburton. I do not know the exact year in which this exchange took place, but John Eliot died at the Priory of St. Germans, having given it the name of *Port Eliot*, in 1565. An account of that transaction is to be found in Carew's Survey of Cornwall, published about 1580.* Chalmers, in his Biographical Dictionary, speaks of the family of Eliot of Port Eliot, and those of Heathfield and Minto, to be descended from a Sir W. Aliot, who came over with William the Conqueror, but this account is merely traditional, and cannot be borne out by proof. The Heralds' Visitation of Cornwall made in 1602, and preserved in the Heralds' College, gives the armorial bearings of the family, the shield containing twelve quarterings,—a proof, at a time when pretensions to Heraldic honours were minutely scrutinized, that the origin of the family could not have been very recent."

* The first Edition of Carew's " Survey," appears to have been in 1602. It was probably *written* about the time his Lordship notices.

I noticed, vol. ii. 277, from the Report of the High
Sheriff of Cornwall, and the Commissioners returning a
nihil, when sent to inquire into the lands and goods of
Sir John Eliot, and also from what he had himself declared I surmised, either that means had been resorted to,
to screen his property, or that Eliot was a man of ruined
fortunes. I derived my information from a Manuscript
to which I referred.

On this Lord Eliot remarks, " With respect to Sir
John Eliot's ruined fortunes, I must be allowed to call
in question the accuracy of this supposition. The lands
attached to the Priory of St. Germans were of considerable extent; they have descended from father to son to
the present day, and now form a considerable portion
of my father's property—I am certainly at a loss to account for the report of the Sheriff and Commissioners,
of which I was ignorant, and can only suppose that he
must have conveyed his estate to his son."

This perplexing incident in Sir John's history, has
been perfectly cleared of any doubts, since I have perused his correspondence. The apparent destitution of
Sir John, which startled his Lordship, was solely a contrivance to elude the gripe of the Law. A letter addressed to his cousin Boscawen, which I have printed,
fully explains " this management of his poor fortune,
which through the disturbance of these times I may not
call my own." Sir John grants an allowance of 200*l.* per
annum to his youngest son for travelling abroad. This
was no mean expenditure; Sir Symonds D'Ewes, was
allowed at college only 50*l.* a year, at a time his father
was one of the Six clerks in Chancery, with an income
of 3000*l.* a year. I find Sir John in the Tower ar-
ranging leases for tenants, through the medium of his
relatives, who held his estates in trust. He subscribes

letters to a confidential servant, " Your loving Master."
Nor does Sir John, abstracted as we shall find him in
his platonic ethics, evince any deficient shrewdness in
worldly affairs; take his opinion on one of the Tenant's
request to have a wall rebuilt to which Sir John was
not liable—" There would be more charity than wisdom, in this." It appears that none of the estates were
forfeited, nor probably any of the amercements paid.
The vote of 5000*l.* afterwards granted by the Parliament to his sons, was probably a mere party object;
and seems to have been a remuneration for a loss which
had never been experienced.

An important circumstance in the developement of
Sir John Eliot's personal character, was his extreme
irascibility. I ascribed much of the turbulence of his
genius to his hot temper, and I conveyed an idea of
one of these eruptions of passion by the extraordinary
incident of Sir John's quarrel with the Moyles, when
" in the hour of reconciliation, with wine before them,
Eliot treacherously stabbed the father in the back."
This is the most painful incident in the life of Eliot; and
as he is held to have been a martyr in the cause of freedom, party writers, as Mrs. Macaulay and Mr. Brodie,
in alluding to several anecdotes of his outrageous violence, for several are noticed, are pleased to say of those
who have handed them down to us that " the charges in
which they have indulged, do not rest on satisfactory
evidence." I was satisfied with the evidence I adduced,
—namely, that of the very person who had received
the blow, and told the particulars to his grandson, the
learned Dean Prideaux, from whom Echard received

it: I consider the fact is now confirmed by a curious apology sent by Sir John Eliot to Mr. Moyle, which Lord Eliot discovered among some family papers. I transcribe this singular document with his Lordship's observation.

APOLOGY OF SIR JOHN ELIOT.

MR. MOYLE,

I doe acknowledge I have done you a greate injury which I wish I had never done, and doe desire you to remit it, and I desire that all unkindnesse may be forgiven and forgotten betwixt us, and henceforwarde I shall desire and deserve your love in all frendly offices, as I hope you will mine.

JO. ELYOTTE.

Witnesses.

WILLIAM CORYTON   NICHOLAS NICOLLS
BEVILL GRENVILL   EDWARD CARTER
DEGORIE TREMAYNE

There are two other names which I cannot read; among those above, are persons distinguished in those times, and in Parliament.

On this document Lord Eliot observes, with a due feeling to his great ancestor,—" I do not know whether you will agree with me in thinking, that the language in which it is couched would hardly lead one to suppose that it was addressed by an assassin to his victim. It appears to me to be an acknowledgment of a hasty and unpremeditated act of violence, but not one which precluded in the writer's opinion the possibility of a restoration of friendly feeling between him and the injured party."

I perfectly agree with his Lordship, that this extraordinary apology was not written by a man who had stabbed his companion in the back ; nor can I imagine, that after such a revolting incident any approximation to a renewal of intercourse would have been possible. It is therefore evident to me, that this apology was drawn up for some former " great injury," whatever it might be—but it surely confirms the recorded tale. The apology was accepted, and it was "*in the hour of reconciliation*, with wine before them," that the treacherous blow was struck. We remain, however, in ignorance of the cause of this implacable hostility, as well as of another far more important to learn, his personal invectives against the Duke of Buckingham. I discover by Sir John's letters, that on the death of Buckingham there was a suit pending, and accompts to be settled, between " My Lord Admiral," and Sir John. There is also a letter of Selden from the Temple, dated November 1628. It relates to "a Patent of Sir John's, delivered to him in a box," for the purpose of Selden's examination whether the death of the granter made it void. This evidently was Buckingham—one of his earliest companions and apparently his patron. We know too, that Eliot was at court—there was a connection with Buckingham and an intercourse with the royal circle, for Sir John was well known to the King, which in the short life of this declamatory patriot are both remarkable.

In consequence of what I noticed of the singular portrait of Sir John Eliot, of which the late Mr. Belsham had informed me, representing the Patriot with " A Comb in his hand," in which some mysterious allusion to his neglected state had been imagined, more particularly as Sir John had desired his posterity to preserve this very Portrait as " a perpetual memorial of his hatred of tyranny"—Lord Eliot with the same continued zeal, sent to Town from Port Eliot two portraits of the Patriot, taken at different periods of his life—both undoubted originals. I have been favoured with a view of them. They should never more be separated. The one represents Sir John in the vigour of life, with a ruddy complexion; the more interesting portrait bearing the melancholy inscription that it was *painted a few days before his death in the Tower*, betrays the last stage of atrophy or consumption. The contraction of the pallid face placed by the side of the broad and florid countenance of his early manhood, offers a very striking and pathetic image of mortality.

The mystery attached to "the Comb" is perfectly cleared on an inspection of the Tower-portrait. Sir John is painted in a very elegant morning-dress, apparently of lace, holding this huge and clumsy instrument of his coiffure. · It was the bad taste of the artist, which produced this impertinent accompaniment; the picture though somewhat hard and stiff, has a great appearance of truth.

CORRESPONDENCE.

I said in the second volume of these Commentaries, p. 283, " During his long imprisonment in the Tower, Sir John Eliot found, as other impetuous spirits have, that wisdom and philosophy have hidden themselves behind the bars of a prison window; there, his passions weaker, and his contemplation more profound, he nobly employed himself on an elaborate treatise on " The Monarchy of Man."

When this was written, I was unacquainted with that series of correspondence, chiefly from the Tower, which Lord Eliot has since confided to my care. · Nothing less than the abundant zeal which we mutually felt, for a very memorable character imperfectly known in our history, could have induced his Lordship to have exerted no ordinary pains, and me to undergo a slight martyrdom of patience, in conning the alphabet of Sir John.

Sir John Eliot, who loved the labours of the pen, preserved copies of his own letters, and many of those of his correspondents have been bound in the same volume; among these are the illustrious names of Hampden, Selden, and Hollis; the name of Pym does not appear.

The Correspondence will not throw any light on public affairs, or on the political life of Eliot. Not a single political allusion passes between Hampden and Eliot. The subject appears to have been studiously avoided. Eliot probably dreaded that his papers might be unexpectedly searched; and it was not without difficulty that some of the letters reached the imprisoned patriot. It is to be regretted that we learn nothing of Sir John's preceding life. He tells his sons that it had been a busy one. There is no evidence of Sir John's disposition to rhyming in his Correspondence; his harsh imprisonment in the Tower had infallibly awakened that propensity, had he ever possessed it. I therefore do not know how to account for the satires said to be composed by him against the Duke of Buckingham. We find in the letters an abundance of philosophy, of the most abstract and elevated ethics; a singular mixture of the dogmas of the Porch, and the faith of Christianity. His classical attainments were considerable; his style of composition is Ciceronian; it is sometimes exuberant, and sometimes it requires great attention not to complain of its obscurity. But he aimed at a splendour to which he often reached; and the fortunate passages of his eloquence had been rarely equalled by others in his day. He was a votary, perhaps a victim to Stoicism; he had filled his mind with sublime reveries; and the stoical philosophy which he so ardently cultivated, may have offered consolations in a dungeon. His scholastic erudition injured his genius; in the Treatises he has left, he advances no position but on some authority; and Hampden, to whom Eliot sent his writings for revision, in performing the critical office with infinite delicacy, advised his friend not to bind up the flowers of others so much, as to draw from his own fertile invention. More than one large Treatise, are the fruits of his imprisonment, and remain the monuments of the greatness of his mind.

The letters of Sir John Eliot, which I have selected, appear to me to exhibit some novel and singular traits in his own personal character—in his chastised mind, abstracted from the ungoverned passions of society. The lofty strain of morality which he addresses to his sons, is at least admirable—it came from one who formerly had not been himself so familiar with that theory of morals, which charmed him in the dreary years of his confinement. The last days of Eliot seem to have been touched by a more melancholy tenderness,—the secret precursors of a life about to cease; the meltings of his unbroken mind.

I have preserved every letter of Hampden, of whom I have never met with any other writings. They delight from the charm of his manner, and the strong feelings which evidently dictated them. They are usually com-plimentary or consolatory; some bear a deeper in-terest; and all are stamped with the character of a superior mind.

(Eliot Papers, 34.)

[This letter, which I could not venture to curtail, is a most un-common address of a Father to his Sons. It not only conveys to us some particulars of the memorable writer himself, but dis-plays at full the singular state of his mind—the high tone of his philosophical conceptions. The style seems too elaborate for ordinary day-life, but many reflections show the writer had been schooled by experience while he lectures on a sublime theory of morals.]

SIR JOHN ELIOT TO HIS SONS.

SONNS,

IF my desires had been valuable for one hour, I had long since written to you which (what) in little, does de-liver a large character of my fortune, that in nothing has allowed me to be master of myself. I have formerly been prevented by imployment, which was so tyrannical on my time, as all minutes were anticipated; now my lea-sure contradicts me, and is soe violent on the contrary, soe great an enemy to all action, as it makes itself un-useful—both leisure and business have opposed me either in time or libertie, that I have had noe means of expression but my praiers, in which I have never failed to make God the witness of my love, whose blessings I doubt not will deduce it in some evidence to you.

And now having gotten a little opportunity (though by stealth) I cannot but give it some testimony from myself, and let you see my dearest expectation in your good, in which both my hopes and happiness are fixt as in their sphear, which moves with your endeavours though guided by the influence of a greater power.

It is no small satisfaction to me when I have intelligence of your health, and I bless Heaven for it as some
effect of my petitions; but to hear of the progress of
your learning, of your aptness and diligence in that,
of your careful attendance in all exercises of religion,
and the instruction and improvements of your minds,
which are foundations of a future building, this does
infuse another spirit to me, and extends my comforts to
a latitude that hardly is expressible. I cannot but in
general thus discover it, partly to intimate the pitch of
my affections, that your course may rise with it; partly
to represent your owne example to you, that you digress
not from that rule which practise and experience continually must better.

It is a fine history well studied, the observation of
ourselves, the exact view of our own actions to examine
what has past, it begets a great knowledge of particulars, taking of all kindes; and gives a larger advantage
to your judgments truly to discriminate, for it carries
a full prospect to the hart which opens the intention,
and through that simplicity is seene the principle of each
motion which shadows or dissembles for us the good or
evil. From thence having the trew knowledge of particulars what we have done and how; and the judgment
upon that, what our workes are to us; then come we to
reflect upon ourselves for the censure (judgment) of any
action wherein every little error is discovered, every obli-
quity is seene, which by the reprehension of the conscience (the most awefull of tribunals) being brought to
a secret confession, drawes a free repentance and submission for the fault, and soe is reduced to conformity
again: this fruite has the study of ourselves, besides
many other benefitts. The varietie of contingeancies
and accidents, in our persons, in our fortunes, in our

friends, are as so many lectures of philosophie, showing
the doubtful being and possession we have here, the uncertainty of our friends, the mutability of our fortunes,
the anxieties of our lives, the changes and vicissitudes
they are subject to, which make up that conclusion in
divinity that we are but pilgrims and strangers in this
world; and therefore should not love it, but our rest
and habitation must be elsewhere.

If I should take occasion from myself to dilate this
point more fully, what a catalogue could I give of instances of all sorts! What a contiguity of sufferings of
which there is yet no end! Should those evills be complained? Should I make lamentation of these crosses?
Should I conceave the worse of my condition in the
study of myself that my adversities oppose me? Noe!
I may not—(and yet I will not be so stoical as not to
think them evils, I will not do that prejudice to virtue
by detraction of her adversaries). They are evills, for
I doe confess them, but of that nature and soe followed,
soe neighbouring upon good, as they are noe cause of
sorrow, but of joy; seeing whose enemies they make
us, enemies of fortune, enemies of the world, enemies of
their children, and to know for whom we suffer; for
Him that is their enemy, for Him that can command
them whose agents only and instruments they are to
work his trials on us, which may render us more perfect
and acceptable to himself should these enforce a sorrow
which are the true touches of his favour, and not affect
us rather with the higher apprehension of our happiness.

Amongst my many obligations to my Creator, which
prove the infinity of his mercies that like a full stream
have been always flowing on me, there is none concerning this life wherein I have found more pleasure or ad-

vantage than in these trialls and afflictions (and I may
not limitt it soe narrowly within the confines of this life
which I hope shall extend much further) the operations
they have had, the new effects they worke, the discoveries they make upon ourselves, upon others, upon all ;
shewing the scope of our intentions, the summe of our
indeavours, the strength of all our actions to be vanitie ;
how can it then but leave an impression in our harts,
that we are nearest unto happiness when we are furthest
off from them, I meane the vaine intentions of this world,
the fruitless labours, and indeavours that they move,
from which nothing soe faithfully delivers us as the
crosses and afflictions that we meet, those mastering
checks and contraventions that like torrents break down
all outward hopes ?   This speculation of the vanitie of
this world does not only shew a happiness in those
crosses by the exemption which we gain, but infers a
further benefit in that by a nearer contemplation of ourselves ; of what we doe, consist, what original we had, to
what end we were directed, and in this he whose image
is upon us, to whom we doe belong, what materials we
are of; that, besides the bodie (which only is obnoxious
to these troubles) the better part of our composition is
the soule, whose freedom is not subject to anie autho-
ritie without us, but depends wholly on the disposition
of the Maker, who framed it for himself, and therefore
gave it substance incompatible of all power and dominion but his own.

This happiness I confess in all the trials I have had
has never parted from me (how great then is his favour
by whose meanes I have enjoyed it !) The days have all
seemed pleasant, nor nights have ever been tedious ; nor
fears nor terrors have possest me, but a constant peace
and tranquillity of the mind, whose agitation has been

chiefly in thanks and acknowledgments to Him by whose grace I have subsisted, and shall yet I hope participate of his blessings upon you.

I have the more enlarged myself in this, that you might have a right view of the condition which I suffer, least from a bye relation, as through a perspective not truly representing, some false sence might be contracted. Neither could I thinke that altogether unusefull for your knowledge which may afford you both precept and example. Consider it, weigh it duly, and when you find a signe or indication of some error, make it an instruction how to avoid the like; if there appears but the resemblance of some virtue, suppose it better, and make it a president for yourselves ; when you meet the prints and footsteps of the Almightie, magnify the goodness of his providence and miracles that makes such low descents ; consider that there is a nature turns all sweetness into venom, when from the bitterest hearbs the bee extracts a honie. Industry and the habit of the soule give the effect and operation unto all things, and that to one seems barren and unpleasant, to another is made fruitfull and delightsome: Even in this, by your application and endeavour, I am confident may be found both pleasure and advantage. This comes only as a testimony of my love (and soe you must accept it, the time yielding noe other waie of demonstration), and by this expression know that I daily praie for your happiness and felicity as the chief subject of my wishes, and shall make my continual supplication to the Lord, that from the riches of his mercie he will give you such influence of his graces as your blessing and prosperitie may satisfy and enlarge the hopes and comforts of

Your most affectionate Father.

Tower, 8 July, 1629.

(Eliot Papers, MS. fol. 173.)

[The present seems to be the first letter Hampden wrote to
Eliot; the address being more formal than the others.]

NOBLE SIR,

I HOPE this letter is conveyed to you by so safe a
hand that yours will be the first that shall open it, or if
not, yet since you injoy as much as without a contradiction you may the liberty of a prison, it shall be no
offence to wish you may make the best use on't: that
God may find you as much his now you injoy the bene-
fitt of secondary helpes, as you found hime yours while
by deprivation of all others you were cast upon his immediate support. This is all I have or ame willing to
say, but that the paper of considerations concerning the
plantation might be very safely conveyed to mee by this
hand, and after transcribing should be as safely returned
if you vouchsafe to send it mee. I beseech you present my service to Mr. Valentine, Mr. Long my countryman if with you, and lett mee be honored with the
stile of

Your faithfull friend and servant,

JNO. HAMPDEN.

Hampden, December 8th.

(Eliot Papers, fol. 23.)

[This is a complimentary letter of Hampden; but the mention
of Sir John's sons and his " papers" gave it some interest to the
father and the author.]

About 1628 or 9.

SIR,

IF my affections could be so dull as to give way to a
sleepy excuse of a letter: yet this bearer our common
friend had power to awaken them, and command it, to
the public experience of whose worth in doing, I can

now adde my private of his patience in suffering the miseryes of a rough hewn entertainment: to be tolerated by the addition of your sonnes company: of whome if ever you live to see a fruite answerable to the promise of the present blossoms, it will be a blessing of that weight as will turne the scale against all worldly afflictions, and denominate your life happy.

I returne your papers with many thankes which I have transcribed, not readd; the discourse therefore upon the subject must be reserved to another season: when I may with better oportunity and freedome communicate my thoughts to you my friend. Till then with my salutations of all your society, and prayers for your health I rest,

Your ever assured friend and servant,

JOHN HAMPDEN.

Hampden, January 4th.

(Sir John Eliot's MSS. fol. 56.)

[The following letter shows that Sir John's estates were placed in trust to save them from a legal seizure, or amercement.]

TO MY COUSIN BOSCAWEN.·

SIR,

HAVING a great confidence in your worth, as I find you to have been selected by my father-in-law, I have presumed likewise for my self to name you in a trust for the management of that poor fortune, which through the disturbances of these times I may not call mine own. As it concerns a prisoner, I cannot doubt your readiness to take such an object, from your charity: but the interest of my children being present likewise in the necessity of orphans, and their extraction from your blood and kindred, give me no less assurance in your love than my libertie might impart. Your trouble will only be for the sealing of some leases now and then, upon compositions of my tenants, for which as there is occasion, I have appointed this bearer, my servant, Maurice Hill, to attend you, to whom your dispatch in that behalf shall be a full satisfaction of the trust.

Tower, 28th February, 1630.

(Eliot MSS. fol. 94.)

[Eliot remonstrates with his son, on some remissness in his studies. He opens with some very exalted ideas of a platonic cast; and impresses the necessity of " Privacy, as the nurse of Studies." At the close the idea of *Intention* is remarkably used.]

RICHARD,

THAT your studies may not want occasion, if my letters do impart it, I shall often solicit you as now to the intention of that work, hoping more often by that means to hear again from you, for till the last conveyance I had no little doubt, after so long a silence, where you were, or whether you were or no; but now your paper has resolved me with some satisfaction to my hopes, that the reflection of your virtues will in time afford me both comfort and confidence; comfort in your happiness and confidence against all accident. For as my hopes so my fears have their chief place in you, (you and your brother, for you two I make but one in respect of the spirit and affection which shall always be between you,) who as in order and expectation you are first, are likewise the greatest object of my care, the success of which will stand for a pattern and prediction to the rest. Therefore you must endeavour to make this precedent exact, that shall have transition to others, and not to frame it to the common models of the time, but *contrarium mundo iter intende*, like the *primum mobile* and first shadow, thought for whole worlds, the generality of men, as the less orbs make their revolutions irregular; then let your motions have that regularity and fulness, as no others may impair them.

In this case it will not be enough to abandon some acquaintance, but to leave all; I mean the pleasure of society, that *esca malorum*, as Cicero calls it, and to retire wholly to yourself. Virtue is more rigid than to be ˙taken with delights; those vanities she leaves, for these she scorns herself; her paths are arduous and rough, but excellent, and pleasant to those who once have past them. Honour is a concomitant they have to entertain them in their journey, nay it becomes their servant, and what is attended by all others, those who travel in that way have it to wait on them. And this effort of virtue has not, as in the vulgar acceptation, its dwelling on a hill, it crowds not in the multitude, but *extra conspectum*, as Seneca says, beyond the common prospect, for what is familiar is cheap; and those things are always in greatest admiration which are least seen; the desire giving lustre to the object, *majus è longinquo reverentia*, saith Tacitus, all glory is heightened by the distance, not of place but time, that it is rarely seen makes it more glorious and admirable, which without a want and expectation, would be lost, at length neglected, as a prophet is not honoured in his country. Apply this then to yourself, for we may compare Mantua with Rome. Would you have estimation among men (for honor is no other), there are two ways to gain it, virtue and privacy, and the latter is an inducement to the former; for privacy is the only nurse of studies, studies of virtue, therefore for virtue or for honor's sake. What is most happy for yourself is most precious with others, where that it may follow you, follow not that which flies when it is pursued; for shadows and honor, are in that quality alike, if not the same.

But I doubt there are shadows of those shadows that are followed; something less than honour, while the sub-stance and virtue is neglected. How comes it else that your tutor should complain you are careless and remiss? It cannot be when there is true affection, there should be indiligence and neglect; when studie is declined the desires are alienated from the virtue, for no ends are attained without the means; and the neglect of that shows a diversion from the other. If it be since my last, I must resume my fears, that though your own judgment did not guide you, my cautions should be lost. If it should be hereafter when that advise, those reasons and the commands, and authority of a father (a father most indulgent to the happiness of his child,) which I now give you to redeem the time is spent; to redeem the studies you have missed, and to redeem yourself who are ingaged to danger, or that hazard and adventure. If these make no impressions, and these must be read in the characters of your course, if they work not an alteration, if they cause not a new diligency and inten-tion, an intention of yourself, and intention of the object, virtue; an intention of the means, your study, and an exact intention of the time to improve it to that end, I shall then receive that wound, which I thank God no enemy could give me, sorrow and affliction of the mind, and that from him from whom I hoped the contrary — but I still hope, and the more confidently for the pro-mise which your letters have assured me. Let it be bettered in performance by your future care and dili-gence, which shall be accompanied with the prayers and blessings of

Your most loving Father,
JOHN ELIOT.

Tower, 7th of November, 1630.

To R. ELIOT.

(Eliot MSS. 108.)

[On the removal of his lodgings in the Tower. These occasion no alteration in his mind. Sends some " light papers" for Sir Oliver Luke's corrections.]

SIR J. ELIOT TO SIR OLIVER LUKE.

SIR,

My manie troubles of removing have a while hindered me from writing to you. The lodging which I had upon my first remove before Christmas being again altered, soe as I may saie of my lodgings in the Tower as Jacob for his wages, Now then ten times have they chaunged it, but, I thank God, not once has it caused an alteration of my mind — so infinite is that mercie which has hitherto protected mee, and I doubt not but I shall find it with mee. The greatest violence of that storme is like to fall on Valentine, he being retrencht of that libertie he had, which maie be some prejudice to his business. It threatens likewise some dropps on Mr. Selden, and has stopt the discharge was looked for — being yesterday, his day of appearance in the court, but the judges would not quit him, and therefore continued him again on baile for a while longer, that they might further advise therein.

*   *   *   *

When you have wearied your good thoughts with those light papers that I sent you, return them with the corrections of your judgment. I may one day send you others of more worth, if it please God to continue me this leisure and my health, but the best can be but broken, and in patches from him that dares not hazard to gather them. Such thinges from me falling like the leaves in Autumn soe variously and uncertainly, that

they hardly meet again — but with you I am confident
what else my weakness shall present will have a faire acceptance.   Your charity is my assurance in this point,
of which being most deserving as of your praiers, I rest,

Your most affectionate servant,

JOHN ELIOT.

Tower, 25th January, 1631.

(Eliot Papers. 110.)

[Eliot complains of a difficulty in receiving letters.   He alludes
to some rumours of his liberation, and closes not without hope of
rejoining the Grenville family.]

TO MR. GRENVILLE.

Tower, 31st January, 1631-32.

SIR,

THE restraint and watch uppon me barrs much of
my intercourse with my frends, while their presence is
denied me, and letters are soe dangerous and suspected,
as it is little that way we exchange; soe as if circumstances shall condemn me, I must stand guiltie in their
judgments, yet yours, though with some difficultie I
have received, and manie times when it was knocking at
my door, because their convoy could not enter they did
retire again, wherein I must commend the caution of
your messenger; but at length it found a safe passage by
my servant, made mee happie in your favour, for which
this comes as a retribution and acknowledgment.

For those rumours which you meet that are but
artificial, or by chance, it must be your wisdom not to
credit them; manie such false fires are flying dailie in
the ear: when there shall be occasion expect that intelligence from frends, for which in the meene time you do
well to be provided, though I shall crave when that dispute falls properlie and for reasons not deniable, a change
of your intention in particulars as it concerns myselfe, in

the rest I shall concur in all readiness to serve you, and in all you shall command me who am nothing but as you represent. My humble service to your ladie, and tell her that yet I doubt not to kiss her hande—make much of my godsone.

(Eliot's MS.)

[Eliot describes the beginning of his fatal disorder, which he thought originated only in colds.]

TO KNIGHTLEY, HIS BROTHER.

Tower, 15 March, 1631-32.

FOR the present I am wholly at a stand, and have been soe for this fortnight by a sicknesse which it has pleased my Master to impose, in whose hands remain the issues of life and death. It comes originally from my colds, with which the cough having been long upon me causes such ill effects to follow it, that the symptoms are more dangerous than the grief; it has weakened much both the apetite and concoction, and the outward strength, by that some doubt there is of a consumption, but we endeavour to prevent it by application of the means, and as the great physition, seek the blessing from the Lord, &c.

About a week after, he says his health is amended except the hoarseness and some remainder of the cough, which he expects the season will remove.

[He philosophises with good humour on his doctors. They had already considered his illness to be consumption.]

TO HAMPDEN.

Dated 22 March, 1631-32.

LATELY my business hath been much with Doctors, so that but by them, I have had but little trouble with myself. These three weeks I have had a full leasure to do nothing, and strictly tied unto it either by their direction or my weakness. The cause originally was a cold, but the symptoms that did follow it spake more sickness; a gradual indisposition it begot in all the faculties of the bodie. The learned said a consumption did attend it, but I thank God I did not feel or credit it. What they advise as the ordinance that's appointed I was content to use, and in the time I was a patient suffered whatever they imposed. Great is the authority of princes, but greater much is their's who both command our purses and our wills. What the success of their government wills must be referred to Him that is master of their power. I find myself bettered, though not well, which makes me the more readie to observe them. The divine blessing must effectuate their wit— it is that medicine that has hitherto protected me, and will continue me amongst other affairs to remain

Your faithfull friend and servant,

J. E.

(Eliot's MS. Letters, 119.)

[Hampden sends some observations on his younger son, John Eliot; and on his elder, respecting some irregularity at College. At the close, Hampden gives some opinion of Eliot's manuscript.]

HAMPDEN TO ELIOT.

SIR,

I HOPE you will receave your sonnes both safe, and that God will direct you to dispose of them as they may be raised up for his service and to your comfort.

Some words I had with your younger sonne, and given him a taste of those apprehensions he is like to find with you, which I tell him future obedience to your pleasure rather than justification of past passages must remove. He professeth fair; and the ingenuity of his nature doth it, without words; but you know vertuous actions flow not infallibly from the flexiblest dispositions; and love's only a fitt subject for admonition and government to work on; especially that which is paternal. I confess my shallowness to resolve, and therefore unwillingness to say any thing concerning his course, yet will I not give over the consideration, because I much desire to see the spirit rightly managed. But for your elder I think you may with security return him in convenient time, for certainly there was nothing to administer feare of a plott; and in another action that concerned himself, which he'll tell you of, he received good satisfaction of the Vice Chancellor's faire carriage towards him.

I searched my study this morning for a booke to send you of a like subject to that of the papers I had of you, but find it not; as soon as I recover it I'll recommend it to your view. When you have finished your other parts, I pray think mee as worthy of the sight of it as your former, and in both together I'll bewray my weakness to my friend by declaring my sense of them. That I did see is an exquisite nosegay composed of curious flowers, bound together with as fine a thredd; but I must in the end expect honey from my friend somewhat out of those flowers digested, made his own, and giving a true taste of his own sweetnesse, though for that I shall awaite a fitte time and place. The Lord sanctify unto you the sournesse of your present estate and the comforts of your posterity.

Your ever the same assured friend,

April 4th. J. HAMPDEN.

(Additional MS, 5016.)

[At the British Museum, which I accidentally discovered in a box. This letter never reached Eliot, it was intercepted.]

JOHN HAMPDEN TO SIR JOHN ELIOT.

NOBLE SIR,

'TIS well for me that letters cannot blush, else you would easily reade me guilty. I ame ashamed of so long a silence, and know not how to excuse it, for as nothing but businesse can speake for mee, of which kinde I have many advocates, so can I not tell how to call any businesse greater than holding an affectionate correspondence with so excellent a frend. My only confidence is I *pleade* at a barr of *love*, where absolutions are much more frequent than censures. Sure I am that conscience of neglect doth not accuse me; though evidence of fact doth. I would add more, but the entertainment of a stranger friend calls upon me, and *one* other *unevitable* occasion; hold mee excused, *therefore*, deare friend, and if you vouchsafe mee a *letter*, lett mee beg of you to teach me some thrift of time, that I may imploy more in your service, who will ever be

Your faithful servant and affectionate friend,

JO. HAMPDEN.

Commend my service to the soldier if not gone to his Colonel.

Hampden, March 21, 1631-32.

To my honnored and deare friend Sr John Eliott, at his lodging in the Tower.

(Eliot's MSS. Letters, fol. 126.)

[This animated letter of Hampden relates to Sir John Eliot's Sons. He describes the promising character of Mr. Richard Eliot.]

SIR,

I AME so perfectly acquainted with your cleare insight into the dispositions of men, and ability to fitt them with courses suitable, that had you bestowed sonnes of mine as you have done your owne, my judgment durst hardly have called it into question, especially when in laying downe your designe, you have prevented the objections to be made against it: for if Mr. Richard Eliott will in the intermissions of action adde study to practice, and adorne that lively spiritt with flowers of contemplation, he'll raise our expectations of another Sir Edward Verre, that had this character — all summer in the field, all winter in his study, in whose fall fame makes this kingdome a great looser: and having taken this resolution from Counsaile with the highest wisdome (as I doubt not but you have), I hope and pray the same power will crown it with a blessing answerable to your wish.

The way you take with my other friend declares you to be none of the Bishop of Exeter's converts, of whose minde neither ame I superstitiously: but had my opinion been asked I should (as vulgar conceipts use to do) have showed my power rather to raise objections than to answer them; a temper between Fraunce and Oxford might have taken away his scruple with more advantage to his years: to visite Cambridge as a free man for variety and delight, and there intertained himselfe till the next Spring: when University studys and peace had been better settled then I heare it is; for although he be one of those that of his age were looked for in no other booke but that of the minde would be found no ward if you should die to-morrow: yet 'tis a great hazard mee thinkes to send so sweet a disposition guarded with no more experience amongst a people, whereof many make it their religion to be superstitious in impiety ; and their behaviour to be affected in ill-manners : but God, who only knowes the periods of life, and oportunityes to come, hath designed him (I hope) for his owne service betime, and stirred up your providence to husband hime so early for great affaires, then shall he be sure to find hime in Fraunce, that Abraham did in Terar and Joseph in Egypt, under whose wing alone is perfect safety.

Concerning the Lord, who is nowe reported to be as deepe in repentance as he was profound in sinne : the papers, &c. : I shall take leave from your favour, and my streight of time to be silent till the next weeke, when I hope for the happinesse to kisse your handes, and to present you with my most humble thankes for your letters, which confirm the observation I have made in the progresse of affections : that it is easier much to winne upon ingenious natures than to meritt it. This they tell mee I have done of yours, and I account a noble purchas, which to improve with the best services you can command and I perform, shall be the care of

Your affectionate friend and servant,

JOHN HAMPDEN.

Hampden, May 11th, 1631.

Present my services to Mr. Long, Mr. Valentine, &c.

Do not thinke by what I say that I am fully satisfied of your younger sonne course intended, for I have a crotchett out of the ordinary way, which I would have acquainted you with if I had spoken with you before he had gone, but am almost ashamed to communicate.

(Eliot Papers, fol. 132.)

HAMPDEN TO ELIOT.

SIR,

I RECEIVED your commands by the hands of Mr. Wian,* and was glad to know by them that another's word had power to commaund your faith in my readinesse to obey you, which mine it seems had not. If you yet lack an experience, I wish you had putt mee upon the test of a worke more difficult and important, that your opinion might be changed into beliefe. That man you wrote for I will unfainedly receive into my good opinion, and declare it really when he shall have occasion to putt me to the proofe. I cannot trouble you with many words at this time: make good use of the bookes you shall receive from mee, and of your time; be sure you shall render a strict account of both to

Your ever assured friend and servant,

JOHN HAMPDEN.

Present my service to Mr. Long. I would faine heare of his health.

Hampden, June 8th, 1631.

(Eliot Letters, No. 135.)

[In this letter to the famous Holles, he does not darkly hint at the danger of his correspondence. Six months elapsed before Eliot received the answer. Both parties agree that they can only safely communicate by their hearts.]

SIR JOHN ELIOT TO D. HOLLES.

SIR,

THROUGH a long silence I hope you can retaine the confidence and memoire of your frende. He that knows

---

* Sir John had written a letter of introduction for Mr. Wian to Hampden. Wian was his Proctor.

your virtue in the generale cannot doubt any particular of your charitie. The corruption of this age, if no other danger might occur, were an excuse, even in business, for not writing. The sun, we see, begets divers monsters on the earth when it has heat and violence; Time may do more on paper; therefore the safest intercourse is by harts; in this way I have much intelligence to give you, but you may divine it without prophesie. 'Tis but the honour and affection which I owe you contracted in these sillables.

Your most faithfull frind and servant,

J. E.

Tower, 23d June, 1631.

(Eliot Letters, 159.)

WORTHY SIR,

I AM confident you believe I have returned you a thousand of thancks, and as many answers to your loving letter, since you were pleased to honour me with it, as that before I did as many times visit you with my best well-wishing thoughts, and entertaine you with the offers of my faithfullest services, and that all this entercourse hath been really and truly acted, being done by the hart, which is both (as you say) the safest, and indeed alone real : for that is, though perhaps it appeare not, whereas great outward professions many times appeare when thei are in substance nothing. You and I have found this to be trew philosophy, which as your wisdome will make use of to discerne a superficial frend, so lett your goodness do the same to judge aright of his silence and of all his actions, who is without complement,

Your most faithfull and affectionate
frend and servant,

D. HOLLES.

1 need not express here my desire to be remembered
to the rest of our fellowes, nor need I name them.

Dameram, (query ?) 26th Dec. 1631.

(Eliot's MS. Letters, 140.)

[This is a literary letter, replete with delicate hints and nervous
criticism ; it conveys a high notion of the good taste and the good
sense of Hampden.]

HAMPDEN TO SIR JOHN ELIOT.

SIR,

YOU shall receave the booke I promised by the
bearer's immediate hand. For the other papers, I presume to take a little, and but a little respite. I have
looked upon that rare piece only with a superficial view,
or at first sight, to take the aspect, and proportion in the
whole : after, with a more accurate eye, to take out the
lineaments of every part. 'Twere rashness in me,
therefore, to discover any judgment before I have
ground to make one. This I discerne, that 'tis as complete an image of the patterne as can be drawne by
lines. A lively character of a large minde. The subject, method, and expressions, excellent and homogeniall,
and to say truth, (sweet heart,) somewhat excceding my
commendations : my words cannot render them to the
life ; yet, to shew my ingenuity rather than wit, would
not a less modell have given a full representation of that
subject ? Not by diminution but by contraction of parts.
I desire to learne, I dare not say. The variations upon
each particular seem many. All I confess excellent.
The fountains are full ; the channel narrow ; that may
be the cause, or that the author imitated Virgil, who
made more verses by many than he intended to write,
to extract a just number. Had I seen all his, I could
easily have told him make fewer ; but if he had bade

me tell which he should have spared, I had been apposed : so say I, of these expressions. And that to satisfy you, not myselfe, but that by obeying you in a command so contrary to my own disposition, you may measure how large a power you have over

J. HAMPDEN.

Hampden, June 20, 1631.

Recommend my service to Mr. Long ; and if Sir Oliver Luke be in town, express my affections to him in my words. The first part of your papers you had by the hands of B. Valentine long since. If you hear of your sons, or can send to them, let me know.

(Eliot Papers, 130.)

[This is a curious letter of one of the country gentlemen, of Sir John's party, who gives an account of the commissioners for Loan-money. He " would not be complimented out of his money," and exults on " holding his hands fast in his pocket."]

MR. SCAWEN TO SIR JOHN ELIOT.

THE seconde fearfull commission is now past, and since by your servant you are pleased to demand it of me, I will present you with the relation of the progresse of it.

We were all called together (but in severall days following) at Bodmin. After the commission was read, we were like to depart without as much as any speech offered us ; much tyme was spent in straining courtesy between the son and the father, and I think we had bin deprived of the expectation had not the courtier brought down some of his court-phrases in exchange for the mony. I interpreted their longe silence to the best, thinking they meant by it, that they thought the matter such as no Cornish man would open his mouth in it, and therefore fittest for a stranger, who, for aught that I could perceive, directed his words more to those that should have spoken, than to us that should have heard.

We were directed the first day, that such as would not compound, should give their answers in writing; a course which, if they had held thorough, would have proved little to their advantage. The hundred of East was first called in, which (making choice of the pistors and men fittest for composition) they made pretty store of mony, till St. Germans, according to the direction giving their several papers, had shewn the way of non-composition, (for of twenty-eight returned, not one compounded). Landrake and Landulph followed the president, upon which they thought it best to finish that day's service without calling out that one hundred. The West hundred had not many: Pyder and Stratton very few; Powder somewhat more; but the greatest proportion raised came from Penrith and Kerrier, Trigg and Lesnewth, they being under the command of the Castle, they thought it not wisdom to hold out. The total amounts to not more than 2000 pounds, of which the most of it comes from the meaner sort of people, and such as, I presume, scarce have the value. Some with great words and threatenings, some with persuasions (wherein Sir B. did all) were drawne to it. I was like to have been complimented out of my mony; but that knowing with whom I had to deal, I held, whilst I talked with them, my hands fast in my pocket.

You will wonder to hear what things we had here returned for Knights: but that nothing is now to be wondered at.

If any thing lie here wherein I may serve you, I shall take it an honour to be commanded; and be assured, that as you suffer for others, so there are some others that suffer for you, amongst which is

Your servant,

W. S.

SIR JOHN'S ANSWER ABOUT THE LOAN-MONGERS AT BODMIN.

June 21, 1631.

SIR,

I THANKE you for your intelligence of the late passages at Bodmin, wherein some satisfaction does arise, that though that country have not all the wisdom that they should, yet they are not in as great stupiditie as some others, but divide between folly and abjection. I am glad to hear you neighbours at St. German's doe so well, and by your example make themselves good presidents for others. Those that broke that rule will have occasion to repent it, when they shall see their gain only in the loss of their own monie, which may work a better circumspection for the future. Though I am at a great distance from you in my person, my affection is still with you; and as I wish your happiness, my indeavours shall be readie to procure it. I praie, as to yourself whom I would have confident of this truth, give it in assurance to the rest, that in all things which may level with my power, none shall be more industrious to that service than   J. E.

(Eliot Papers, MS. fol. 146.)

[A complimentary letter, with the present of a small buck, from Hampden.]

DEAR SIR,

I RECEIVED a letter from you the last weeke, for which I owe you ten, to countervaile those lines by encrease in number that I cannot equall in weight: but time is not mine now, nor hath bene since that came to my hands, in your favour therefore hold mee excused. This bearer is appointed to present you with a buck out of my paddock, which must be a small one, to hold proportion with the place and soyle it was bred in. Shortly, I hope (if I do well to hope) to see you ; yet durst I not prolong the expectation of your papers.

You have concerning them layde commaunds upon mee beyond my ability to give you satisfaction in ; but if my apology will not serve when wee meete, I will not decline the service, though to the bewraying of my owne ignorance, which yet I hope your love will cover.

Your ever assured friend and servant,

JNO. HAMPDEN.

Hampden, July 27, 1631.

(Eliot Letters, 152.)

[Eliot's advice to his younger son John on travelling to Italy. Hopes he will avoid " the territories of the Church," and forbids his entrance into Spain. At that period so universal was the dread of relapsing into Papistry.]

TO JOHN ELIOT.

SONNE,

I HAVE received and considered of your letters which mention your desire and reasons to pass speedily into Italy. Good company, I knowe, is a choise thinge, and as a pleasure so an advantage in your travells, which I presume you studie, not for name only, or the affection of some title, but as it meetes with virtue, and then it's truly valuable, that being the crowne and dignity of all honor. The oportunity I confesse which such company does present is a fair motive for the journey, but the time I doubt not yet seasonable to answer it. Autumn in those parts is most dangerous to strangers: the abundance of their fruites, the corruption of their aer through the strife of heat and moisture, and the natural disposition of all bodies to sicknesse and infection in the return of blood, makes it at first more fearful; besides, the plague has raigned generally in that country, and some townes still are visited, by which both the aer and houses may be yet suspected, untile some frosts correct them. I leave to your better consideration to resolve to stay till Spring.

That reason which you give for the advantage of the language, has its truth meerly the contrary; for if without knowledge in the French you first shall seek the Italian, that will be then less pleasant and soe more difficult, by which the more necessary will be left, to be then gained when perchance there will be leasure for it: whereas if you shall gett againe some perfection in the French, and then gett into Italie, what you then lose will be regained againe at your returninge homewards, and you become a master in the tongues. This winter spent in France I hope will be enough for preparation, and then at springe you may pass from thence to Italie.

For the danger that's pretended in your travells in those parts only with private company, I am confident there is no reason, but what the sickness may occasion, and that admits no priviledge. The territories of the Church I hope you will avoid (those I confess are dangerous, as all Spaine, which by no meanes I can allow you ever to enter), but other parts are free, and peaceable as in England, where with discretion you may as much rely on your safetie, for the present troubles in France I conceive little cause of doubt. To strangers they impart noe hasards or adventures, more than voluntarily they insure, but such advantage of knowledge and experience they may yield, which I did think the hope and spirit of that gentleman from whom you received that argument would not have declined.

Thus much in answer to your letter, which I make only on advise. I wonder you never wrote since your being over of Monsieur Durant. His wife inquires here for him, whom I would gladly satisfie, as know how you have agreed. Be careful in your religion, make your devotions frequent, seeke the blessing from above, drawe your imitation to good patternes, lett not vaine pedantries deceive you, prepare your estimation by your virtue, which your own carriage and example must acquire, wherein you have assistants in the most earnest prayers and wishes of

Your loving Father,
JOHN ELIOT.

Tower, 1st September, 1631.

(Eliot Papers, MSS. fol. 163.)

[Hampden sends news, and highly compliments the genius and studies of Eliot.]

SIR,

IN the end of my travailes, I meete the messengers of your love, which bring mee a most gratefull wellcome : your intentions outfly mine that thought to have prevented yours, and convince mee of my disability to keepe pace with you, or the times. My imploiment of late in interrogatory with like affairs hath deprived mee of leisure to complement, and the frame of depositions is able to justle out the style of a letter. You were farre enough above my emulation before ; but breathing now the same ayre with an ambassador, you are out of all ayme.

I believe well of his negotiation from the large testimony you have given of his parts, and I beleeve the

King of Sweden's sword will be the best of his topicks
to persuade a peace.

'Tis a powerful one now if I heare aright: fame giving Tilly a late defeate in Saxony with 20,000 losse;
the truth whereof will facilitate our worke. The Spaniard's curtesy being known to be no lesse then willingly
to render that which he cannot hold. The notion of
these effects interrupts not our quiett, though the reasons by which they are governed do transcend our pitch;
your apprehensions that ascend a region above those
clouds which shadow us, are fitt to pierce such height;
and ours to receave such notions as descend from thence;
which while you are pleased to impart you make the de-
monstrations of your favour to become the rich posses-
sions of

Your ever faithfull friend and servant,

JOHN HAMPDEN.

Present my service to Mr. Long.

Hampden, October 3.

God, I thanke him, hath made me father of another
sonne.

(Eliot Papers, 168.)

[Sir John seems in the following letter somewhat doubtful of a
political apostacy in his friend and fellow-sufferer, Valentine, who
he confesses has "his jugglings."]

SIR JOHN ELIOT TO THOMAS GODFREY.

Godfrey dates from Grantham.

* * * * * *

VALENTINE after his long travails did betake himself
to rest, so as in a month or more, being at his lodging
near the Gate-house, noe friends might see him but
whom his Greatnesse would admit. Sicknesse was pretended, but there were that thought it counterfeit and

affected ; and yet there be that hold his dissimulation worthie punishment. Really I believe him (his juglinge set aside) in the same state he was, both in bodie and in businesse, for though the charge of the Attorney may have changed something in his favour, his fortune is not altered, but the expectations are the same, and as the virtue, such may be the man. This is all I can tell you of him, unless by supposition I could judg him in his reservations and retirement, knocking at some back-door of the Court, at which if he enter to preferment you shall know it from

Your faithfull friend and servant,

J. E.

Tower, 8 November, 1631.

(Eliot Papers, 179.)

[Of all these letters the present seems the most beautiful, the deepest feelings are revealed in the most simple language. It is pathetic—it is even awful, when we find that it was the close of Eliot's correspondence, and the description of the emotions of his departing spirit. Hence the religious consolations ; the mournful happiness which cheered the consumptive and weary prisoner, who was now anticipating that after-state, to which he was fast approaching.]

TO HAMPDEN.

SIR,

BESIDES the acknowledgment of your favour that have so much compassion on your frend, I have little to return you from him that has nothing worthy of your acceptance but the contestation that I have between an ill bodie and the aer, that quarrell, and are friends as the summer winds affect them. I have these three daies been abroad, and as often brought in new impressions of the colds, yet body and strength and appetite I finde

myself bettered by the motion. Cold at first was the
occasion of my sickness, heat and tenderness by close
keepinge in my chamber has since increast my weakness.
Air and exercise are thought most proper to repaire it,
which are the prescription of my Doctors, though noe
physick. I thank God other medicines I now take not,
but those Catholicons, and doe hope I shall not need
them: as children learn to go, I shall get acquainted with
the aer, practice and use will compasse it, and now and
then a fall is an instruction for the future. These va-
rieties He does trie us with, that will have us perfect at
all parts, and as He gives the trial He likewise gives the
ability that shall be necessary for the worke He will sup-
plie, that does command the labour, whose deliveringe
from the Lion and the Bear, has the Philistine also at
the disposition of his will, and those that trust him, under his protection and defence. O! infinite mercy of
our Master, deare frend, how it abounds to us, that are
unworthy of his service! How broken! how imperfect!
how perverse and crooked are our waies in obedience to
him! how exactly straight is the line of his providence
to us, drawn out through all occurrents and particulars
to the whole length and measure of our time; how perfect is his hand that has given his Sonne unto us, and
with him has promised likewise to give us all things—
relieving our wants, sanctifying our necessities, prevent-
ing our dangers, freeing us from all extremities, and
died himself for us! What can we render? what retribution can we make worthy soe great a majestie?
worthy such love and favour? We have nothing but
ourselves who are unworthy above all, and yett that as
all other things is his; for us to offer up that, is but to
give him of his owne, and that in far worse condition

than we at first received it, which yet (for infinite is his goodnesse for the merits of his Sonne) He is contented to accept. This, dear frend, must be the comfort of his children; this is the physic we must use in all our sicknesse and extremities; this is the strengthening of the weake, the nuriching of the poore, the libertie of the captive, the health of the diseased, the life of those that die, the death of that wretched life of sin, and this happiness have his saints. The contemplation of this happiness has led me almost beyond the compass of a letter; but the hast I use unto my frends, and the affection that does move it, will I hope excuse me. Frends should communicate their joyes: this as the greatest therefore, I could not but impart unto my frend, being therein moved by the present expectation of your letters, which always have the grace of much intelligence, and are happiness to him that is trulie

Your's,

J. E.

Tower, 29 March, 1632.

Had Charles the First been as intimately acquainted with the nobler aspirations of Sir John Eliot in his prison, as the reader is now enabled to be, the severity of that imprisonment had perhaps been mitigated. But Eliot, who seems to have been far more a man of sensation than a philosopher, in the active period of his life; that period when he struck at a Moyle, and when his personal rancour broke out against his former friend Buckingham, had committed even a less pardonable irruption of his irascible nature. Eliot had implicated the King's connivance at the rumoured poisoning of his royal father. He alluded to something " which he feared to speak and feared to think." The harshness of Charles the First towards Eliot, and Charles is not accused of cruelty even by his enemies, indicates a cause of offence, either of a deeper dye, or of a more personal nature, than probably we have yet discovered.

END OF THE FOURTH VOLUME.

LONDON:

PRINTED BY SAMUEL BENTLEY,

Dorset Street, Fleet Street.

CPSIA information can be obtained
at www.ICGtesting.com
Printed in the USA
BVHW04*1154160818
524721BV00012B/419/P